STRATEGY, EVOLUTION, AND WAR

STRATEGY
FROM APES TO
EVOLUTION
ARTIFICIAL INTELLIGENCE
AND WAR

KENNETH PAYNE

Georgetown University Press / Washington, DC

Library of Congress Cataloging-in-Publication Data
Names: Payne, Kenneth, 1974– author.
Title: Strategy, evolution, and war : from apes to artificial intelligence / Kenneth Payne.
Description: Washington, DC : Georgetown University Press, 2018. |
Includes bibliographical references and index.
Identifiers: LCCN 2017057435 (print) | LCCN 2018012277 (ebook) |
ISBN 9781626165816 (ebook) | ISBN 9781626165793 (hardcover : alk. paper) |
ISBN 9781626165809 (pbk. : alk. paper)
Subjects: LCSH: Strategy. | Strategy—Psychological aspects. |
Artificial intelligence—Military applications.
Classification: LCC U162 (ebook) | LCC U162 .P39 2018 (print) | DDC 355.02—dc23
LC record available at https://lccn.loc.gov/2017057435

19 18   9 8 7 6 5 4 3 2   First printing

Printed in the United States of America

Cover design by John Barnett/4eyesdesign.com.

For Valerie Payne-Morris

CONTENTS

INTRODUCTION

THIS BOOK EXPLORES THE EVOLUTIONARY BASIS OF HUMAN STRATEGY IN war and considers the prospects of a radically distinct approach to strategy using artificial intelligence (AI). Strategy is defined here as the purposeful use of violence for political ends. This definition sharpens the focus onto war and away from other human endeavors that may require a similar aptitude for planning imaginatively to realize goals.

My conclusion is that strategy is soon to undergo something of a dramatic transformation because machines will make important decisions about war and will do so without input from human minds. The results may be dramatic—including a shift in the utility of deterrence, a profound reordering of existing power balances, and challenges to the notion of the "warrior." AI will likely enhance the power of the offensive side in conflict and will make decisions about escalation in nonhuman ways at a pace that is inhumanly fast.

I take an evolutionary approach to understanding strategy—seeing it largely as a product of our intense and complex social relationships. Living in a group entails cooperation and shared planning about future goals—especially when it comes to conflict with other groups. This process of negotiating goals within a group and working together to achieve them is what we call strategy, particularly when it involves goals that conflict with those of rival groups. Until now, all strategy has been inherently biological—connected intimately to our evolved origins as social primates. Our decision-making, conscious and otherwise, is informed by our human biology and the motivations that derive from it. I describe this evolutionary process in the first third of the book; in the second part I explore how the arrival of culture has modified this evolutionary process. The last third is an exploration of how artificial intelligence might change this biological essence and radically alter the essence of strategy.

Human strategy reflects the human condition—starting with the basic reality that we are social and embodied agents. We are motivated to reproduce and survive and have evolved a series of subordinate goals and procedures to enhance our prospect of survival. Warfare between groups of humans is the consequence of this biological imperative, even if the links sometimes seem obscure or tangential. Moreover, the prospect for violent conflict has shaped the evolution of our minds, including the evolution of human consciousness. It has given us an acute sensitivity for what other humans might think or want. We are emotional, and these emotions act as an important heuristic, streamlining our decision-making process in ways that have proved adaptive.

We will see that much falls out of the difference between these basic human realities and the realities of machines. What machines might seek to achieve and how they go about achieving it are not necessarily akin to the situation we face. Indeed, I suggest that there will be radical differences and large strategic consequences. One caveat: rather than creating a danger from AI acting strategically *on its own account*, the main effects of AI are likely to be felt from AI acting *in our interests*, which may produce rapid power shifts and unintended consequences. Even so, AIs will challenge some of the fundamental tenets of strategy—including the importance of mass, the dominance of the defense, the utility of surprise, the efficacy of preventive warfare, and the link between a society's values and the way in which it approaches strategy. All of these are possible with technology not far distant from what is available today. This is not to say that the onset of more advanced AI than that, capable of dealing flexibly with real-world situations, will not entail serious dangers, nor that it might not generate some internal motivations of its own. But even then it might not look much like the malign, anthropomorphized versions of AI that populate alarmist science fiction and journalistic accounts.

To give some idea of the argument that will follow: I suggest that there have been two macro-level "revolutions" in human strategic affairs—the first, when our species underwent some sort of cognitive transformation, which seems to have gathered pace somewhere around one hundred thousand years ago; the second, now under way, in which artificial intelligence will profoundly alter the way in which cognition shapes strategy. AI has the potential to affect humans more broadly than just in strategic affairs, of course—reshaping our societies, our bodies, and perhaps even our minds as the distinction between it and human and intelligence breaks down. But these possibilities are of interest here primarily insofar as they have an impact on strategic affairs.

My argument stresses continuity in strategic affairs, from the evolution of human intelligence to the advent of AI. Not everyone is convinced. Take the basic question of violence and human nature. Despite increasingly persuasive evidence about violent human prehistory, there remains a school of thought that war is a modern phenomenon distinct from the more peaceful way humans lived in our evolutionary past

(Fry 2007). This thinking suggests that modern civilization, rather than our evolved human nature, has unleashed the scourge of war, waged with powerful modern weapons, for material gain. Others, like Harry Turney-High, allow that "primitive" man was violent but argue that the wars of modern states are qualitatively different and altogether more serious than the wars of states of the past (Turney-High 1971). Not only were primitive warriors ill-disciplined and ill-equipped, he suggests, but they were motivated by existential passions—including the rather Freudian motive to release pent-up frustrations by fighting: violence as stress relief. For Martin van Creveld, too, primitive war differs from those of modern states in its instrumental-ity—with modern states applying reason and logic when it comes to the use of violence (van Creveld 1991). I disagree. There is great continuity in human affairs to set against the compelling differences between cultures, and these often reflect the influence of our evolved psychology. "Primitives," as much as "moderns," are driven to fight for reasons that can be instrumental, existential, or some mixture of both.

Other writers stress the linkage between strategy and particular manifestations of culture—especially the sorts of weapons involved (Fuller 1946). Certainly there is rich variation in human culture that has resulted in the kaleidoscopic character of warfare. This presents a problem for all theorists seeking to identify general pat-terns from the particulars of history. My answer to this challenge is similar to the one advanced by Carl von Clausewitz, who discerned continuity in the psycholog-ical factors that underpin strategic behavior. One difference with Clausewitz is the connection made here to the evolutionary basis of those psychological attributes. In particular, they are connected to the need to cooperate and generate scale.

The Big Battalions

Strategy is a rich and diverse activity with many subtleties. At its core, how-ever, strategy entails an adversarial and dynamic relationship between at least two groups. There are many possible goals in life and many possible approaches to realizing them. These variations of strategy flow from one big driver: the ad-vantages that accrue to scale when human groups fight using simple weapons. The essence of strategy for early man was to concentrate force in time and space against weaker enemies. If a favorable local force ratio could be constructed, then victory would likely follow. Hence the predominance of raid and ambush as tactics in warfare of hunter-gatherer communities, and also of chimpanzees.

This need to generate mass created in humans an incentive for cooperation in large groups—including, eventually, groups far larger than the small, mostly

kin-based bands in which early humans spent most of their days. And there was sufficient intergroup conflict to exert a powerful evolutionary pressure. There are other
reasons than warfare to cooperate more intensely and in larger groups—hunting, as
Robert Ardrey has argued, is one candidate, though the skills of ambush are similar, whatever the prey (Ardrey 1976). More broadly, cooperation of all sorts allows
comparative advantage for mutual gain via specialization, with individuals making varied contributions to the public good. Imitative learning and communication
creates the possibility for cumulative cultural knowledge far greater than one individual can acquire. Still, the evidence increasingly suggests that intergroup conflict
in prehistory was sufficiently pervasive to be an important catalyst for cooperation
in itself. This conflict provided a powerful selection pressure—selecting, that is, for
the willingness to cooperate with nonkin in larger groups.

This need to generate scale in combat reinforced the advantages of communication via sophisticated language. Integral to that was the need to speculate on
what others were thinking—a skill psychologists refer to as the "theory of mind."
It required imagination, not just to think about the goals of others but also to
conceive of possible futures around which to orient action. In short, group conflict fostered a particular sort of human intelligence that was intensely social and
flexible, and capable ultimately of scaling up to groups far larger than the small,
mostly interrelated bands of other primates.

This is the social brain theory of human evolution, which is increasingly ac-
cepted in evolutionary psychology. But it comes with an added twist: the sort
of intelligence that we developed was strategic, and from the beginning it was
shaped by the need to think about coordinating the behavior of groups in deadly
competition with others.

Strategies of the Strong and of the Weak

Of course, strategy entails much more than generating mass. Sustaining it over
time, via logistical support, remains a challenge even in the era of the modern
state. It would have been particularly problematic in the resource-scarce environments of many hunter-gatherer communities of history. Controlling the activities of large groups would also have proved difficult in the absence of effective
communications and the hierarchy needed to compel obedience. Without more
formal hierarchies or a means of imposing discipline, tactics in battle were fairly
rudimentary. There might have been a logic for ever-larger groups—and even,
as human evolution progressed, for the cognitive capacity to form multiple and

flexible group identities. But the practical matter of assembling large communities and generating effective fighting power from within them would have been challenging. Napoleon Chagnon, in his long-running anthropological study of the war-like Yanomamö people of the Amazon, found that villages larger than around 150 people either fissioned into smaller settlements or required the fierce and tyrannical leadership of an unusually brutal headman to keep order (Chagnon 2014). That number is evolutionarily significant, as we will see.

Additionally, while large groups have a theoretical advantage in conflict, weaker parties might still offset these advantages. If strategy were only about accumulating scale, it would be a comparatively straightforward proposition. But smaller groups can sometimes win. Doing so, however, also requires cooperation and trust, the same basic building blocks that underpin the creation of large groups. The means of defense might include deception, maneuver in space, fortification, or the clever use of terrain. Fighting in close formation of disciplined warriors would serve a similar purpose—anything to defend against force being concentrated against isolated defenders, with each in turn being defeated.

Once weapons technologies became more sophisticated, they could affect the balance between attackers and defenders, further complicating the essential advantages of scale. In rare film footage from the 1960s, Robert Gardner captured a set piece battle between rival groups of hunter-gatherers in Papua New Guinea that neatly illustrates the problem of concentrating force against a dispersed enemy formation armed with projectile weapons (Gardner 1963). Gathering together created a large target for hurled spears, so the fighters remain dispersed. The problem was further compounded by the inability of commanders, watching on from a short distance, to coordinate their nominal subordinates. Such coordination might have allowed maneuver and the use of terrain to flank enemy defenses, but there is little evidence of that in Gardner's footage. Pitched battle looks dramatic, and accumulated casualties exert a dramatic toll on belligerent societies. These are certainly not purely ritual confrontations; they are in deadly earnest. Still, the risks of pitched battles are severe and the difficulties of strategic command are pronounced—it is much better, then, to surprise an unprepared enemy in raiding before their defensive weapons (shields, armor, spears, or walls) can be brought to bear.

The dramatic footage from New Guinea, as with Chagnon's research in the Amazon, is a window into earlier human warfare, and worth keeping in mind. Strategy, it shows, does not simply devolve into accumulating a large force with which to annihilate smaller groups in battle or ambush. Even small groups benefit greatly from the intense cooperation and specialization that mark human cultures, to the point at which they can, and have, repeatedly seen off formidable adversaries. The point is that the pressures of conflict that arose during the evolution of *Homo sapiens* created a powerful motive for cooperating more intensely in ever-larger groups of unrelated confederates. When weapons were primitive and used at arm's length, mass really mattered. When weapons grew more sophisticated—the result of the cultural expertise unleashed by intense cooperation—strategy grew increasingly complex. But it was still often about assembling a favorable local force ratio. Isolated fighting units cannot readily fend off concentrations of comparable enemy units.

The rich panoply of strategic behaviors we engage in today flows from the strategic intelligences that prehistoric violence prompted. Without underplaying the remarkable diversity unleashed by culture, human strategy remains fundamentally informed by the evolved psychology of prehistory. In his principles of war, Antoine de Jomini identified the importance of scale and of concentrating force (Jomini 1992). Clausewitz, too, focused on mass, which might be concentrated against the enemy's "center of gravity" (Clausewitz 1993). These, though, were only starting points for strategy. Victory might often go to the larger force, but even when it didn't, evolutionary psychology often still had something to contribute to understanding why.

Mind Reading and Deception

"Theory of mind" entails having beliefs about the beliefs of others. This complex skill, which humans seem to possess to a greater degree than any other animal, is the basis of much strategic intelligence. It also unleashes complex culture acquired through social learning. We can learn not just blindly by unreflective mimicry, or by "aping," as we sometimes disparagingly put it (and perhaps unfairly given that other apes also seem capable of more sophisticated learning), but rather by discerning what another person is trying to *achieve* and adopting approaches that are best suited to realizing it. We certainly can imitate, but we can also seek to understand what others intend; having seen this, we can combine actions in novel combinations to realize a goal.

Theory of mind is also intimately connected to communication, including through our uniquely rich human capacity for language. Our language is capable of abstract representation—using words as symbols for objects but also for immaterial ideas, including ideas about beliefs. We can imagine the interior lives of others, even when they are not physically present, and can communicate this to our peers, spinning stories and communicating the ideas that are the basis of our human culture. Language becomes a way of constructing and navigating a rich social world.

Orienting around what other agents are doing is a common feature of biological life, especially among social animals. But humans take this general notion of social cognition to a highly sophisticated level. Theory of mind is like a Russian doll with an instinctive empathy at its core—an unconscious emotional sensitivity to the fate of others. Other social animals also demonstrate this instinctive sensitivity—and it might be one of the drivers of altruistic behavior (de Waal 2017). On top of that, however, is another layer: of reasoning about others' minds and communicating with them. Here, too, some mammals—especially great apes—have demonstrated some abilities. But for this outermost layer, with its capacity to imagine abstract others, we seem to surpass all other species. When it comes to AI and strategy, one of the big questions is the extent to which machines will need a similar capacity in order to navigate a social world on our behalf.

The other thing that theory of mind gives is scope for lying and deception. We, probably uniquely, understand that others can hold false beliefs, and that in some circumstances we would do well to deceive them. This ability, imperfect though it is, is the best counterfoil to mass and concentration in strategy—the rapier to set against the bludgeon. Lying is a high-stakes gamble within groups of über-cooperators since they are always on the lookout for shirkers and interlopers (Trivers 2013). But the payoff in adopting deception can be significant.

The complex repertoire of strategic behaviors described by classical strategists—surprise, maneuver, and deception—are all of a piece. They entail being able to do what the other side does not anticipate, in large part because of humans' ability to imaginatively "get inside" the heads of others and understand what they believe. The great works of classical strategy, from Sun Tzu and Machiavelli through Clausewitz and Jomini, and into the modern era of Thomas Schelling and Bernard Brodie, all explore the idea that beliefs, especially false beliefs, are the basis of shrewd strategy. Deception, feints, ruses, surprise, and even the term "stratagem" itself carry the connotation of exploiting the false beliefs of one's opponent.

This ability to exploit weakness rests on a keen appreciation of the situation—or, most accurately, the social situation. Understanding the situation, including gauging the beliefs and intentions of other actors, is the cornerstone of modern British military thought. The "indirect way of war"—a phrase employed by British strategist Basil Liddell Hart—is another staple of classical strategy that reaches back to the precepts of Sun Tzu (Liddell Hart 1967). "Know yourself, and know your enemy," as that author put it, and you will avoid defeat (Sun Tzu 2014).

Adherents of the indirect approach seek to avoid the brute strength of an adversary and exploit their own comparative advantage. Doing so often requires an astute reading of enemy strengths and the ability to exploit the enemy's weaknesses. But we are imperfect judges of the interior lives of others, as we will see, particularly when those others belong to different cultural groups.

One important additional strategic dimension that flows from theory of mind is the balance between escalation, coercion, and deterrence. Strategy, since it is competitive and adversarial, is inherently about responding to and shaping the intentions of others. This requires, at a minimum, an attempt to understand the motivations of antagonists—the better to understand what it will take to change their minds. This, too, is a core theme in classical strategic theory. Clausewitz and Schelling, for example, both see war as a test of will, or resolve—a special sort of conversation through violence (Schelling 2008; Clausewitz 1993). Stephen Rosen similarly sees combat as entailing an exchange of information about the motives of the belligerents: what they want and how hard they will fight for it (Rosen 2005). Only in the actual fighting itself is such information manifest; but the strategist must gauge all this beforehand and discern between simple posturing and genuine intention.

Strategy, when seen like this, is an intensely psychological activity. Lawrence Freedman has described it as the construction of power in the moment, which captures some of this contingency and complexity (Freedman 2013). Strategy demands a fine judgment of what others are thinking, the better to coordinate with allies and compel adversaries. Advantages accruing from scale are clearly only a starting point for explaining strategic intelligence.

In sum, intense cooperation is the hallmark of human society and an important feature of strategy, whether fighting on the offensive with large forces, or on the defensive, seeking to exploit whatever means are available to prevent the enemy concentrating force and defeating you in detail. If a group finds itself in competition with others, it must weigh what it will take to change those others' minds. Strategy thus entails careful thinking about coercion, escalation, and deterrence.

These themes run through our evolved existence. All social life in biology requires individual organisms to respond to the behavior of others. For humans, the solution to this challenge has come via an internally generated theory of other minds; an imperfect yet still powerful way of navigating competitive, dangerous environments. Partly this is an instinctive and subconscious process—one that, for example, sees us conform automatically to the norms of those within our circle while acting more warily and less generously to outsiders. Partly it is also a matter of conscious reflection and rumination; a capacity for elevated reasoning, thinking about our thinking, that really sets us apart from other animals.

Evolution (Over)Simplified

The argument so far boils down to the importance of warfare as a catalyst for the evolutionary processes of ever-deepening sociability in humans. Enough danger from intergroup violence and enough return from scale and we have a plausible engine for the development of theory of mind, intense cooperation, and expanded social groups.

Two theories are useful in exploring this dynamic, and I explore both in the chapters on evolutionary psychology that follow. The first is a mathematical model developed by Frederick Lanchester, based on the logic that larger groups have a disproportionate advantage in combat. Only ever an idealized abstraction (Lanchester employed it to understand aerial combat in the Great War), this model has been enthusiastically embraced by both military theorists and biologists to describe "warfare" in the animal kingdom and among early human groups (Lanchester 1916).

The second theory, or collection of theories, might loosely be described as the "social theory of intelligence." This has been advanced by a range of scholars across disciplines, including psychology, neuroscience, anthropology, and archaeology. It suggests that our minds, including our conscious minds, evolved to help us navigate our social world. Of particular importance is the idea from evolutionary psychologist Robin Dunbar that we have evolved a neural capacity for a particular size of social group—some 150 people, by his reckoning (Dunbar 2014). A large brain comes with the cost of very high energy demands, but there are obvious constraints on how much time is available for foraging, let alone the amount of food available in the local environment.

Set against this are the very substantial evolutionary gains from social cognition—the ability to speculate about the internal states of other minds and to ruminate on oneself via metacognition. Human-level consciousness confers the ability to imagine others' viewpoints, including those of people not present. We can also visualize possible futures for ourselves and imagine the attitudes of absent ancestors, even deities, all knitted together in one social universe. Clifford Geertz and Napoleon Chagnon both liken human culture to a spider's web in constant flux (Geertz 2010; Chagnon 2014). It is this dynamic web that we evolved to track. And, while Dunbar reckons that his smallish number echoes into the modern world of Facebook friends and mobile phone texting, this sort of cognitive flexibility has allowed us to escape the narrow confines of kinship bands to form vast social networks stretching across time and space. Moreover, we have developed another equally remarkable ability to belong to multiple distinct social networks at once, each with its own set of attendant norms (Tajfel 2010). To do these things requires a powerful imagination—one that is predicated on understanding the minds of others.

Such bold claims about the evolution of strategy and human intelligence oversimplify matters considerably. The notion of a cognitive revolution in early humans, for example, elides a number of possibly related evolutionary developments that scientists are only now beginning to understand and about which much uncertainty remains. My argument is accordingly speculative, even though it draws on similar themes from the research of many others.

Consider the evolution of language as an important element of that cognitive "revolution"—but one about which much remains unclear. Dunbar, in his gossip theory of language, suggests that human language evolved as an aid to social interaction and for monitoring group dynamics, especially one's own place within the group (Dunbar 2004). The ability to speak and the subjects about which we spoke likely coevolved, with the range of abstract concepts becoming richer as sociability deepened (Seyfarth, Cheney, and Bergman 2005; Pinker and Bloom 1990). Recent research indicates that other great apes have some capacity for language. Rocky the orangutan learned to emulate human vowel sounds (Lameira et al. 2016). Koko the gorilla communicates via sign language with her longtime human friend, a skill also exhibited by some captive chimpanzees, most famously one called Washoe (Patterson 1978; Griffin 2001). These apes demonstrate that language, like much else in human behavior, may not be as uniquely human as we might suppose. But the other great apes lack important dimensions of sociability, notably the ability to adopt another's perspective with the same acuity we possess. This might limit their abilities to have, much less communicate, complex abstract ideas about their social world. Human language, with its rich vocabulary, highly developed semantics, and complex grammar is—to the best of our present understanding—unique. And it seems intimately connected to our social world and our theory of mind.

Still, the communicative ability of apes suggests that the roots of human language reach back much further into human prehistory than has been supposed and certainly a long time before the cultural explosion that we witness in the production of complex social artifacts, like tools and musical instruments, during the last one hundred thousand years. Notwithstanding the difficulties of adducing evidence from a scanty fossil and genetic record, there is some agreement that language has a long history in human evolution—to which the linguistic abilities of our fellow great apes adds considerable support. Dunbar and colleagues argue for a lengthy gestation of linguistic and social abilities, perhaps stretching back hundreds of thousands of years into antecedent species of hominids like *Homo erectus* and even before our split from Neanderthals some four hundred thousand years ago (Gamble, Gowlett, and Dunbar 2014). The production of cultural artifacts in the last hundred thousand years represents an intensification in the exploitation of evolved capacities rather than the generation of wholly new attributes. We might have been capable of multiple, flexible group identities and high degrees of intentionality (that is, the ability to mentally represent others, even absent others) well before the appearance of complex cultural products.

Perhaps. Just when these distinctively human attributes emerged and at what pace they developed remains uncertain and subject to debate. My description of a "cognitive revolution" nonetheless provides a neat shorthand for a package of developments in humans that have to do with their social world. Perhaps this shorthand is too neat, or perhaps the "revolution" proceeded in incremental stages. The vast complexity of the human brain and the richness of human experience and creativity should put us on our guard against accepting the twin dangers of neuro-reductionism and "just so" stories from evolutionary psychology. Reductionism entails taking a behavior and linking it to particular structures in the mind, and in so doing overlooking the rather complex processes of the human mind about which there is still considerable uncertainty. A very recent mapping of the human brain identified a total of 180 distinct brain regions, nearly one hundred of which were, astonishingly, altogether new (Glasser et al. 2016). Moreover, the processes of the brain, while they involve specialized regions, are typically the product of dynamic networks of neurons, often vast in number and densely interlinked, including via reciprocal loops. Our present capacity to understand such networks is limited, among other things, by the rather blunt sensors at our disposal, including fMRI, which uses a large magnet to measure blood flow, thereby indicating which regions are particularly active. We should exercise caution lest we rightly be accused of spouting "neurobollocks"—a popular insult in the field.

As for "just so" stories of evolution, the tendency is similar: find a modern-day behavior and connect it to a plausible-sounding evolutionary theory. Often such theories have a lot to do with sexual dynamics—such as the idea that women prefer deep-voiced men and good dancers because those are indicators of testosterone, which in turn predicts who will defend offspring from predation, including from rival males (Collins 2000; Hugill et al. 2009). But perhaps those voices evolved to intimidate other men so as to better compete for scarce resources, including women (Puts et al. 2016). Experimental evidence supports both theories, and perhaps it's both. Another suggestion: the human fist evolved to better punch rivals, and the face to better deflect the blow (Horns, Jung, and Carrier 2015).

This contrasts with another theory, that the human face is the product of self-domestication—becoming progressively less aggressively masculine and ape-like.

There is an inevitability to such speculation. We cannot, after all, return to the Paleolithic era and observe how different traits fared as they evolved. We possess only patchy insight into the evolutionary environment: via fossils, archaeological excavations at early human sites, modern ethnography with extant hunter-gatherer communities, studies of other primates (especially the great apes, our closest genetic relations) or, more recently, genetic analysis. Furthermore, the picture is constantly changing, as with a recent finding of human remains in Morocco that predate our earliest known human remains by one hundred thousand years (Hublin et al. 2017). There have apparently been several bottlenecks in our lineage since that time, limiting our genetic diversity so that we humans are more genetically homogenous than chimpanzees. Further complicating the picture we also know that some of our ancestors have interbred with at least two other *Homo* species—with many western Europeans having Neanderthal genes and some Asia-Pacific dwellers possessing DNA from another extinct and largely unknown hominid, currently called Denisovans (E. Harris 2015; Rutherford 2016; Bowden et al. 2012). These and other dramatic discoveries make human prehistory seem more recent, rather fragile, and continually lucky. The genetic record shows that we parted company from a common ancestor with chimpanzees some six million years ago, yet here are some profound developments happening in only the last hundred thousand years. This is worth keeping in mind for a later discussion about why only humans, among all the primates, developed a rich culture, including tools and language.

In any event, the lesson is to treat such "just so" theories sensitively—as theories, with some supporting evidence but with a degree of uncertainty. We must beware of cherry-picking evidence from the already imperfect record to fit our theory. We can develop a view that human conflict and social life relates somehow to the uneven distribution of food resources, as primatologist Richard Wrangham does, or, as Dunbar explains, that language evolved as a way of managing inter- and intragroup conflict (Wrangham 1996). We can, with both these theories, adduce a considerable volume of evidence to build a convincing argument. But nothing is certain.

Enter Culture

Our evolutionary history produced a powerful, socially skilled brain that dramatically changed human existence, endowing us with the cognitive flexibility to survive and prosper in all manner of physical environments. The knowledge that we acquired could be shared with group members via complex language. Culture in these large nonkin groups was both a badge of membership and a way of generating and sharing ideas. Specialist knowledge was possible. We developed an ability to produce sophisticated artifacts, including tools and weapons. Once we had these, the basic parameters of strategy became greatly more complex.

This cultural phase of human evolution occupies the second part of the book. How best to meaningfully compress some twenty thousand years or so of strategic activity by greatly differing cultures into only a few chapters? My approach is thematic and includes the following themes:

- War drove cultural development by reinforcing our tendency to cooperate in groups against outsiders that is the evolved basis of strategy.
- For encultured humans, technology, warfare, and society are dynamically interlinked. The ways in which societies enact strategy are shaped by culture; but cultures are fluid, and ideas can cross between them. Fighting itself provides an important motor in copying what works. This malleability and dynamism complicates the notion, popular in international relations scholarship, of a static (or at least sticky) and homogenous "strategic culture" that shapes how groups conceive and enact strategy.
- Technology (and, more broadly, specialization within societies) complicates the basic logic of evolved strategy. With sophisticated weapons, the advantage traditionally enjoyed by larger forces in primitive conflict can be offset, sometimes entirely. Combat by cultured groups is frequently a "combined arms" activity in which different weapons and different types of warrior are employed in concert in an effort to asymmetrically offset the advantages of the adversary.
- Culture enlarges both the geographical and temporal scope of strategy. Culture permits the formation of large groups with sophisticated technologies capable of campaigning via interlinked action over extended periods of time and across large distances. Chimpanzees fight rival groups over months and years, but humans with sophisticated culture can do more than repeat the same small-group tactics. Strategy might be less a matter of generating power in the moment—there can be planning for future campaigns, resources must be husbanded, and finances can be channeled in particular directions. Here strategy shades into planning and the range of options multiplies dramatically—a combinatorial explosion of strategic options is possible.

- Strategy retains important links to its evolutionary setting despite its rich variety. In important ways, strategy remains an inherently psychological activity. Partly this link is about the way we make strategic decisions via an evolved, intensely social psychology. This, for example, entails favoritism for insiders and prejudice against outsiders; or, for another example, an evolved self-aware consciousness with which to manage social dynamics of our group.

  Partly the link to evolution concerns the broad approaches to strategy. There are still echoes, however dim, of the two modes of fighting common in prehistory. On one hand are the enduring gains from concentrating large forces against smaller ones. On the other are the strategies of offsetting this strength—especially via deception, hardening, or dispersal to avoid overwhelming strength being concentrated against isolated individuals who can be annihilated in detail. The possibilities for both basic approaches are shaped by the culture of the belligerent societies, including their respective technologies. The efficacy of each approach will vary widely, too, with the local balance between attack and defense shifting accordingly.

  At the same time, war retains its essence as a struggle for influence—and here, too, we can detect its psychological inheritance. Encultured strategists, like their forebears, must weigh the costs of coercing or deterring the enemy and the risks of escalation. Strategy is an imaginative, inherently psychological act involving sophisticated theory of mind. Strategists create and employ power that is perceived by adversaries; strategists attempt to gauge how that will be perceived and acted on.

  Modern, encultured war is in some senses a much more complicated affair than that waged by hunter-gatherer societies—with campaigns sustained over long periods; waged by more organized, professional, and disciplined forces; and sometimes commanded by leaders with specialized strategic knowledge. But underpinning this complexity is our evolved psychology.
- An assessment of culture must also address "rationality." The aspiration to use force instrumentally is an important part of strategic behavior. But this rationality of a very human kind, in which knowledge, including of what we want, no less than how to get it, is uncertain. Decisions are often made using evolved cognitive shortcuts rather than a detailed appraisal of the situation in hand.

These themes run through three chapters, appearing in each. They are on, in order, warfare and strategy in ancient Greece; Napoleonic times; and lastly the nuclear age. This is well-thumbed territory—but there are good reasons for that, having to do with available evidence and the weight of existing analysis. Moreover, while these examples may be familiar to some readers, I hope that seeing them in the light of our evolutionary psychology will add freshness to the analysis.

The three cases also have the added merit that they are widely different societies—with different technologies, social relationships, and strategic challenges—and yet they nonetheless show continuity in approaches to strategy. Notwithstanding this manifest cultural variety, we find the same evolved cognitive responses. Accordingly, the main conclusion here is that strategy in all its myriad cultural manifestations retains a core psychological essence unaltered by even the most radical technologies invented.

A preview of the argument to come might be useful. The example of Greece and the ancient historical world shows that warfare had become complex. Alliances of groups, each with different strategic attributes, were capable of waging sustained campaigns against one another. The combat was frequently "combined arms" with different types of warriors and different approaches to employing them, both singly and in concert. Moreover, strategy was about more than just fighting. Rather, it was about generating fighting power with which to coerce enemies. We see that the morale of the civilian population matters, as does the group's economic capacity to sustain campaigns over an extended period and at range.

One technology—the "hoplite panoply"—serves to illustrate two big ideas: that there is a relationship between culture, technology, and the style of fighting (which may work in both directions), and that the power of the offensive can be blunted by canny defenders (in this case using shields and close formation to limit the ability of attackers to concentrate force, à la Lanchester's square law). The defense has other good options too—in its use of fortification and depth to avoid pitched battle, for example.

A second technology developed in this era, writing, offers additional points. Writing was the first information technology, a far distant precursor to the AI of today. It provided a way to further entrench the gains of culture—allowing for ideas and specialized knowledge to be created, shared, and stored. In a sense it *augmented* the evolved intelligence of humans. The effect on strategy was profound and far-reaching, not least because strategy itself became a subject for authors. Writing greatly facilitated metacognition, or the reflective thinking about thinking and the sharing of ideas between and within communities. It catalyzed rationalism, in the sense that it allowed the rigorous examination of ideas against evidence. Epistemic communities, including in strategic affairs, emerged. In contrast to the shifting and ephemeral nature of oral communication in preliterate societies, writing allowed a more considered and more rigorous examination of ideas.

Napoleonic warfare and Carl von Clausewitz's strategic thought provide several additional observations that complement my broad thesis. For one thing, Lanchester is again relevant: Napoleon demonstrated an instinctive mastery of concentrating force in space and time and of exploiting the resultant shock to defeat shattered enemy forces in detail. Next is the idea that culture shapes warfare in ways that are not merely technological. Ideas about how to use force can be as important as the weapons technologies themselves. This is demonstrated by France's tremendous martial advantage arising from a new expression of nationalism and from the ability of commanders to harness this advantage in battle, particularly via the use of the column and mission command to empower subordinates.

And last, the period sheds further light on the balance between offense and defense—and in particular Clausewitz's striking observation that the defense is stronger than the attack (Payne 2016; Paret 2007). Clausewitz, whose writings offer frequent psychological insights, suggests that the inherent advantages of the offense can be offset by clever defenders. He was especially struck by the gains inherent from defending home turf—from the sense of belonging, as exemplified by Spanish guerrillas in the Peninsular wars, which he mistakenly describes as a novel form of warfare. If the tremendous fighting power generated by the patriotic French conscripts demonstrated an enduring advantage from scale, the partisans contrariwise illustrated the varied strategies of the weak to avoid concentration. Both styles of warfare showed the enduring strategic benefits of social cohesion via our peculiarly human über-cooperation.

Like Thucydides before him and Schelling after, Clausewitz was part of a literary tradition of thinking conceptually about strategy and, moreover, of thinking about it in psychological terms. Clausewitz's writing, moreover, reflected the intellectual tensions of his day between scientific understandings of human psychology and the more emotional and spiritual currents of the Romantic movement.

The final chapter considers the development of nuclear weapons. If any technology were going to challenge the established psychological foundations of strategy, surely it would be the hugely devastating thermonuclear bomb. Here again there are several important additions to the overall idea under development that is that technology, and culture more broadly, affects but does not radically transform the evolved psychological essence of strategy.

Certainly many strategists thought nuclear technology *was* revolutionary and transformative of existing strategic precepts. So vast a force could now be concentrated by an attacker as to obliterate any organized defense. Lanchester's square law would be validated in such circumstances: defensive formations, fortifications, and dispersals would all be useless. But in the next instant, Lanchester's precept might be rendered wholly redundant: if the defender was similarly equipped and managed to survive in some measure, then the attacker could in turn be devastated by a huge concentration of force. Defense through denial was not a possibility; instead, defense would rest more assuredly on deterrence via the threat of punishing reprisals. This seemed a radical departure necessitating new approaches to thinking about strategy. Defense would henceforth be achieved by the threat of punishment rather than denial—and that threat would somehow need to be credible (Jervis 1989).

In the United States this fostered attempts to understand strategy via the use of quantitative analysis—especially game theory. Underpinning some analyses was a conception of actors as abstractly rational, possessed of clear, ordered preferences and a "perfect" knowledge of the options. This seemed to offer the prospect of a more rigorous, scientific basis for strategy and reflected wider currents in the social sciences of the day. In a sense it was a particular cultural expression of thinking about force—a reasonable abstraction rather than an accurate reflection of how strategy would be made and enacted, even with nuclear weapons. It lent real-world deliberations about an unprecedented and horrific form of warfare a semblance of rigor and cool-headed detachment.

Not everyone was convinced. For Schelling in particular, strategy remains resolutely psychological, nuclear or otherwise (Schelling 2008). Schelling certainly used game theoretic examples but abjured the mathematical modeling and retained the human dimension in decision-making. This turned out to be more representative of nuclear strategy in practice, as a review of crisis decision-making during the Cuban Missile Crisis confirms. Defense via the threat of punishment was inescapably psychological. Like all previous strategy, it would require a careful appraisal of the antagonist's motivations in order to gauge what they wanted and how badly. That is, it would rest on "theory of mind" calculations using a combination of cognitive processes, some instinctive and emotional, others more detached and reasoned. Coercion, deterrence, escalation, deception: all the basic ingredients were still present in nuclear strategizing. Herman Kahn, a prominent nuclear theorist of the day, had posited carefully calibrated "ladders of escalation" with distinct thresholds of violence (Kahn 1960). But when a real crisis came, there was a good deal more uncertainty and ambiguity about the intentions and resolve of the enemy.

After all, if there was perfect information ahead of any conflict—about the capabilities or intentions of an interlocutor—there would be no need to fight, since the outcome could be anticipated and a bargain reached on the basis of that foreknowledge (Fearon 1995). Instead, rather than a rational, abstracted science, nuclear strategy remained ineffably psychological.

Enter AI

The last part of the book describes the ways in which artificial intelligence will constitute a second cognitive revolution in strategic affairs. The strategic studies literature has only recently turned its attention to modern developments in AI, although there has been much intriguing thought coming the other way—from AI specialists concerned about the threats their research poses.

Science fiction, of course, has long been versed in the martial uses of AI. The Off World Replicants of *Blade Runner* were my first introduction to the idea of warfighting AI; later I plundered my father's shelves of science fiction, including Arthur C. Clarke's *2001: A Space Odyssey* and Isaac Asimov's classics, with his famous rules for robots. The film *Tron* left me wondering whether it would really be possible to upload a human into a mainframe and emulate the human brain electronically on silicon hardware. Later still came the faithful cyborg of *Aliens*; the *Terminator* (whose AI is far more plausible than his time travel); and then the sinister Agent Smith, human avatar of the machines running *The Matrix*. Intelligent machines, Hollywood said, would be curiously human and thus capable of conscious reflection and intrinsic motivation (usually to do us harm). Often, the only thing missing was emotion—a concession to their alien nature.

This fictional world at its best is philosophically stimulating—as with the films *Ex_Machina* and the manga cartoon *Ghost in the Shell*, which both pose profound questions about what it means to be alive and sentient. Indeed, *Ex_Machina* was written under the guidance of Murray Shanahan, an eminent professor of cognitive robotics, and was based on his work on embodied intelligence (Shanahan 2010). Many questions were raised by these thoughtful films: Would an AI experience the world in the same way that humans do? Would it feel emotions? Would it even need a body, or could it float free in some disembodied network, like the Puppet Master of *Ghost in the Shell*? Above all, what would motivate such an AI? Would those motivations bring it into conflict with humans?

All this science fiction has fed into some popular stereotypes of an AI future. Sometimes it is a dystopian future—as with AI posing a threat to existing jobs and social structures (Ford 2015). Sometimes it is the possibility of AI adopting malign behaviors. *Tesla's* Elon Musk likened it to summoning a demon, and Stephen Hawking thought it could spell the end for humanity (Gibbs 2014; Cellan-Jones 2014).

Another, perhaps more immediate fear is the possibility of AI drones killing innocent bystanders (in another fictional scenario, this time from *Robocop*). Hundreds of scientists signed an open letter calling for the international prohibition of weaponized AI. Perhaps some of them failed to appreciate that it already exists in automated missile control systems, like the American *Patriot* batteries and *Aegis*-equipped air defense ships (P. W. Singer 2011). The fear here is not of AI developing a "mind" of its own and being a sentient strategic actor with interests that conflict with ours, but rather of AI being used to wage war on our behalf—potentially a more merciless, uncontrollable war.

The public discourse on AI is reminiscent of the alarm at the prospect of strategic air power during the interwar years (Overy 2013). Parallels also exist with the onset of the nuclear age and the ultimately fruitless search for effective civil defenses to address public anxiety about nuclear conflict. Now AI and war have crossed into the public consciousness, feeding off and into the bleak Hollywood vision of the future.

In the last part of the book I consider the likelihood of these alarmist visions materializing and explore their strategic implications. When he first heard of the atomic weapon, strategic theorist Bernard Brodie declared that everything he had written hitherto was obsolete (Zellen 2012). It was not, at least from the perspective of the underlying psychology of strategy. Similarly profound changes seem afoot with AI; certainly there is much breathless hyperbole, and the pace of research goes some way to substantiating the excitement and anxiousness. The strategic implications will likely be substantial, even if for some time to come there will be considerable continuity in strategic affairs. Nonetheless, AI deserves the tag of being "revolutionary" because, unlike nuclear weapons, it will entail decision-making of a distinct, nonhuman variety.

The part on AI is broken into two chapters, the first of which looks ahead into the near future to explore the development of AI that is already feasible and in some cases beginning to feed into strategic affairs. After an overview of the technology underpinning modern AI, this section explores the implications of "tactical-level" systems using AI that is already here, or readily feasible, and that is capable of carrying out military tasks "autonomously." Many of these systems will utilize an approach known as "deep learning," which, superficially, is modeled on the neuronal basis of human brains. This approach to AI has been responsible for some exciting breakthroughs during the last decade or so. Algorithms have proved adept at "learning" how to perform tasks with great precision, speed, and memory. These distinctive features of modern AI will permit some compelling strategic advantages under certain circumstances. Tactical weapon systems employing this sort of AI will be able to make local decisions without higher-level input and will outperform humans attempting to do likewise.

There are some important strategic implications here, especially when thinking about the psychological basis of strategy. These platforms will still be wholly reliant on human input to provide their overarching mission and rules of engagement. Strategy at the highest levels will continue to be shaped by our evolved psychology. It will be adversarial, violent, political, and social. It will still entail judgment about risk and uncertainty, with plenty of scope for chance. Familiar approaches of concentrating force at a decisive point, using speed and surprise, and maneuvering in time and space will be employed.

Nevertheless, this sort of AI will fundamentally alter some established strategic principles. For example, the speed and automaticity of its decisions will challenge the ability of human strategists to control the action by issuing initial guidance that can anticipate subsequent developments. Among the possible consequences are unintended escalation and failed deterrence, as machines make judgments about violence along wholly nonhuman lines, without recourse to human-like "theory of mind" calculations and risk parameters.

Another consequence of these tactical AI systems will be dramatic shifts in military power, as states possessing even a marginal technological advantage in AI are able to overwhelm less-able enemies. Tactical AI could render much conventional, non-AI force obsolete. Additionally, such systems will change the assessment of risk in warfare and perhaps reduce the threshold for violence among states possessing it. It will transform the way in which fighting power is constituted, diminishing the importance of morale and cohesion. It will alter the ways in which armies are constituted and commanded, perhaps changing the relationship between society and the use of force on their behalf.

Finally, there may be some dramatic implications for the way in which Lanchester's square law is made manifest. Because of their advantages in speed, precision, and pattern recognition, tactical AI systems will heavily favor the offensive and the side making the initial move in any conflict. These systems will be able to maneuver rapidly from distributed networks to accurately deliver concentrated force against enemy actors, benefitting from overwhelming local force ratios. Moreover, unlike human actors, such AI systems will not be affected by the psychological factors that, as Clausewitz argues, seem to limit the advantages of attacking forces in favor of the defense. The fighting power of tactical AI, by contrast to humans, will not depend on the sort of instinctive cohesion that is especially potent when under attack.

These tactical AI systems will, additionally, challenge the ability of defenders to employ their established tactics of delay, denial (through hardening, dispersal, or hiding), maneuver, and deception. Defenses will be fixed by pattern recognition and be vulnerable to "first strike" by rapidly concentrating automata seeking to seize the initiative and cycle decisions with tremendous speed. The overall strategic balance might therefore tip further toward the offensive, especially when attackers enjoy a marginal qualitative advantage. One possible salvation for the defense lies in present-day AI's vulnerability to "spoofing" through the creation of noise. Decoys are a mainstay of defense—and in the near future it may be possible for defending AI systems to create enough clutter on the battlefield to offset the pattern-recognition abilities of attacking AI.

A more profound break with existing strategic principles will come only when AI has achieved full autonomy, both in terms of goals and execution, a possibility considered in the second chapter on AI. This would require a generalist AI capable of applying its learning flexibly across a variety of tasks—something well beyond the capabilities of existing AI. This sort of artificial intelligence will be marked by two key attributes: its degree of cognitive flexibility, in contrast to the more brittle and narrow skill sets of tactical AI, and its degree of autonomous motivation. But there are other attributes of human intelligence that such artificial general intelligence (AGI) need not emulate in order to qualify, namely, theory of mind, emotional cognition, and human-level consciousness. It is possible, however, that some types of AGI might possess these abilities—a consideration that I make in concluding the book.

The two issues of autonomy and cognitive flexibility run through my analysis of AGI. First comes flexibility. This is about tackling different challenges with the same cognitive package and also about the ability to manage concurrent tasks, especially when they are in tension. The more flexible the intelligence (in the sense of being able to make useful decisions in a variety of contexts), the more scope there is for tension and the need to arbitrate between goals. Modern AI, of the deep-learning variety, is rather narrow and inflexible. Today the same basic algorithm *could* handle a variety of tasks, but once trained to optimize outcomes in a particular domain it is not possible to apply general lessons to another domain. In humans, complex skills can be developed with limited training experience and repackaged across domains. But without laborious retraining the skilled chess-playing AI cannot be usefully reapplied to poker, still less to flying an aircraft. This sort of transferable learning would, by contrast, be a hallmark of AGI. And like humans, that AGI will need to negotiate and "satisfice" between goals.

Second is autonomy. Humans certainly don't enjoy full autonomy, given the myriad unconscious influences on their decision-making, including social influences and the deep underlying evolutionary imperative to replicate. So "full autonomy," whatever that might be, need not be a prerequisite for AGI. Indeed, an AGI that is given goals by outside actors will still have to decide how best to pursue them and how best to resolve any tensions between them. This is especially true when considering social relations between multiple agents, whether artificial or human. That itself constitutes autonomy of a sort.

Autonomy relates to *motivation*, and humans are motivated at a very deep, fundamental level by the goals of evolution: survival of the individual agent in order to reproduce. Humans, like other biological agents, have evolved distinctive ways of addressing this problem, relying in part on our intense sociability. This gives us a whole range of intermediate motivations that shape our behavior, conscious and otherwise. AGI might be social, too. But it would not necessarily be social in the same way humans are—using the same cognitive processes that we do. It would certainly lack the biological imperative—even when loose analogies are available from "genetic algorithms" that combine to produce more effective "offspring." So its goals would be given exogenously, at least in the first instance, by its designer. An AGI might then experience something akin to intrinsic motivation but only if it has to develop subordinate goals in order to successfully navigate its environment. In a sense this would be similar to humans, whose evolutionary goals are given exogenously but whose repertoire of behaviors is arbitrated, at least in part, by myriad internal processes according to internal motivations. Autonomy, in other words, can only ever be partial—for both humans and AGI alike. Moreover, motivations that emerge within the AGI might be unanticipated by designers and not entirely welcome.

Flexible skills and the possibilities of greater autonomy, including the possibility of developing sub-goals, will be signature achievements of AGI. But to what end? My answer involves a discussion of meaning. For humans, choosing between possible goals depends on the value we place on goals, or what they "mean" to us. On one dimension meaning is about the relationship between concepts. Humans are excellent at combining and recombining dense networks of related concepts, including linguistic concepts. Machines are becoming increasingly good at this, including via "thought vectors" that represent ideas in numeric code. But there's another dimension to meaning that relates to value, including the value that might accrue from some particular action. In humans this value is inextricably linked to our emotional, embodied feelings. Machines might model such attributes. But because they lack the biological basis of emotions, even an emotional "module" would not feel like much to a machine—it would just be a way of prioritizing information and arbitrating between it, perhaps based on signal intensity or some sort of weighting. Would a machine be able to grasp "meaning" in the human sense? And without such meaning to arbitrate its actions, how would a flexible machine intelligence choose what to do from the wide range of goals it could conceivably pursue? In the "toy universe" of the tactical, inflexible AI, it might be as simple as maximizing a score or value—the sort of logic that also animates simple economic models. But in a far richer world, the AGI will need some way of dealing with complexity, and it must be able to do so rapidly.

The lessons here for strategy are profound: machines, at least as we presently understand them, will navigate between goals according to principles that are inherently inhuman. We may try to encode our own values into machines *ex ante*, taking account of all foreseeable contingencies. But the world is too complex and we do not know our own minds well enough for this to produce a satisfactory answer. What chance has the machine got of matching our unfolding preferences? Among the strategic implications are questions related to the ethics of armed conflict but also to the direction of campaigns. Again, there are significant questions here about the predictability of an AGI charged with enacting strategy and about our ability to correctly anticipate possible decision points that may arise in the future, giving the machine guidance on how to act on our behalf.

To conclude the analysis, I consider those human aspects of general intelligence that an AGI need not, but might, possess—and consider their strategic impact. Human intelligence is distinguished by many features, and prominent among these are "theory of mind," an emotional palate, and self-aware consciousness. These are all evolved and embodied solutions to particular challenges, and there's no obvious way in which an AGI running entirely on nonbiological architectures could somehow acquire them. The conclusion of the book, however, suggests a practical way that an AI might acquire those processes without developing them autonomously: by integrating with biological intelligences. How would this be done? It's a far distant prospect that today is only obscurely visible and contains many uncertainties. Such an AGI will emerge not by raw engineering but by incorporating human intelligences, in essence modifying what it is to be an individual human by adding in the cognitive strengths of machine-learning AI to greatly boost human cognition. Perhaps this could even happen by merging human and machine intelligences together as a collective. Such a scenario seems to me more plausible than engineering a super-AGI from the ground up; and some relevant technologies are already progressing. We can imagine a spectrum of augmented general intelligences, with one end having a more human flavor, centered on individual human cognition, and the other having more machine-like intelligence. Even that's not the end of the possibilities, however, since the sort of "mind-merging" technologies now in their infancy may change the balance between individual and social intelligence in radical new directions.

These ideas raise important ethical questions, not least about what it means to be a person, which has implications for ethics and the laws of armed conflict. As for strategy, the ramifications are likely significant too. The altogether inhuman calculations of an AGI will be modified, but so too will the evolved psychology that has underpinned human strategy for the last few millennia.

Here, at the frontiers of modern research on the mind, we are so far beyond the knowable that it's difficult to hazard much insight about strategy, except perhaps in its broadest sense. Strategy would still be a social endeavor that requires coordination within social groups. It would demand flexible intelligences that are able to anticipate how others might act and to imagine what they might want in the future. Seeing strategy from this elevation allows us to see again the core elements that run throughout human history. Indeed, in endowing machines with human-like properties—consciousness, emotion, empathy, and so on—it's hardly surprising that the result would be strategic intelligences, interacting strategically, along somewhat familiar lines.

Still, in the particulars of strategy there could be radical changes. When would groups risk escalation or be deterred? What would be the balance between defense and offense? The basic psychological foundations of strategy would be altered by AGI of the sort imagined here. But so, too, would the bases of our existing social life. On whose behalf would strategy be conducted? Humans have developed a bewildering variety of cultures and organized their social lives in groups that range in size from the small hunter-gatherer band to global superpowers. Underpinning all this has been the capacity for flexible and abstract group identities. One thing that has radically changed the character of human groups has been their dynamic relationship with technology. We might expect AI of whatever flavor, but especially of the sort that is highly flexible and can augment human cognition, to produce new social groups. With scope for new agents and new social structures, the space for possible strategy is large and only hazily visible.

PART I

The Evolution of Strategists

CHAPTER 1

Defining Strategy as Psychology

WHAT DOES IT MEAN TO SAY THAT STRATEGY IS PSYCHOLOGY? SOME definitions are in order, starting with strategy itself. My view of strategy extends over the long term, connecting prehuman life with artificial intelligence. Yet strategy as a distinct and coherent activity is sometimes seen as a more recent development, reflecting the increasing complexity of warfare in Enlightenment Europe of the eighteenth century. Larger armies, with more specialized skills, required professional generalship, not just to manage the action on the battlefield but to make practical use of violence for some wider aim. Strategy in this sense is intimately connected with the era of Clausewitz and Napoleon, although that didn't stop Clausewitz and his peers from reaching for more generalizable themes that might be applicable across a range of cultural and historical circumstances. This era also intensified the intellectualization of strategy as the *study* of war (as opposed to its practice), and Clausewitz himself epitomizes the process. Strategy emerged as a distinct academic discipline, one that could be subjected to the analytical rigors of natural science, after the style of the times—certainly one that drew on themes from philosophy and history (Gat 2001).

The etymology of the word "strategy" is much older, dating back to classical Greece of Thucydides and reflecting both the institutionalization of command and the increasingly technical challenge of command in war and battle (Heuser 2010). The wars of states, even early modern ones, required organization far beyond those of the hunter-gatherers or nomadic pastoralists. Strategy in turn demanded abilities beyond the battlefield—albeit that commanders could still be expected to lead from the front, at great personal risk, like their premodern antecedents. There were forces to raise, logistics to organize, and domestic politics on a larger canvass with which to reckon. Generalship nonetheless remained intimately connected with battle until Napoleon's time, with the emperor himself embodying the supreme political and military power of the French state. Thereafter, however, the appropriate separation of policy and strategy became a key debate in strategic discourse and is still a hardy perennial of staff college debates.

In the modern era, the term "strategy" has gained widespread usage in domains far beyond its military origins, especially in business and politics. As a result, as Hew Strachan notes, strategy has sometimes lost some of its coherence (Strachan 2005). And in the military domain, its meaning has changed too—strategy has been forced upward and outward by the development of a subordinate "operational" level of war during the twentieth century, largely as a consequence of the increasingly professionalized and specialized skills associated with modern industrial warfare and the huge resources and long-term planning that go into facilitating it. Additionally—in Western democracies, at least—operational warfare interposes a barrier between civilian political oversight and the activities of uniformed military. The result has sometimes been frustration on all sides: among the uniformed military who chafe at interference in properly tactical affairs by inexperienced politicians and the politicians who meet the resource demands of their generals only to be frustrated by the failure to attain the overall goals of strategy. Whatever its benefits, the "operational level" also obfuscates the essential Clausewitzian notion that war is politics all the way down. At the same time, it pushes strategy away from the action, both in time and space—stretching that intimate connection between political goal and violent activity.

Yet there is considerable value in trying to extend the scope of strategy beyond the conventional, historical usage, as Lawrence Freedman does in his wide-ranging overview, taking into account a broader epistemological basis for understanding strategy than most orthodox treatments (Freedman 2013). Freedman, like me, begins in evolutionary history by appraising the strategic interactions of other primates. He then ranges broadly, taking in business theory and the development of social sciences as well as more traditional military affairs. This has the great advantage of seeing strategy in its broader human context—of adversarial, competitive relations. Some of the psychology underpinning these may be similar, regardless of the particular competitive context. My focus, in contrast, is more narrowly on strategy *in conflict*. In this particular context, strategy is the purposeful use of violence for political ends. This definition is sufficiently broad to extend the scope of strategy beyond our species, and even beyond biological life, while still retaining a connection to its violent essence.

Enter Evolution

Evolutionary psychologists suggest that the goals we seek and the ways we seek them are ultimately connected to the onward propagation of genes (Dawkins 1987). This need not necessarily entail reproduction itself, since the continuation of the genes of kinsfolk who share genetic code will be almost the same, albeit in directly diminishing proportion to how closely related they are (Hamilton 1964). The result is the possibility of altruism (sacrificial behavior) toward others who share our genes, thereby explaining the suicidal behavior of social insects.

This basic underlying motivation is common to all biological life. But strategy is not common, at least not in the sense of the term employed here. Evolutionary processes have worked on humans to produce unique characteristics, most notably a sophisticated "theory of mind." These attributes in turn create the possibility of a rich human culture and localized patterns of behavior and thought (Barkow, Cosmides, and Tooby 1992). Theory of mind—the ability to intuit, albeit imperfectly, what others are thinking—is the basis of our tremendous adaptability and evolutionary success as a species. We have specialized in social brains—and later I'll argue that the threat of war was an important spur to that specialization. Cooperation amid sometimes violent competition is perhaps the key driver of human evolution. This delicate balance between competition and cooperation is the essence of politics. Thus "man is by nature a political animal," in the title of Peter Hatemi and Rose McDermott's account (Hatemi and McDermott 2011).

Other organisms must interact with their environments, which contain an array of hazards, including others of their own species. Yet while they may learn from that interaction via feedback loops, there is often a degree of automaticity to such behavior that disqualifies it from being strategic in a human sense. Some social animals may possess something like our theory of mind and be able to produce something akin to our strategic behavior. But there are still profound qualitative differences between their social strategizing and ours.

Some modesty about human strategizing is in order. In common with other animals, human evolution has done a good deal of the "learning" on our behalf, even though such embodied, hardwired adaptations can be limiting when the environment changes in any profound way. But humans also possess additional cognitive flexibility, thanks to our intense sociability, especially with nonkin. The possibility of parochial altruism for kin and "reciprocal altruism" for nonrelatives endows human strategy with a richness lacking even in other primates. Who should we trust to help us? Who may take advantage of us? We spend a good deal of our time reflecting on our relations with others and discussing it via our unique linguistic abilities. We also possess some uniquely human abilities for metacognition and rational reflection, via our conscious mind, which I discuss further in the next chapter.

These attributes endow human strategy with rich variety and an ever-changing character. Yet, despite this tremendous variety, the foundations of strategy remain inescapably psychological, because strategy entails pursuing selfish goals in an arena with other similar minds. The need to think strategically drove our evolution down particular pathways. If we see strategy as instrumental or purposeful, political, social, and violent, one master theme unites these, whatever the local context: strategy is, at its core, a psychological phenomenon (Payne 2015b).

Allowing that strategy is inherently psychological enables us to extend our understanding of warfare beyond the modern industrialized world, to earlier and radically different cultural expressions of strategy, including in human prehistory. It even allows us to extend our discussion beyond human experience to that of human ancestors and of other social animals that engage in something like strategic behavior. And, in the other direction, it allows us to peer into the future to explore the impact of artificial intelligence on strategic behavior.

Consider, for example, the psychological concepts of perception, judgment, curiosity, creativity, and imagination. All are integral to strategy and all elevate it above the automated, routinized response of simpler organisms in making decisions about how to respond to environmental competition in realizing goals. The extent to which a machine would be able to evince creative decision-making or be motivated by curiosity is the subject of cutting edge AI research. While there is considerable uncertainty about the prospects for AI of this sort, framing the issue in this way permits a more rigorous discussion than commonplace and breathless hyperbole about "machines destroying humanity."

One caveat: the distinction between human and other animals is not entirely clear cut. This question of psychology separates the war-like activities of an ant colony from those of a chimpanzee community. But what about the distinction between humans and chimps? Chimpanzees follow similar (but not identical) motivations and ways as do human communities (Wrangham and Glowacki 2012). For the ants, behavior is situationalist—driven by immediate environmental cues (Gordon 2011; Keller and Gordon 2009). Primates, by contrast, seem able to take a step back and reflect on group dynamics, including the perspectives of others. Still, even chimpanzee strategy is qualitatively different from human strategy because humans have a more sophisticated theory of mind.

Strategy Is Purposeful, Even If We Don't Know It

So strategy is both psychological and shaped by our sociability. And we can discern other broad features, applicable across species and human history. One is that strategy aims at some goal. The violence entailed in strategy is instrumental—it seeks to achieve something, rather than being nihilistic. That something need not be material gain, like resources or territory. These are the most obvious evolutionary imperatives, along with the opportunity to reproduce. But the goals of strategy could also be more existential in nature—and even then they may nonetheless have evolutionary value (for example, if resultant behaviors confer status or if it boosts resilience). Complicating things still further, sometimes the goals may be obscure to the strategists themselves (Payne 2015c). Indeed, decision-making can be shaped in the moment by a plethora of unconscious stimuli that influence how we decide to act and to what end (Eagleman 2011).

Sometimes the connection between our goals and the replication of genes is obscure. Consider religious motivations—the desire to please the gods through virtuous behavior, for example. The propensity to believe in supernatural, personified deities and to follow their dictates may be the result of an evolved tendency to see human-like agency lying behind events. That tendency could be the by-product of our extremely useful ability to imagine other minds, including minds not physically present. Moreover, imagining active deities, or even absent ancestors looking on from a distance, is an effective way of strengthening group identity and policing norms (Johnson 2016). These are adaptations that on the whole serve us well in an intensely social environment in which intuiting the intentions of others is of critical importance for our own well-being (Epley 2014).

Thus, any argument that strategy is instrumental clearly needs some caveats. Neither the purpose nor the ways in which strategy is pursued may be entirely clear to the conscious human agent who feels he or she is in control. Indeed, the promptings of our unconscious mind—quick, adaptive, and cognitively efficient—likely evolved ahead of our rich conscious human experience.

Even after we have acted, any attempt to intuit why we behaved in a particular way is tricky—plenty of reasons might occur to us as we consciously construct a plausible, satisfying narrative to retrospectively account for our behavior. Perhaps it's not entirely unjust to suggest that the conscious mind, the one conducting an internal monologue, is rather more a rationalizer than a rationalist. So, while we may flatter ourselves that we are conscious, deliberative agents who purposively shape our own destinies toward some clear end, our unconscious minds are typically hard at work applying evolved heuristics or simplified models to stream-line decision-making (Kahneman 2011). A powerful experiment by Benjamin Libet demonstrated this by showing that the motor neurons of a participant begin firing in preparation to move his hand well before the conscious decision to actu-ally move the hand was under way (Libet 1999). This is often (and in my view erroneously) seen as a challenge to free will, but at the very least it demonstrates vividly the activities of the unconscious mind and the arrival, sometime after that fact, of conscious awareness and conscious justification. Strategy, this view of the unconscious mind suggests, is sometimes improvisational and discerned through a glass darkly. It unfolds in real time according to a logic that is often dimly per-ceived, in pursuit of goals that are likewise obscure.

Meaning and Prestige as Strategic Goals

Can we say more than that the goals of strategy are related to evolution? Or even that they are sometimes obscure and even unconscious? Yes, but only by keeping our focus on the intensely social world in which we evolved. Of course humans need to be concerned with security, access to food, and reproductive success. Yet our intensely cooperative and encultured evolution has imbued human existence with a bewildering variety of possible additional goals, including some that at first blush seem to run directly counter to evolutionary logic (e.g., celibacy among priests or the desires of a kamikaze or modern-day suicide bomber). Even here, however, an evolutionary account is possible. It's just that the intermediate goal (extreme group loyalty) that serves the ultimate evolutionary goal (survival in a dense social network) is manifest in counterintuitive, and perhaps ultimately counterproductive, ways. Once again, strategy falls out of our social existence and the need to fit in and to understand what others want.

Two prominent social goals that animate strategic behavior are a search for meaning and a desire for prestige (Maslow 1968; Frankl 2011). The search for meaning, a distinctively human trait, reflects humans' ultrasociability and draws on our conscious capacity for abstract expression, communication, and self-reflection. If we don't understand what others intend or grasp how we fit into our larger social universe, we are disadvantaged. Moreover, this search for meaning fits well with the view of consciousness as rationalizer. We are motivated to construct a plausible and satisfying account of our own behavior. But satisfying in what ways? There are a number of possibilities. Leading contenders are the narratives that paint us in a favorable light: as being in control (an agency illusion); as likely to succeed (an optimism bias); and as rationalizing away failures and setbacks (Sharot 2012).

There is an important emotional dimension to meaning, for humans. On one dimension, meaning is relational—about categories and how they relate to one another. Intelligent machines are able to grasp this sort of categorical meaning and are getting better at it every day. But the emotional dimension of meaning is distinctively biological—an embodied response to a living organism's interaction with its environment. This is true of "basic" emotions that we likely share with many other animals, such as fear or rage, and is also true of the rich palate of social emotions that we derive from our interactions with other humans.

On prestige as a core human motivation, it's useful to distinguish between a dominance hierarchy that is common to primates and other social species, and a prestige hierarchy that is a distinctively human trait (though perhaps not exclusively so). Pronounced variations in the social lives of the great apes, species that are often compared with humans, have been observed. Chimpanzees and gorillas, for example, have distinctive social organization and reproductive strategies. They also have clear dominance hierarchies in which males compete to gain primacy, in part for access to food and in part for access to fertile females. Becoming the alpha male in a community of chimpanzees is a goal worth fighting for and sometimes even risking survival. Humans also compete for dominance—with physical attributes and displays contributing to establishing status. Napoleon Chagnon famously found that Yanomamö men who had killed were far more likely to be married and have children than those who had not (Chagnon 1988). Physical dominance persists as a factor even in modern, liberal, and ostensibly meritocratic settings. Business leaders are taller than average, and studies have found that women prefer men with deep voices or men whose dancing indicates higher testosterone levels.

Status can evidently still be earned from physical dominance. Yet humans also afford prestige to themselves and others that is not solely based on a capacity to inflict great violence. Jane Goodall noted how Mike, one of the chimpanzees she was following, attained alpha status by grabbing some gasoline cans and making a tremendous racket with them—that is, using tools to enhance his display (Goodall 1991). Here can be seen the rudiments of prestige: the use of tools or skill in a way that gains status. Our human prestige hierarchies are elevated to greater levels of abstraction, and the connection with dominance is often negligible. But prestige is a signal of cooperative value; we emulate successful behavior, as all advertising executives know, and we seek to gain the trust of prestigious individuals.

Social psychologists often ascribe human behavior in groups to the desire for status or esteem because, from an evolutionary perspective, being valued by the group brings rewards. In our rich and diverse human culture, exactly *what* will earn prestige is open to a degree of local interpretation, as anyone boasting of skill in alchemy in modern-day academia might attest. More broadly, however, prestige rests on the possession of skills that are valued, scarce, and difficult to acquire—or at least the appearance of possessing such.

Culture gives us a bewildering variety of possible ends, both individually and on behalf of the group. These concrete ends (to get the job, learn a musical instrument, see the world) are pursued in the interest of intermediate objectives (meaning and prestige) that in themselves are evolutionarily important. No wonder human strategy is so complex! And no wonder that there is an enduring debate about the causes of conflict. Conceiving of strategy as resting on evolved psychology draws attention to material motivations—for food, sex, territory, or physical security. From the outset, however, our intensely social world presented more subtle goals to track, reputation and status included.

Status also applies collectively. The concept of a "national interest" animates many modern accounts of international affairs, especially those with a "realist" bent. Usually this is taken to mean a focus on securing the state against physical threat. The implication is that statesmen ought to focus narrowly on the power of rival groups in order to make sure that their own relative power does not lag behind. This may allow a parsimonious view of state behavior, but it bears little relation to the actual goals or behaviors of human society. One leading classical realist, Hans Morgenthau, posited the existence of a psychological basis to international relations. But his view of psychology concentrated on dominance hierarchies, which he attributed to an innate "will to power" in men (Morgenthau 1954). Morgenthau's narrow interpretation of what motivated humans largely overlooked cooperative tendencies and prestige hierarchies. And yet, if the imperatives of international society were as obvious as many realists supposed, there would scarcely be the need for the constant cajoling by realist thinkers like Morgenthau for political leaders to pursue the national interest and to guard against the insidious danger of letting their values cloud judgment.

The modern psychologically informed view of group behavior is, by contrast, more empirically robust and nuanced. If we allow that the group itself is constituted in large measure by its culture—the shared ideas about who it is and what it does—then it is impossible to conceive of interests as separate from values. This point is recognized by no less a realist than Henry Kissinger, notwithstanding Kissinger's realist inclinations not to let moral values override more pressing strategic concerns. The most concise statement of the matter comes from Ned Lebow, writing that "our interests depend on identity, and identity in turn depends on community" (Lebow 2008, 354). How we behave is shaped by what our culture defines as appropriate, honorable, or prestigious.

Another layer can be added to this complex of social motivations: connecting meaning and prestige with the desire to belong. Social and experimental psychology provides much evidence that shows our bias toward salient in-groups, the ways in which we see seek justice for our group and empathize more with in-group members, and our intense unease at being excluded from groups (Brewer 1999). Threats to our own lives accentuate the extent to which we identify with the group, as predicted by terror management theory; it is as though our search for individual meaning becomes intimately bound up in the narrative and identity of the group (Solomon, Greenberg, and Pyszczynski 1991). Group prestige is closely identified with our own prestige.

This all makes for a much richer tapestry than the blunt "will to power" that underpinned Morgenthau's essentially Nietzschean analysis. Yet it all starts with the same evolutionary pressures that shape our need to connect socially. Belonging, identity, and meaning combine to motivate human social behavior, including in competition with other groups. Indeed, as adherents of self-categorization theory argue, the in-group itself is typically defined in contrast to out-group identity, so that the potential for conflict is inherent in the way in which humans categorize themselves socially (Turner 1987). Because our ability to intuit what others intend is somewhat haphazard, theory of mind notwithstanding, we might easily misread the ambiguous behaviors of other groups (Mercer 1996). At this point our prickly desire for status and justice kicks in.

In sum, understanding the evolved psychology of humans, including the profound need to belong to a society, can help us understand much of our strategic behavior, including our intergroup and interstate behaviors. No wonder "realists" in international relations need constantly to urge a focus on security: leaders in the real world seem easily distracted by projects of personal prestige or by their moral codes. But if prestige is integral to evolutionary success, serving as a complement to or even a substitute for dominance through brute force, then such seemingly obtuse behaviors become readily explicable.

Strategic Violence

This book focuses on strategy in a narrow sense—one that is authentic to the military etymology of the word. Of course, as Strachan and Freedman observe, that focus has widened in the modern era so that pretty much any situation, especially one marked by competition and complexity, calls for a strategy. This is particularly true in the business world, which has adopted the term wholeheartedly—perhaps even in the unconscious hope that some of the positive characteristics of the military might enhance their own image, such as its dynamism or even the macho, dominance hierarchy of the warrior. Strategy in this guise retains some of its key elements, including of choosing between conflicting goals, determining the best path ahead, or marshaling scarce resources. It can be oppositional and antagonistic, too, just as it can be for card players sitting across a poker table or teams mixing it up on the rugby field. But strategy as it pertains to war is distinguished from the other variants by collective violence—whether actually inflicted or merely threatened.

This is a Clausewitzian point too. He placed battle and fighting at the center of his theories of war, in part to contrast the earlier era that had prized maneuver and other stratagems by which rulers could attain goals without risking valuable resources in battle. But even in that more genteel eighteenth-century Europe, violence never disappeared. The relative importance of battle might shift with changing cultural circumstances, but the violence itself remains the distinctive feature of strategy. In the nuclear era, strategy often focused on the threat of violence rather than its actual employment—the "grammar" of strategy (Clausewitz's term) took on a distinctive feel even though the essential "logic" of violence remained. Strategy, as ever in human conflict, retained its connection to the possibility of killing. In the conception popularized by Thomas Schelling and other nuclear weapons strategists of the twentieth century, strategy is a special form of communication: communication by violence.

This definition is deliberately flexible—it allows comparison between illiterate groups of hunter-gatherers and space-age superpowers. It brings the "wars" of chimpanzees within the ambit of strategic studies but perhaps not the wars of ants. Violence, even instrumental or purposeful violence, is insufficient as a marker of strategy. To be sure, ants live intensely social lives that sometimes entail great violence against rival colonies. They meet my yardstick for strategy insofar as they fight collectively with other groups of their species. These "wars" of annihilation might even be adjudged "political" without doing too much damage to the term, since they are driven by the ultimate issue of who gets what. Ants, like other individuals in resource-constrained environments, are driven to maximize their chances of reproductive success—which requires food and security from predation. As agents responding to environmental inputs, including social interaction with conspecifics, ants might strike biologists as strategic actors.

Still, by itself, that social violence is not enough to count as strategy. The strategic machinations of chimpanzees and humans possess a cognitive flexibility and sophistication that makes them altogether qualitatively different from those of ants. The politics of the ant colony are more basic than those of social primates because ants, while sometimes locked in conflict with rival groups, do not conduct their social lives within the colony along the same lines as apes (that is, via intricate patterns of interrelationships featuring cooperation and conflict or reciprocal altruism and exploitation). They are small individual cogs in a large collective, all in the service of the nest and its queen, whose DNA they share. They do not exhibit the sort of cognitive flexibility that typifies human strategy—encompassing planning, imagination, and communication.

Ants, by contrast, are executing more predictable routines in consequence of immediate prompting from their environments that produce particular behavioral responses. Their goals in warfare are tightly linked to the evolutionary imperatives of resource possession and genetic advancement. Humans may share the same ultimate motivations, but humans can attain them via a broad range of intermediate and proximate goals—through revenge, for example, or through the desire to win prestige—because they live in a social world that is characterized by greater cognitive capacity to reflect on what others intend.

So, savage brutality and wars of annihilation are insufficient evidence for strategy, which additionally requires politics and minds. Ants instinctively responding to immediate environmental prompts in ways that have hitherto proved adaptive may produce complex behaviors—but these are merely instinctive, innate, and essentially mindless. Similarly, ant-like artificial intelligence can execute strategy, but it cannot devise it in the sense the term is used here. The social world of the ant or automaton does not require a theory of mind or an attempt to gauge what other individuals want. This theory of mind is the basis of politics, at least for politics broadly defined as the negotiation between agents in a society whose goals conflict. Without politics like this, there is no society on behalf of whom strategy is enacted. Ant society is a collective of individual agents—but the autonomy of these agents is more basic and constrained than the autonomy of agents in human or chimpanzee societies.

We might perhaps shift our perspective upward from ant to colony to see the agent-environment boundary as circumscribing the colony itself rather than the individuals it contains. The automatic behaviors of individuals within an ant collective produce an intelligence that is *distributed* across the group. Together the group exhibits complex behaviors that are beyond the ability of any one member—a "hive mind," to mix species in the metaphor. But even then this hive mind lacks the capacity for self-reflection that typifies human strategy.

Thinking of strategy in these abstract terms—social, political, reflective, violent—opens the possibility to consider a startling new development: an artificial intelligence that in both motive and method may depart radically from biological modes of strategic thought. Will the social lives of AI agents be closer to that of ants or chimps? Perhaps both are possible. Or perhaps they will be entirely different altogether.

Uncertainty and Chance

One final dimension of strategy is that it involves decisions made amid uncertainty. Carl von Clausewitz wrote, "In the whole range of human activities, war most closely resembles a game of cards" (Clausewitz 1993, 97). Note that he did not reference chess, a game that often strikes people as a decent analogy for strategic affairs and which was for many years the benchmark test for artificial intelligence. Card playing is an analogy that faithfully captures some important aspects of strategy: poker is certainly dynamic, with each new card changing the balance of possibilities, although being iterative it is somewhat less dynamic than the more fluid proposition of war itself. Poker is also adversarial, and the stakes involved can be very real to the high-stakes gambler. Like war, cards involve incomplete information: the actors do not know exactly what cards the others possess, and they do not know how sensitive to risk other players are. Poker and war are both bound with chance—the odds are so complex as to be incalculable. Unlike chess, poker involves imperfect and asymmetrical knowledge on both sides. And it's an emotional proposition, especially if the stakes are high.

In the final analysis, however, card games lack two key elements of strategy: they are not violent, at least not ideally, and they do not typically involve collective decision-making. Accordingly, there is no agent-principal problem of the sort that marks real-world strategy, where groups have to come to some agreement about what goals to produce and then, typically, must delegate responsibility for executing the agreed-on approach to some subset of the group.

Imperfect though it is, Clausewitz's famous analogy is a favorite of mine, perhaps because of the place of chance in strategic affairs. Yes, there are probabilities and calculations to be made. But knowledge is necessarily imperfect in a game of poker, even if you are a devil of a card counter. The analogy of war and poker is intriguing when it comes to artificial intelligence, not least because the complexity of the game seemed to be beyond machines. If they could win against humans at poker, how far might that reveal something important about their strategic potential? Modern AI can comfortably beat humans at chess and has solved checkers (making it impossible to beat). It comfortably outperforms humans at many classic 1980s arcade games. Even at Go, the board game popular in east Asia where there are myriad possible moves (more even than atoms in the universe), a modern AI can now routinely beat the very best human adversary (Tromp and Farnebäck 2007; Silver et al. 2016). Poker was thought by many to be beyond an AI—but recently an AI took on and beat high-class human poker players over an extended series of games (Metz 2017). It was a startling achievement, given the complexities and asymmetries involved. In both Go and poker showdowns, AI players made moves that surprised observers by departing radically from strategies that most expert humans would make.

However, the poker analogy goes only so far. War is an even more complex proposition since a range of possible objectives exist—and even the protagonists themselves may not know what they want until put to the test, still less what an adversary is after. Thus strategy contains an intensely improvisational and dynamic quality, not least since prior to the application of force (or a threat) it is impossible to gauge with any degree of certainty what the effect will be on adversary behaviors. Strategy lacks the structure of the poker game, which is where Clausewitz's great analogy ultimately comes up short. There can be no "solving" human strategy through the "brute force" of huge computing power, or even via the sort of probabilistic reasoning employed by a champion poker AI.

Clausewitz employs two additional analogies that chime with the analysis here: he likens war to a duel and to a wrestling match. Both of these capture the idea that violence is intimately connected to strategy. The duel is especially insightful because it suggests a role for honor—a key motivation in strategy, whether we explicitly acknowledge it or not—and for rules. The antagonists understand that they must behave in a certain fashion appropriate to the situation. They may be combatants, but they are also members of a collective society, bound by that society's norms and obligations. What, specifically, is considered honorable and what rules and rituals must be followed may vary widely between cultures. The wrestling match analogy, by contrast, suggests that violence can break these bounds of convention. Anything goes, in a passionate struggle to dominate. Caught up in the intensity of the moment, we might well lose sight of the original dispute or the goals for which we embarked on war. Along those lines, Clausewitz balanced the rationality of war against its emotionality, or logic against passion.

Each of the three Clausewitzian analogies captures something of war and the strategy that shapes it. Strategy entails violence; it is social and emotional; it involves making decisions where the odds are uncertain. And so it is inescapably psychological.

Conclusion: Strategy as Art

The argument throughout this book is that strategy has evolved, first as an expression of human evolution and then—with increasing variation and complexity—in response to our "cultural evolution." The great cultural variety in strategic behaviors is a function of our evolved disposition to form cultures. Now we stand on the cusp of nonbiological cognition as a result of artificial intelligence.

There is another commonplace analogy, this time between art and strategy. Both activities were unleashed by the cognitive explosion described earlier. Neanderthals may have produced art, but no animals we know of can be said to do so, even if chimpanzees "paint" and engage in seemingly ritualistic behaviors (Kühl et al. 2016; Lincoln 2005). This analogy with art is worth further reflection since the two activities draw on similar cognitive abilities, including imagination and improvisation. They are always nested within a social context, but they also act to shape that context. It is a cliché to think of war as art, thanks largely to Sun Tzu and myriad successor theorizers that use the same *pro forma* title: *The Art of War*. Clausewitz, notwithstanding his landmark attempt to discern regular patterns underlying war, was very much of the view that theories about war leaned more to art than science. Like art, strategy evolved in humans as the answer to a particular problem—how to conduct lives of intense sociability. In both cases the group and the search for meaning underpinned its development (Dutton 2010). Much in strategy falls out of that sociability—both when it comes to the goals for which we fight and the ways we do so. Sociability, we will see, helps explain the importance of scale, the utility of surprise and deception, and the propensity to escalate, especially in response to challenges to esteem—all enduring features of human strategy.

There is a connection between our human evolution and our strategic behaviors, however distant our modern, liberal social world seems to be from the world inhabited by the hunter-gatherers of early human history. At a deep foundational level the instincts selected over millennia that favor the onward propagation of our genes continue to motivate us and shape our behaviors today. We can trace the roots of human propensity for organized social violence to the inclination to fight for access to important resources, including food, territory, and, for males especially, sex. Similarly, we can trace the evolution of the pronounced human tendencies for altruism and empathy to the need to work closely and harmoniously within our social groups, including with nonkin members.

An AI, at least one that operates on nonbiological "hardware," need not necessarily share these dispositions. Consider the possibility of its possession of a fundamental, often unconscious desire to advance its "genetic code." Perhaps we can think of its evolving algorithms as somehow synonymous with our DNA. I disagree, but even then there is no a priori reason to suppose that this might involve the same competitive resource struggles between and within "species" of AI as that which guides human behavior. An AI need not, therefore, be subject to the same proxy motivations—the desire for status or the need to control scarce resources, including reproductive resources. In sum, the world of the nonbiological AI need not have as its foundational premise the sometimes intense competition for "survival of the fittest" gene. The same is not true, however, of AIs that function as an amalgam of digital and biological systems—and in this increasingly plausible world of augmented humans (and other biological species, too) we might expect strategy to retain something of its evolved dimensions. That possibility is what concludes my study of evolution and strategy, but I start with the first cognitive "revolution": the evolution of the human mind.

CHAPTER 2

Evolutionary Strategy

STRATEGY IS INTIMATELY CONNECTED TO OUR HUMAN PSYCHOLOGY. Both human goals and the ways humans go about realizing them are heavily influenced by our evolved biology, part of which is our evolved psychology. The notion that our minds, just like our bodies, are the product of evolution has been gaining ground in recent decades. This contrasts with an earlier scholarly tendency—especially prominent in the social sciences—to see human minds as extensively molded through exposure to culture. In this view, our very sense of reality was largely the product of social knowledge (Berger and Luckmann 1991). Many researchers across different disciplines stressed the primacy of experience in shaping behavior, with the attendant notion that minds are a highly labile tabula rasa (Pinker 2003).

This approach was appealing since it chimed with a progressive, meritocratic understanding of development and education. Adherents of this "cultural turn" emphatically and correctly rejected the deterministic flavor of many earlier attempts to apply evolutionary theory to human behavior—notably the pernicious logic of social Darwinism. The idea that humanity could be classified by race, gender, class, or nation was especially repugnant in the aftermath of genocidal world conflict, as was the attendant idea that social groups themselves were the category that was the subject of natural selection—each pitted in zero sum conflict for the "survival of the fittest."

This social "constructivist" view rapidly gained ground in international relations theory during the 1990s, just as developments in biology, genetics, archaeology, and anthropology were shifting the focus back toward an evolutionary perspective. That shift was slow in coming. In the scholarly climate of the 1970s, the first serious attempts to revive evolutionary thinking in the social world via what was termed "sociobiology" ran into controversy (Wilson 1980). Its cause was undermined by flatly dubious suggestions that sociobiology could account for differences in intelligence between races or in mathematical ability between genders (Herrnstein 1994). Evolutionary psychology applied haphazardly and without rigor to controversial topics has often served to entrench existing prejudices rather than to uncover the ways in which evolution actually shapes modern social conditions. Thankfully, much of the heat has now left the debate, in large part because the evidential bar is rigorously enforced but also because the consensus view has shifted. It now allows a more nuanced view in which genes are important influences on behavior but rarely in a deterministic manner. Instead, the mainstream view is that they create tendencies, or repertoires, of possible behaviors.

Violent Human Nature

Unease with crude social Darwinist thinking perhaps fed the view commonly found in academic anthropology that humans were an essentially peaceful species whose war-like behavior was a modern artifact. Dating at least to Jean-Jacques Rousseau's view of a pacific "state of nature," this anthropological weltanschauung gained ground in the twentieth century, especially during the deep pessimism of the inter- and postwar years when the fruits of modernity seemed most dubious (Rousseau 1984). Lawrence Keeley offers a succinct account in his compelling rebuttal, *War before Civilisation* (Keeley 1996). Seeing war as a modern cultural artifact rather than as an inherent feature of human nature still appeals to some scholars (Fry 2007, 2015). But, as with the "blank slate" view of human nature, the rosy take on premodern culture has lost ground in recent decades.

The evidence against it is incomplete but cumulatively persuasive, from animal comparisons, where it transpires that chimpanzees are far from peaceful cooperators; from ethnographic studies of modern hunter-gatherer communities, which have found dramatically high levels of casualties amid endemic warfare; to the archaeological record—sparse though it is—where evidence of violent deaths abounds (Diamond 2013; Wrangham and Glowacki 2012; Gat 2006). A powerful case can be marshaled that lethal intergroup conflict has been a long-standing feature of human behavior. Where there is intergroup violence, there is scope for strategy.

What does it mean to say that strategy in modern humans reflects human evolution? It says more, surely, than that early mankind practiced strategy; rather, my argument here is that mankind's evolution was in large measure shaped by the need to do strategy effectively. Strategy and human evolution are inseparable partners. The sort of cognitive processes we possess are intimately connected to the need to coordinate effectively to deal with the threat of predation, especially by other humans. Enlightenment philosophers like Rousseau liked to speculate about a "state of nature" in which man existed before modern society came into being. Radically different conclusions were conceivable, such was a scarcity of knowledge about prehistory. Famously, Thomas Hobbes saw the state of nature as a violent place—all against all—while for Rousseau the situation was the opposite (Hobbes 1982).

But this debate itself was fundamentally flawed: there never was a "state of nature" before some sort of "social contract" emerged to regulate the behavior of men in larger societies. The modern debate about violence is different. There is no similar view of man leading an atomized life, away from community, just a debate about the parameters of that community life. Hobbes, it transpired, was closer to the mark, insofar as prehistoric life could be highly violent and unstable. But his view was incomplete: prehistoric life also contained the seeds of a more peaceful world to come because of the need to cooperate, and thus understand, what others intended.

Dunbar's Number

Early human communities likely looked a bit like modern hunter-gatherer communities: humans lived in fairly small groups, many related to some degree; they fragmented into ever smaller groups to forage and hunt during the day but came together in larger bands at night for security. On occasions, even larger groups would meet—to manage their relations together in the same territory, arbitrating disputes, and perhaps intermarrying. This sort of fission-fusion society is common to other species, including other primates. In humans, the exact parameters might vary depending on the physical environment, such as the amount of resources versus the density of the population subsisting off it. Clues as to the size of early human communities come from the excavation of their settlements but also from an inventive study of brain size.

Robin Dunbar and colleagues argue that there is a relationship between cognitive architecture and the capacity of a primate to sustain social relations. Specifically, they argue that the size of the neocortex positively correlates with the number of individuals with whom the animal can map meaningful social relations (Dunbar 1992). When graphed, the result is a clear linear relationship between neocortex size and social group size. Extrapolating from their graph suggests that for humans, the "natural" size of a social group is about 150 individuals, which has become known as Dunbar's number. We need to extrapolate because human society no longer conforms to the parameters of the relationship—at least, not in an immediately apparent way. Modern human groups come in all sorts of sizes, and humans evince a capacity for tremendous flexibility when it comes to forging collective identities. Nonetheless, Dunbar and colleagues detect the influence of this evolutionary constraint on social network size in some modern-day settings, including mobile phone usage and online social networks (Miritello et al. 2013). Others have observed how the structures of modern armed forces operate on similar lines (Payne 2015a; Junger 2011).

In fact, the focal group of hunter-gatherer societies—kinship bands that spend much of their time together—are often smaller than the headline number of 150; it is somewhere in the range of 30 to 50 people. Napoleon Chagnon's research with the Yanomamö people of the Amazon found that larger groups almost always split into smaller, neighboring settlements, usually over some grievance (Chagnon 2014). Dunbar's number suggests an upper limit of what is cognitively possible for humans. For a society to function together, the members must be able to gauge the motivations of other people within the group and they must have some understanding of how each person fits within that group. This social networking requires what psychologists call a "theory of mind": the ability to conceive of an interior life in another individual. This ability need not be entirely conscious, since many of our intuitions about other people occur subconsciously, including those related to sexual attraction and aggression. Humans have a sophisticated ability to intuit what others might be thinking, though we often make mistakes in doing so, some systematic (Epley 2014). We are able to conceive of several orders of "intentionality"—we are not just aware that an interlocutor has a mind but that this mind might be thinking about someone else who has a mind, and that that person in turn might be thinking about someone else again. Going beyond this level of intentionality (I know that he knows that she knows that he knows) is impossible for most of us but, in any event, this is sufficient to map the social dynamics of small groups of the sort that Dunbar identified.

The point is that even before their emergence as a distinct species, our ancestors were living in groups, and those groups existed in relationship with other groups that were intensely social. This need to manage relations within and between groups is the very essence of strategy. In the case of humans (and some other primates) it turns out that collective and individual violence is an integral part of these group dynamics. Because violence is an inescapable feature of premodern man's life, thinking about violence (again, not necessarily consciously) has been a feature of our evolution.

Evolved Strategies

What sort of evolved cognitive abilities are relevant to strategy? One primary ability is the capacity to intuit with some degree of accuracy what other people believe. The second is the capacity to deceive others of one's own intentions, the better to mislead and surprise them. A third is the capacity to cooperate effectively with others, which again requires the ability to intuit what others want.

These skills are evident in some degree in other primates, though are most fully realized in humans. Robert Trivers detects their essence in many biological relations between organisms: depressingly, it lies in the ability to deceive (Trivers 2013). Earlier, Trivers had elaborated the mechanism through which humans cooperate with nonkin, which is the basis of our unique ability to extend our social networks far beyond what Dunbar's number suggests is the evolved limit (Trivers 1971). The "reciprocal altruist" cooperates with others at personal cost. The altruist does so in the expectation that, on average, there will be some payback in the future (hence reciprocal) even at risk that their partner(s) may "free ride" off their efforts and not return the favor.

The extent to which an individual cooperates along these lines varies according to individual propensity, cultural and group norms, the probability of payback materializing, and the probability of getting away with cheating or shirking on one's commitment. There is more chance of payback in small communities located geographically close together, where everyone knows everyone else, so that reputations can form and interactions are frequent—as in an early hunter-gatherer community.

A range of implications follows, including a propensity to attribute the behaviors of others to their interior attitudes, even though that may not be warranted. Known as the fundamental attribution error, this cognitive glitch can explain much about strategic misperception (Ross 1977). Indeed, it helps explain our general tendency to see human agency underpinning events even when it does not. Why? Perhaps because being overly sensitive in this way usually pays off: better to be safe than sorry.

We also have an acute radar for deception or inauthenticity—anything that indicates our interlocutor is not to be trusted. Trivers and Dan Ariely separately note our propensity for self-deception about how trustworthy we are: we believe ourselves to be good reciprocal altruists the better to deceive others, as Trivers argues, and the better to balance our cheating with our conception of ourselves as essentially good, as Ariely suggests (Ariely 2012).

Who, then, to trust? Culture becomes a badge of belonging and, as the group expands beyond those one knows intimately, it becomes a proxy for reputation.

This privileges the capacity to recognize and categorize other people as belonging to some group or other. Still, notwithstanding our suspicion of cultural outsiders, we have an inbuilt tendency to overcooperate and err on the side of trusting strangers. Trust is earned through repeated interaction. Yet even in one-shot versions of the "prisoner's dilemma," a famous game theory situation structured so as to favor noncooperative behavior, real-world participants tend to cooperate (in contrast to their utility maximizing "rational" counterparts) (Kiyonari, Tanida, and Yamagashi 2000). Why? It may be that our willingness to do so is in part a consequence of the threat of war. For that to be so, the payoffs from cooperating in an insecure environment must be significant.

In sum, humans have evolved ways of thinking that are at once both embodied and social and reflect the particular contingencies of our evolutionary history. We cooperate with those we know and trust, that is, those who belong to our group. We demand fairness and justice on behalf of our group, and we seek revenge against those who violate group norms. The basic tenets of strategy come from the ways in which our needs in life are realized through the performance of the group—including against rival groups—and of our own standing within the group. For the group to work well we need to understand intentions and cooperate to mutual advantage. Cooperation, deception, surprise: all these are the basis of human strategy.

Of Chimps and Men

Other social primates face similar challenges to humans, but none has evolved the same revolutionary package of cognitive abilities that enables human strategy. There is some debate about what constitutes this package, but constituent elements include a capacity for language, cultural learning (especially tool-making), and a capacity for "mind reading." In reality, the various elements are probably interrelated. They are unified by their connection to our social world. Cooking, tools, language—all freed-up time in the day, facilitated more intense and creative social interactions, and allowed social groups to adapt flexibly to novel environments.

This social motor also connects to our bodily evolution. Evolutionary psychologists speculate about the evolution of the human fist in order to inflict violence and about the shape of the human head as a way of deflecting it (Horns, Jung, and Carrier 2015). Others consider the unique attributes of the human shoulder joint, which is very different in construction from those of the other great apes

(N. Roach et al. 2013). Humans have the ability to throw hard and fast and to perform the complex mental calculations of aiming off to hit moving targets. The human shoulder joint thus highlights the coevolution of mind and body and demonstrates that the human mind is both embodied and encultured. Together these attributes came together in crafting projectile weaponry and in the skill to use it, including in coordination with other hunters and warriors.

Humans are physically weaker than chimpanzees, probably because much of our energy was instead diverted into sustaining increasingly energy-hungry brains capable of managing increasingly social interactions. These social skills readily compensate for our lesser physical abilities. In fact, they are an overcompensation since social collaboration, shared information, and specialization have proved radically more effective than brute force and have allowed humans to extend their range globally and become an apex predator.

By comparison, the other great apes are far less socially sophisticated—though their abilities are nonetheless impressive. Like humans, chimpanzees cooperate, including in hunting and in waging "war" against rivals. They can apparently adopt specialist roles in conducting ambushes of colobus monkeys, funneling prey into the arms of a waiting executioner (BBC Earth 2011). They can use tools, such as swinging branches and clattering tin cans to intimidate rivals, or strip branches to "fish" for termites in termite mounds. Yet there is nothing even remotely approaching the cultural sophistication of humans.

Animal Culture and Intentionality

If we take a broad enough view of culture, we can argue that chimpanzees and other primates—even other mammals, like whales and dolphins—possess culture too (Whitehead 2015). To the extent that culture simply implies learning, whales and dolphins express it in their local dialects and in their use of sponges. Monkeys learn to use stones as tools to gain access to nuts (Shumaker 2011). Chimpanzees employ sticks to "fish" for termites in culturally specific ways that differ from one community to another (Goodall 1991). "Culture" in these very basic senses provides a way of flexibly responding to particular environmental cues. "Learning" a particular culture can be achieved at a basic level by copying what others are doing and at a more sophisticated level by deducing what others are *trying* to achieve. Primates certainly demonstrate imitative learning, even though chimpanzees seem better at it when reared by humans rather than chimpanzees (Tomasello, Savage-Rumbaugh, and Kruger 1993). But there is less certainty about their capacity to learn from watching others trying to achieve something—which is a more flexible and imaginative act that can rapidly produce new, innovative responses.

This sort of learning requires a particular cognitive ability to observe what others are doing and intuit an inner motivation from their behavior—and then innovate new behaviors in order to achieve the same goal. There is intentionality here of a high order: not only must the agent be aware of other agents' behaviors, they also must be able to intuit that those agents are inwardly motivated to achieve a goal. Chimpanzee culture—like that of other socially encultured animals—may not meet such high standards. Equally, there is scant evidence of cumulative culture and the progressive refinement of cultural techniques over generations of learning—another attribute of human culture.

Part of the solution to flexible social learning might be empathy. Another part is an understanding of perspective. Yet chimpanzees possess both these aptitudes to some degree. Empathy involves an intuitive emotional response to seeing another agent's behavior in a given situation. Frans de Waal ascribes empathetic abilities to the chimpanzees he has observed in both captivity and experimental situations (de Waal 2012, 2013). This sort of instinctive response is integral to social relations: a friend is in distress and the chimpanzee automatically comforts it, often through mutual grooming and physical contact. As Dunbar notes, such physical interaction manages the inevitable tensions of social living in small groups. But by the same token it limits the scalability of such groups since the demands of foraging and sleeping leave only so much time in the day for conducting one-on-one grooming sessions (Dunbar 2014). Moreover, empathy is instinctive. Other apes might empathize, as de Waal contends, and respond to the feelings thereby engendered. But such empathy seems innate and instinctive, perhaps working on the basis of "mirror" neurons (the specialized cells in the brain that may reproduce networks implicated in an action just by watching another performing it) (Gallese and Goldman 1998).

A second cognitive feature that promotes learning is the ability to understand perspective. Chimpanzees have some aptitude here, too. Most notably they are able to recognize when others have seen something, such as a hidden stash of food (Bräuer, Call, and Tomasello 2007). Crows show a similar perspective-taking capacity (Cornell, Marzluff, and Pecoraro 2012). There are limits, however: while chimpanzees can deduce what another chimpanzee has perceived, they seem less able to intuit what that *means* to the other individual (Martin and Santos 2016).

We can describe this relative deficiency as being one of "intentionality"—a term that philosophers use to describe our ability to refer to third-party objects and ideas. Chimpanzees seemingly have a clear concept of self, at least as demonstrated in paint spot tests, where the forehead of the animal is daubed with paint, which it then recognizes on seeing its reflection in the mirror (Gallup 1970). But their view on other "selves" is seemingly less well developed (Heyes 1994; Bräuer, Call, and Tomasello 2007).

Humans, by contrast, possess tremendous capacity for reflection on meaning—including what things mean to others. We have a rich theory of mind, or the notion that others actually have a mind that is similar to our own. While far from perfect and typically overestimated, our abilities here have been good enough to allow much deeper social interaction and sophisticated cultural learning. We can see what others intend even if they are unable to achieve it. And we can intuit what they believe.

This is a powerful imaginative act: I know something about your mind by presuming an inner-state as subjectively experienced by you. This distinctive human ability is integral to the construction of richly cultured groups and equally to the generation of sophisticated strategy. It is also suggestive of a sophisticated capacity for *conscious* reasoning. Chimps, self-aware and able to perceive another's perspective, nonetheless cannot do this. We can't ask, and our animal experiments may be overly anthropocentric, but it seems reasonable to conclude that chimps' conscious experience of the world is different from ours and altogether less socially adept.

Neuroscientists searching for the systems in the brain that correlate with consciousness have reached no settled consensus, although there are some good working theories. Chimpanzee brains share some common structural similarities with humans but also many differences (Gómez-Robles, Hopkins, and Sherwood 2013). Differences in the relative size of the prefrontal cortex are likely implicated in the ability for "meta-cognition," that is, thinking about thinking in a self-aware fashion. The human prefrontal cortex is both much larger overall and larger in proportion to the rest of the brain. But more than scale may be involved in achieving reasoning. Specialist areas dedicated to language recognition and generation (Wernicke and Broca's area) may also be involved in social reasoning, and again, there is some evidence of similar areas in chimpanzee brains (Gannon et al. 1998). Anatomically, then, there is considerable uncertainty about the mechanisms that distinguish humans from chimpanzees. But there is, we will see, a strong evolutionary case for how humans developed their remarkable abilities.

Chimps Are "Rational" Strategists, Contra Humans

One further point is worth making about the mind-reading abilities of humans and chimpanzees: it may not always be a strategic advantage to reason as humans do.

This is a finding worth keeping in mind when the discussion later turns to artificial intelligence. In a recent experiment that involved two-player adversarial relations, chimpanzees outperformed their human counterparts. Specifically, they developed strategies that were closer to the mathematically optimum solution to the problem they faced (Martin et al. 2014). The challenge in question pitted two individuals against one another, pressing a left or right button on a touch screen. One player was rewarded if its choice matched its adversary's, the other if it mismatched. All that was required was the ability to anticipate what one's rival would choose next. All players had to go on were the rival's choices in the previous rounds. As an added complication, the payoffs associated with each option could be varied so that one button would deliver larger winnings, provided it was the right option. Chimpanzees had an unerring ability to respond to these payoff changes, strategizing closely to the optimum solution.

Why did the humans fare worse? The study's authors speculated that human capacity for language and categorization had been earned at the expense of pattern recognition and perception, at which the chimpanzees remained adept. This is possible, though it does take a rather zero-sum view of cognitive abilities. I would highlight instead another uniquely human capability—intentionality—as the likely culprit. The human players were trying to put themselves inside the mind of their adversaries. That is, humans were strategizing on the basis of mind reading and not on the basis of probabilities and payoffs. Language and categorization are certainly important features of human cognition in which they surpass other primates (especially when it comes to the categorization of abstract meanings), but they are also manifestations of our intense sociability—the bedrock of which is our sense of others as autonomous agents with their own perceptions and beliefs. So strong is this sense of the inner lives of others that we cannot switch it off and engage in an alternative, more mathematically rational approach to strategy.

What might humans gain from being worse than chimps at finding an optimum strategy in adversarial games like this? The answer lies in the intense sociability of humans, even compared to the obviously social world of their fellow primates. Our theory of mind is the basis of rich cooperative relationships within human society. Being good at cooperating—understanding intentionality and communicating through language—has allowed our group sizes to expand and to forge mutually advantageous relationships on the basis of trust and comparative advantage. As individuals we may not outperform chimpanzees in the narrow ordered universe of two-person strategy games, but then those games differ from many of the real challenges in the social world of humans, where cooperation for mutual gain rather than zero-sum antagonistic relationships are typical.

The headlines of newspaper articles covering this chimpanzee performance suggested an alarming finding: chimpanzees are better strategists than humans. And so they were, in the narrow sense of the game. And in the chimpanzees' environmental niche, some challenges loosely correspond to the sorts of cognition that the chimpanzees in the experiment ably demonstrate. Among humans, however, the typical situation may be rather different.

Social Theories of Cognition

How did we end up with this sort of mind? Dunbar's "gossip" theory of language evolution suggests that language evolved as a means of exchanging information about the attitudes of others in the social world (Dunbar 2004). Language is not a uniquely human ability, but it is allied to other distinctively human cognitive abilities, especially our theory of mind and our ability to comprehend and categorize objects and abstract ideas. As such, it forms part of a package of cognitive abilities that allow us to manage increasingly social lives in progressively larger groups.

The development of gossiping provided a means of making grooming more efficient: rather than a bilateral activity, as with stroking, conversations could be held on a multilateral basis, with three or more participants talking together. This freed up more time for other activities, like eating and foraging more widely. Gossip additionally played an important part in gauging the reputation of others in the group and, perhaps most important, of deducing where one stood (by dint of the quality of social information that others felt inclined to share with you).

Additionally, Dunbar suggests, humans have developed ways of conducting "grooming" still more efficiently via music, singing, and laughter. All these provide a way of enlarging the ratio at which we can provide attention to others (Dunbar 2014). Chimpanzees ameliorate social stresses through one-on-one grooming: in the zoo you can watch their endless quarrels and comforting stroking of one another. But this sort of companionship constrains the scale at which chimpanzees can sustain social groups. Demonstrating by hooting loudly and charging about the social group, as alpha chimpanzees do, provides one way of grabbing everyone's attention. However, while useful for asserting control over disputatious rivals, it's hardly a good way of ameliorating many of the social tensions that build up through time. Humans, in Dunbar's view, have done rather more by joining in shared rituals (there is some recent debate about the possibility of ritualistic behavior in chimpanzee communities), songs, and joking. All these things require a sophisticated and shared understanding of *meaning* that reaches its apotheosis in spoken language.

The sociability thesis for language has plenty of supporting evidence from modern neuroscience, as Matthew Leiberman argues (Lieberman 2015). For example, when our brains are seemingly "resting"—not directly engaged in a particular cognitive task—the systems that remain active are often those implicated in social reasoning. We are, he suggests, engaged in an interior rehearsal of the sorts of social dynamics that occupy us in real life. Supporting evidence abounds elsewhere. The neural systems that fire in response to "social pain," such as exclusion from the group, also fire in response to physical pain (Eisenberger and Lieberman 2004). Whether internal rehearsal in our daydreams, actual rehearsal via play, or the real-life social dynamics of gossiping, humans are brilliant social strategists. Putting all one's eggs into the social-cognition basket via language allowed early humans to break the time constraints of their day—not just in terms of grooming but also via rolespecialization and culture.

Dunbar's thesis offers a plausible account for the benefits of language: gossip facilitates the construction of larger groups that include nonkin. Culture extends the possibility for social identity beyond the core group of mostly interrelated individuals that constitute the small band of hunter-gatherers. We may retain the evolved cognitive architecture that allows us to map the social networks of this small group of somewhere around fifty members, but language gives us the means to extend our network into a larger cultural band.

What is lacking in Dunbar's argument (and the arguments of others who stress a social rationale for language) is an endogenous account of the evolutionary rationale for these larger ultrasocial groups. Where is the big advantage to be gained from intense cooperation and larger groups? My answer is the threat of war, or, more broadly perhaps, the need to defend against predation. Social cognition provides compelling benefits in warfare, delivering scale and the possibility of strategy. There are other possible explanations for the evolution of language, some having to do with cooperation in tool-making and hunting. Others also suggest a social motive—the sort of Machiavellian strategizing in groups that call for local alliances (Carstairs-McCarthy and Bickerton 2007). Again, these motives need not be incompatible since tools are sometimes weapons and the skills of hunting are not dissimilar from the skills of raid and ambush.

Human Strategy Is Conscious

One difference between our cognitive abilities and those of chimpanzees revolves around the issues of consciousness and intentionality. De Waal argues in

Chimpanzee Politics that chimpanzees are strategic actors but that their strategy is largely instinctive and the product of unconscious cognition. De Waal also argues that much human strategy might be made along similar lines, and indeed there is plenty of evidence to suggest this is true. But human consciousness does seem qualitatively different, not least in our capacity to reflect on others' perspectives (Tomasello et al. 2005). This might be the perspective of others in our group, or it might entail reflecting on our future selves—both these activities call for a degree of imagination and cognitive agility. The point is that consciousness is social: it relates to other minds as well as our own.

Thus, human consciousness plays an important part in theory of mind or the process by which we intuit that other people have internal minds much like our own. Part of this process—to empathize with some degree of intentionality—may be instinctual. But consciousness also plays a part in helping us understand that others have beliefs and reflect on what those beliefs might be.

Consciousness is a slippery subject. We must say "human" consciousness because we have yet to find evidence that other species share our particular abilities, although there is plenty of suggestive evidence that some form of conscious experience exists elsewhere (Godfrey-Smith 2017; Griffin 2001). It's a challenging research field, even in humans. From a philosophical standpoint, of course, there is no real way of knowing whether you, the reader, or indeed any other human has a conscious mind like mine—a conundrum that appears in the philosophical literature as that of the "zombie": this someone looks, walks, and talks like a person but has no interior mental state comparable to my own first-person, subjective ontology (Block 2002). The theory of mind is ultimately, for all of us, a matter of guesswork and probability. I deduce that your interior state feels something like mine—we share the same biological architecture and we navigate the same social universe with similar intuitions. However, I have no way of knowing beyond all doubt that your experience of the quality generated by the color "red" feels the same as mine. Still, thanks to technological advances in neuroscience, I do know that seeing red fires similar patterns of neuronal activity in your visual cortex and is associated with the letters that go to make up the word "red." This dense network of associated meanings suggests that, with our similar bodies, including our minds and sensory inputs, we share a similar conscious experience.

But how do I know, in the famous question posed by Thomas Nagel, what it feels like to be a bat (Nagel 1974)? With its different biological sensory inputs, surely the resultant sensation would be extremely different—with no verbalized language in which to articulate conscious thought, what could that conscious sensation of experience feel like? Are bats self-aware, reflective creatures like us, thinking of themselves as individual actors in a subjective, self-referential sense? Nagel's dilemma returns when thinking, later, about artificial consciousness.

As for understanding consciousness in humans, different epistemological approaches are possible. A neuroscientist might look to common brain structures, including the "neural correlates of consciousness," and perhaps identifying at least some sort of animal proto-consciousness (Barron and Klein 2016). Disagreement about which bits of the brain are essential would then ensue (Hill 2016). A philosophical approach might consider how a subjective, first-person experience can arise from matter, and then wrestle with the issues of determinism and free will (Block, Flanagan, and Güzeldere 1997). An experimental psychological approach would seek indicators of reflective consciousness—for example, that I can adopt the beliefs of another person or I can reason logically. And an evolutionary approach would ask which advantages would be served to humans by evolving conscious minds.

Psychology experiments suggest that humans are self-aware, as are chimps and possibly a few other mammals that also pass the "mirror test." What's more, humans possess an unusual ability to reason about "false" beliefs in others by placing themselves in the minds of others, including those not present. This is a higher order of empathy than the instinctive, mirrored feelings for those we are able to see. Higher, too, than the perspective-taking that allows corvids and apes to understand what others can see and intend when they are present—which they demonstrate by rehiding food when others have seen where it is. Humans, this suggests, possess a unique and unsurpassed ability to share psychological states with other individuals: instinctive, certainly, but also reasoned and reflective. Together these abilities indicate that humans can reflect on their own minds and those of others, both of which are vital for mapping complex social worlds rich with abstract meanings. Thus the conscious mind plays an important part in our social cognition. Consciousness is an integral part of this process of reasoning about others and grappling with complex social meanings.

Consciousness as Global Workspace

So consciousness is social: we have ourselves in mind and the minds of others too. There are other important attributes of consciousness, though, which may confer strategic advantages. Notably, it allows us to concentrate attention on particular issues, including issues that extend into the future. And it allows us to recombine cognitions in novel ways, including ways that exhibit creativity and imagination.

To see the strategic benefits of human consciousness in finer detail, consider a prominent cognitive theory of consciousness: the idea that it functions as a "global workspace," a term coined by Bernard Baars and developed by Stanislas Dehaene (Baars 1997; Dehaene 2014). Their theory suggests that a key function of consciousness is to integrate and recombine cognitions, broadcasting the result across the brain. The conscious mind does this by unifying the activities of multiple brain networks, fusing them together as one. A characteristic signal of this is a wide-ranging brain signal that pulses across the cortex, suggesting integration and intense activity among large numbers of neurons, combined in neural networks. Dehaene writes of an "avalanche" of consciousness. This neuronal cascade can be triggered experimentally by presenting subjects with a stimulus for just long enough that it crosses the threshold of conscious awareness. (Masking, or presenting stimuli for less time, incidentally, allows the study of unconscious priming—a vibrant area of current research.)

Gerald Edelman and Guilio Tononi offer a similar concept. Again, there is the notion of neural integration. But they also observe that the array of neural networks contributing to consciousness is highly differentiated (Edelman 2001). The constant dynamism of the conscious mind suggests continual changes in the overall makeup of the conscious workspace. They posit that integration without differentiation would actually result in lost consciousness, with the system blindly pulsing rather than communicating within itself. Nonetheless, they note the stability of consciousness: dynamic and flowing in a stream, certainly, but with a consistent sensation sufficient to generate a stable sense of "self."

What's the point of this consciousness workspace? For Dehaene and Baars, consciousness works as a communications network, broadcasting across the large (physical and conceptual) neural networks of the brain. The workspace is highly reductive, and most information doesn't reach conscious awareness. But what does reach conscious awareness serves to focus attention on some of the most pressing issues facing the organism. It allows the construction of cognitions that are more complicated than typically possible in the more localized networks of the unconscious mind. Among those cognitions would be social reflections about oneself and others.

In addition, consciousness working in this way likely allows information to be shared that is relevant to a broader time frame than the immediate, situationalist responses that typify many unconscious activities. The imagined future, like other thoughts rich in meaning, is constructed in the global workspace by recombining memories and sensory inputs in novel packages. The perspective-taking that is required to imagine our future self is similar to what is required to imagine the interior minds of others—and similar brain systems may be involved. In clever experiments, self-control can be reduced by using transcranial magnetic stimulation (TMS) to inhibit the activities of brain regions associated with perspective taking (of our future selves and of others) (Soutschek et al. 2016). This is just the sort of perspective-taking that troubles chimpanzees and toddlers. TMS, incidentally, validates Edelman and Tononi's point about differentiation because it causes the neurons that have been affected to fire simultaneously, with attendant loss of conscious function.

Another related idea, also commonplace in the neuroscience literature and that chimes with the global workspace, is that consciousness works as a coordinator of brain activity rather than as an executive. A useful analogy might be the leaderless orchestra (jazz, in my imagination). Neuroscientists sometimes talk of the fallacy of the homunculus—the little man inside your mind directing its operations. This is a powerful illusion and the product of our stable, unitary narrative stream; even Joseph Gazzaniga's patients with split-brain hemispheres experienced a unitary conscious experience (Gazzaniga 2011). Instead, we might see consciousness as an improvisation among many parts—which is not to suggest that consciousness plays no part in directing the future actions of the organism or that some brain networks are not more important than others.

Much uncertainty remains. For example, why do some unconscious processes seize the attention of our conscious selves? The brain in toto contains vast quantities of information, processed, for the most part, in parallel unconscious systems. Consciousness, by contrast, is a sequential processor with a relatively small bandwidth for information. Certain brain structures, like the dorsolateral anterior cingulate cortex, might be involved in sorting out what comes to our attention and acting as a sort of alarm system for the conscious mind (Botvinick, Cohen, and Carter 2004).

We can see the conscious mind as a naïve scientist, building a model of the world: when the model doesn't fit new incoming information, our attention is diverted toward the discrepancy. The "reality" we perceive is a projection downward from consciousness and upward from unconscious cognitions vying to cross a threshold. Psychologists talk about the "cocktail party effect" wherein the babble of conversation continues outside of your awareness until someone in the room speaks your name, at which point your attention is seized (Wood and Cowan 1995). These ideas capture two aspects of consciousness: acting as a filter on information by reducing the vast scope available to conscious deliberation and as an active modeler of reality, creating expectations about the future. Both features are useful for our project on strategy. Moreover, the cocktail party effect points again to the importance of social information—especially social information about ourselves.

It also makes sense to talk of the conscious mind actively "recruiting" processes from the subconscious—again, our commonplace language captures this, with the idea of "calling up" memories. Nonetheless, there is still uncertainty about which unconscious cognitions get recruited and when. Their salience, or relevance, may play a part—as judged by similarity to networks already implicated in consciousness. The notion of "mood congruence," for example, suggests that being in an emotional state makes it easier to recall memories with similar associated affect (Bower 1981). Explicit memories themselves offer a good example of the repackaging aspect of conscious recall since such memories are partially encoded and selectively recalled—and subject to considerable evolution and distortion in the process (Loftus and Palmer 1974).

Consciousness blocks out much information, recruits other bits, repackages the entire lot, and broadcasts the whole widely across the cortex. These notions of consciousness—responding, reorganizing, and recruiting new cognitions—point to another feature characteristic of the Libet "free will" experiment and Gazzaniga's research on split-brain patients: that consciousness involves a time lag. The model of reality that we construct in our mind is artful enough to synchronize multiple inputs that arrive at different times and present a coherent and integrated mental image of reality. In this sense we might see the conscious mind not as a rationalist but as a rationalizer of decisions made elsewhere. This is perhaps a disturbing observation for believers in free will—at least free will of the conscious variety. But it makes up for this lag with some dramatic advantages, in particular its capacity to "time-shift" and take a perspective beyond the immediate conditioned responses of the unconscious. Another advantage is in presenting a version of ourselves that is consistent, unitary, and agentic, that is, useful both for our own self-worth and socially, when trying to make sense of what others are thinking.

Much strategic studies literature starts with the intuitively plausible notion that a degree of rationality underpins strategy—and that some of this entails conscious reflection on what the ends of strategy are and how they might be achieved. The process may be somewhat illusory, as Richard Betts argues, with the degree of situational complexity involved and the instinctual responses of humans in the moment undermining any effort at systematic rationality (Betts 2000). Strategy, in other words, may be illusory. What sort of instinctual response undermines this sort of rigorous cost-benefit analysis? To pick just one example, we are apt to heavily discount future gains in favor of short-term ones—which is an impediment to farsighted strategy but which may have paid off in a resource-scarce evolutionary environment fraught with danger. As John Maynard Keynes memorably argued, in the long run we're all dead. So act now, repent later. And yet, Edelman and Tononi argue, one cannot "think" as such without consciousness. If so, the lack of rich consciousness would be a severe impediment to farsighted strategy. Consciousness may be imperfect, in this view, but it is all we have, and it's better than nothing.

This view contrasts with Frans de Waal's earlier idea that the strategizing of chimpanzees and humans alike included much unconscious thinking, either in routinized scripts or as hardwired instinct. It's a false opposition, of course. Much strategy is certainly instinctive and shaped by our evolution. But not all. We have traded (in an evolutionary sense) physical attributes like speed and strength for the considerable advantage of a self-conscious mind. With the flexibility afforded by this, we can engage in complex, logical thought (albeit not in the sense of strict mathematical logic). We can categorize objects and ideas, combine and recombine them, and communicate the result by language, all with bewildering speed. Sophisticated strategy requires this sort of understanding, planning, creativity, and communication—all of which, not coincidentally, pose large challenges for AI researchers. De Waal was correct in *Chimpanzee Politics* about humans and the power of the unconscious brain in strategy, but his view perhaps underplays the distinct strategic advantages that humans gain from their rich self-consciousness.

Those advantages, remember, are primarily useful for navigating the über-social world of large, sometimes nonkin groups. De Waal, thinking about his Machiavellian chimpanzees in Arnhem zoo, argues that the unconscious is strategic. Certainly, but the same is true of the conscious. We evolved the capacity to intuit what others might be thinking and to reflect on what they think about us. Among other strategic benefits of consciousness, such as planning for the future or communicating complex ideas, this ability is singularly useful for a species that generates fighting power from the social cohesion of the group and that is frequently embroiled in violent conflict with conspecifics.

Evolved Consciousness

Consciousness, then, serves both social and integrative functions. When it comes to articulating an evolutionary rationale for consciousness, however, any answer must be speculative because we can see only the results of evolutionary history and must work backward to intuit a logic for its development. Nonetheless, the functional picture described earlier offers a strong and plausible logic. Thus, consciousness might have evolved to track social identity. Indeed, the size of the neocortex, which is strongly implicated in "neural correlates of consciousness," is, as will be recalled from the concept of Dunbar's number, a strong predictor of ability to track social group dynamics.

If it is true that warfare has selected for large, integrated social groups, then consciousness provides an adaptive way of mapping these complex social groups and giving a causal logic for its evolution in humans. This social rationale for consciousness chimes with Lieberman's finding that a brain "at rest" is actually active in networks implicated in weighing social life. It also chimes with Dunbar's gossip theory of language, that the complexities associated with juggling semantic meaning are an intrinsic part of consciousness.

However, this doesn't tell us how consciousness evolved from preconscious brains, nor why other social animals may not have made the leap to human-level abilities to judge social situations. Nicholas Humphrey offers part of an answer to the first question—arguing that self-awareness may have developed out of the brain's internal monitoring circuitry (Humphrey 2011). These would have developed as a way of monitoring the organism's interaction with its surrounding environment, including its social environment. Gradually, Humphrey suggests, these circuits developed a recursive nature as the brain monitors itself monitoring the environment. This self-monitoring recursivity is the basis of the unceasing introspective "stream" of conscious thought. This is meta-cognition, in other words: thinking about thinking. It may account for the qualitative subjective sensation of consciousness, although this is still very far from clarifying how that distinct sensation arises from physical matter. This, of course, is the "hard problem" of consciousness research, and it's not about to be solved here (Chalmers 1995).

It may be that the human brain, as it developed this capacity for monitoring, adapted existing neural circuits and processes. That process of adapting existing systems is common in evolution. Explicit memory, Joseph LeDoux speculates, may have developed in similar fashion by making use of the hippocampus's original function in monitoring the organism's position in time and space (LeDoux 2002).

Why didn't chimpanzees become conscious in the same way that humans did, if it truly is so important for strategy and social relations? After all, chimps fight lots of wars and have complex social relationships. Chimpanzees make tools, and—as de Waal vividly describes—they engage in strategic scheming par excellence (de Waal 2007). Chimpanzees can also learn language from humans and remember it over an extended period (Gardner and Gardner 1969; Dunbar 2004). Yet they cannot use language with the same dexterity that humans do, by employing complex syntax and making reference to a rich range of immaterial concepts. Frans de Waal is in no doubt that chimps feel empathy for fellow chimpanzees in distress—an indicator of shared identity (de Waal 2013, 2010). But on the crucial test of understanding others' beliefs—a key indicator of theory of mind and human-level reflection—chimpanzees have repeatedly come up short.

Richard Wrangham offers a "cooking" thesis that can help account for some of the changes in *Homo sapiens* relative to chimpanzees (Wrangham 2009). Cooking breaks down starch in food, making it more digestible, making it a source of concentrated energy. People switching to raw food diets lose so much weight as to suggest that such diets are not energy efficient, given the adaptation of our digestive systems to cooked food, both meat and vegetable. Less requirement for eating raw food in bulk means more time in the day for other activities, including social and cultural ones. All this extra energy could then be diverted to supporting and enlarging the energy-hungry human brain. This large, social brain could be further fed by making a tradeoff against muscle strength, with chimpanzees much more physically powerful but correspondingly less adept at working together socially. Wrangham and others point to a long period of cooking, beginning—perhaps haphazardly, using accidental fires—very early in our evolutionary history. He estimates some one million years ago. This predates the acceleration of our cognitive and cultural "revolution" in the last hundred thousand years or so. For chimpanzees the evolutionary route stressed individual strength, with some collaboration; for humans the route opened by fire was cognitive dexterity and intense cooperation.

The cognitive explosion in humans was likely caused by interrelated, mutually reinforcing evolutionary developments: fire and cooking, bipedalism for longer-range foraging, collaborative hunting, conceptually and syntactically complex language. There would have been a gradually deepening sociability. And then, perhaps rapidly, a phase transition: after endless millennia of producing the same style of hand axe fashioned from stone, there arose an increasing diversity and sophistication in tools, including weapons, as well as the beginnings of art in painting and musical instruments (B. Boyd 2010; Dutton 2010). Art provides a means of sharing the story of the group; in music and other performance it is a means of extending the grooming circle still further (Gottschall 2013).

The upshot is an evolved brain of remarkable conceptual flexibility that is increasingly social and encultured. Once humans started down this path, a snowball effect ensued. The other great apes are someway toward a similar solution—social and cultured but lacking those final breakthroughs. Chimpanzees may love cooked meat, but they cannot cook it themselves (Warneken and

Rosati 2015). Neanderthals, a *Homo* subspecies, went further still, developing cultures of their own, with tools and perhaps even art, and presumably with the underlying theory of mind to accompany it (Hardy 2004; Rodríguez-Vidal et al. 2014).

Foraging and War

But why go down this path at all? Human sociability and the package of cognitive skills that facilitate it confer many evolutionary advantages. Among these is certainly martial efficacy (Rusch 2014). But we still need some account of why humans developed this package, or why war was such a big deal for humans. Foraging might provide the answer.

With limited intentionality and limited means of communication, the scope of chimpanzee strategy is limited. Still, one should not overstate the case: the Machiavellian mind of the chimpanzee, as well as its tendency for collective violence, is in some respects similar to our own cognitive abilities (Byrne 1989). Chimpanzees evidently conduct raids and can be said to engage in "wars" with rival groups. Perhaps there are similar explanations for our propensity for group conflict.

Scholars have pointed to a variety of motives for human conflict—having to do with male dominance hierarchies, or access to food, territory, or mating partners. Risk taking, male bonding, in-group altruism, and out-group chauvinism are plausible corollaries (Pitman 2010). But other social species, including other great apes, face similar selection pressures and do not, so far as can be determined, respond as chimpanzees and humans do by conducting periodic wars of total annihilation against groups of conspecifics. We need something more to explain the complex web of behaviors involved in war.

Wrangham offers a useful hypothesis in his book *Demonic Males* to explain why chimpanzees are so bellicose; there may be implications for humans too (Wrangham 1996; Wrangham and Glowacki 2012). He suggests that the origins of chimpanzee war lie in the distribution of foodstuffs. Bonobos, a near relative of chimpanzees and an only slightly more distant one of humans, live starkly contrasting lives of relative harmony in groups that are dominated by female matriarchs and in which sex plays an important part in managing social tension. The difference, argues Wrangham, falls out of the environmental niches in which each species lived: for chimpanzees, who competed for food with gorillas, there was a need to forage across a wide territory, and the group would fragment into ones and twos—leaving individuals acutely vulnerable to predation. Bonobos, in the more resource-rich environment south of the Zaire River, could remain in closer proximity; their larger, more cohesive groups, with individuals foraging in close proximity to one another, worked as a deterrent to external aggression. This worked to deter intragroup conflict since an uppity male bonobo would likely be soundly thrashed by a mutually supportive group of females. It also reduced the vulnerability of the group to being picked off, chimpanzee-style, in raid and ambush, where the outgroup attackers enjoy overwhelming odds.

For humans, with a wide hunting and foraging range, especially in open woodland and grassland, the threat of intraspecies predation would be more akin to what chimpanzees faced. Possessing a hunting advantage from their superior stamina, humans would nonetheless risk becoming separated in the course of their extended pursuits and might therefore be vulnerable to predation, especially if these extended pursuits took them into the territory of rival bands. Like the chimpanzee, isolated individuals would be vulnerable to massed attack featuring surprise and the rapid concentration of force. Thus, both humans and chimpanzees may have environmental incentives to wage war on neighboring groups, but humans have an added ability to do so, owing to their evolution of large social brains and the cognitive flexibility to organize for war.

Why the cognitive difference, if similar environmental pressures are at work? Perhaps the threat of predation is lower for chimpanzees. There is still some debate about the frequency of war among chimps that owes something to the small populations under study and the difficulty of observing them continuously in wooded terrain. Nonetheless, when Richard Wrangham, Michael Wilson, and Martin Muller marshaled the available evidence, they found that chimpanzee warfare is frequent and results in proportionately high levels of casualties (Wrangham, Wilson, and Muller 2005). The levels of violence, in fact, are similar to that of intraspecies conflict among humans. Thus, comparatively less warfare among chimpanzees might not be the answer.

A similar conundrum is raised by Dunbar's gossip theory of language: if gossip confers such powerful evolutionary advantages, why haven't chimpanzees developed this last step in theory of mind that would allow them to benefit? There is no settled agreement. The answer may lie partly in the incremental initial gains to be had from any evolutionary development. The genetic record suggests that humans have encountered evolutionary bottlenecks several times. This in turn suggests that the marginal gain from the intensely social evolutionary route may not pay off immediately to the same extent that it will pay off later, once the cultural gains start rolling in. For small groups fighting in real terrain, the theoretical vulnerability of small groups of foragers may not prove decisive on all occasions.

As a broader point about marginal advantages, nonlinear acceleration in co-operation and culture is a feature of human history. For many tens of thousands of years the same basic hand axe litters the archaeological record of early *Homo*. Scant evidence of more-advanced cultural artifacts exists, at least until the last hundred thousand years, when new weapons technologies appear among hunter-gatherer bands. As weapons proliferated and became more sophisticated, these groups expanded into federations and proto-states. This timescale may appear very long from our perspective, but in the grand scale of evolutionary history, where our common ancestor with chimpanzees lived some six million years ago, it is not; ten to fifteen thousand years of civilization is the merest blink.

An alternative explanation for the difference between human and chimpanzee sociability involves the environmental niche within which early humans evolved—perhaps on the shore, certainly in the more-open, less-wooded countryside. Living there might have called more readily for cooperative approaches to social life. Wooded terrain, by contrast, could provide defenders with scope to offset the dramatic advantages of numbers among attackers. Still another difference might be the different child-rearing strategies between the two species. As humans start down the road to more intense sociability, perhaps spurred by the challenge of war, our increasingly large, socially adept brains led to a longer childhood and the need for still greater cooperation—by parents, by extended family, and by others in the small community (Hrdy 2009). Once the ball got rolling, the incentive was to specialize ever further in social cognition. As with cooperative hunting, the social logic of childcare can complement the logic of war in selecting for socially attuned minds. (There is, inevitably, wide scope for debate about which is the key driver, with the answer depending in part on just how violent one assumes human prehistory was.)

One last observation is that while we know that chimpanzees did not proceed down this path of über-sociability, other branches of the *Homo* genus certainly did—Neanderthals, certainly, and perhaps others, like the Denisovans, of whom we are only recently and dimly aware through fossil finds and DNA analysis. There is an element of confirmation bias in our view of intense cooperation as a distinctly human ability, given the extinction of those other strains of *Homo*. It may be, rather, that several species of primates started down this route of more intense cooperation and flexible cognition. Other successors to *Homo erectus* could have used fire and developed cultural artifacts and complex language. But all those subspecies are now extinct; as with many cases of extinct megafauna, the extinction dates to about the same time as the arrival of the *Homo sapiens* diaspora from Africa. Specific narrow advantages seem to have won out, aided by several doses of luck along the way.

As a species, modern humans have been wildly successful in breaking free from niche environments and adapting to a wide range of physical circumstances. In the process we have outlasted many other competing species, including other species of *Homo*, which proved less able to adapt and compete. The fate of Neanderthal and Denisovan humans remains unclear, except that we know there was some interbreeding with humans (Burgess 2016). Nevertheless, the fate of megafauna and apex predators elsewhere soon after their encounter with humans is highly suggestive—in the competition for survival, few could rival *Homo sapiens*. And, while the debate still rolls on over violence in prehistory between groups of humans, the three-pronged assault of primate studies, archaeology, and anthropology is making an increasingly persuasive case for a more bloody view of mankind's history than seemed likely just decades ago.

War Makes the Group and the Group Makes War

There is one further piece in the picture painted here of an evolved human capacity for strategy. It is that group size confers disproportionate advantages in warfare. Moreover, there was probably enough violence to select for individuals that could not only cooperate intensely, through language and theory of mind, but that could also cooperate broadly. That would permit large groups, including many nonkin individuals, perhaps even including many strangers to whom one's only affinity would be cultural. Size mattered.

Here is the evolutionary thesis for strategy so far: conflict itself is a powerful influence on natural selection in humans. For this to have been the case, there would have to be a considerable amount of violence between groups in prehistory. The evidence suggests there was. Moreover, this conflict provides a powerful motor for the cooperative behavior that Robert Trivers identifies. It creates two forces with important strategic implications: first, the pressure of warfare favors societies that better regulate free-riding and police antisocial elements. At the extreme, this may lead to the weeding out of malevolent characters. Wrangham and others have argued that it produces a process of "self-domestication" akin to that seen in other animals that humans have selectively bred to suit our purposes, like cattle, or that have self-selected to live alongside us, like dogs (Cieri et al. 2014; Hare, Wobber, and Wrangham 2012). Second, the pressure of conflict favors larger groups: people who are capable of agglomerating in groups larger than their kinship bands will do better, on average. Together these factors explain the emergence in humans of large groups of increasingly social cooperators.

The irony is that warfare ultimately produces individuals who are more social and less belligerent. Culture, the shared idea of who "we" are and how "we" ought to behave, becomes the badge of group membership. Psychopaths can remain in small numbers within such populations, perhaps because it remains a viable reproductive strategy in large groups of unsuspecting and instinctive cooperators. And dominance hierarchies remain part of our evolutionary legacy, as one can see from watching the mannerisms of some overly self-assured major generals. But prestige hierarchies become relatively more significant since the ability to master complex skills is an integral part of cultural life. These large and rich cultures produce complex artifacts, especially weapons and knowledge, that further enhance fighting power. In short, intergroup war was an important engine of human evolution that produced large groups constituted along flexible lines.

Scale and Lanchester's Law

In the Paleolithic era and in the context of lower population numbers, smaller group sizes, and incessant warfare among hunter-gatherers, the survival of genes was intimately bound up in the survival of the group. It was touch and go: humans have been through several genetic bottlenecks, suggesting that the survival of the entire species, let alone particular groups, was on several occasions a close-run thing (Harris 2015).

With this sort of competitive pressure at work, any advantage in conflict would exert a powerful selection influence on human evolution. Frederick Lanchester's laws, originally developed in the context of aerial combat in the Great War, provide a mathematical proof in support of the timeworn notion in strategic studies that scale matters (Johnson and MacKay 2015; MacKay 2006; Lanchester 1916). Lanchester's laws come in two flavors: the linear law, which holds that combat power increases in linear fashion where combat is a parallel series of one-on-one duels (so that having a few good fighters might be disproportionately more advantageous than having many average or poor fighters, because the skilled warrior can dispatch enemies sequentially), and the square law, whereby combat is properly a group activity in which fighting is all against all and combat power increases geometrically with scale. Size matters in both circumstances but disproportionately so in cases of the square law, where multiple fighters can be brought to bear on an isolated individual. Even a skilled fighter will be hopelessly outmatched by a group of less-skilled rivals. Real-world combat is unlikely to reflect the abstract parameters of the models; in actual fighting, some individuals will be unable to engage the enemy owing to topography of the battlefield or obstructions caused by other fighters. So, at best Lanchester's laws are illustrative approximations of a general tendency.

One vivid illustration of Lanchester's square law in action comes from the team version of mixed martial arts combat, which can be viewed on YouTube (caution is advised for sensitive viewers) (Team Fighting Championship 2014). The bouts start as parallel individual combats, but when one fighter is defeated, his victorious opponent can go to the aid of another team member and turn that bout into a two-on-one contest. This lopsided fight is most likely to end in the defeat of the outnumbered fighter, and the two victors can then join another fight, with almost certain consequences. Once even a small quantitative advantage is gained in the first victory, the contest, having begun evenly, accelerates rapidly to a conclusion.

Dominic Johnson and Niall MacKay persuasively argue that Lanchester's square law applies to human evolution, such that over a period of many thousands of years groups that could cooperate in sizable coalitions would win out over those that did not, provided they could engineer circumstances in which their numerical advantages might be brought to bear and they could fight in ways that avoided single combat. Conversely, the numerically weaker side might try to negate this advantage by engineering a situation wherein combat more closely resembles the linear law situation—using terrain or fortifications to create a choke point—as the Spartans did against the massed Persians at Thermopylae—or by using disciplined ranks, with each protecting the next man, as with hoplite warfare. Once the lines are broken, the square law comes into play: mass can be concentrated against individual adversaries and an enemy can be defeated in detail, with one man swarmed by many at a time. Being a skilled warrior in such circumstances would be of limited avail. Projectile weapons, which allow the concentration of force from distance, would perform a similar function—force could readily be devastatingly concentrated against one target.

Chimpanzee conflicts attest to the importance of scale and lend support to the notion that Lanchester's square law might be useful in understanding human conflict. The apes are evidently risk-averse when it comes to combat, which in their case is mostly unarmed and thus conducted at a range that exposes belligerent participants to great personal risk. As Johnson and MacKay observe, the square law suggests that the prospect of being killed diminishes markedly with scale when combat is all-against-all in similarly nonlinear fashion to the increase in fighting power. As a result, chimpanzees favor the tactics of raid and ambush, using surprise and numerical advantage to overwhelm adversaries while minimizing the personal risk of combat.

When it comes to the fighting, then, Lanchester's square law has applicability to both species. Some evidence suggests it also applies to the wars of ants, especially when smaller species go up against larger rivals (McGlynn 2000). While chimpanzees exhibit some limited flexibility in constructing ambushes (possibly even adopting different roles, as seen in one "funnel"-like ambush), there are marked strategic constraints imposed by their more limited social capacity. Humans, by contrast, have the capacity for a richer palate of action, especially once they start fashioning sophisticated weapons. In particular, they have a greater ability to coordinate their actions, thanks to their highly developed theory of mind and their specialized language skills. Moreover, these cognitive skills enhance their ability to monitor and punish free-riders who might be tempted to shirk the dangers of battle. Warrior codes and rituals attest to the close linkage of status and honor with performance in battle. The social pressure to perform honorably is intense, and failure to do so risks humiliation, ostracism, or worse.

Once humans began fashioning offensive weapons and increasing their lethality, Lanchester's square law became even more relevant: one-on-one combat is less likely when one can be picked off at range by concentrated fire from multiple attackers. Nonetheless, the tactics of raid and ambush remained dominant features of strategy, offsetting as they do any attempts to enhance the defense—for example, through fortification. Pitched battle is certainly possible, as testified by vivid film footage and ethnographic evidence from hunter-gatherer societies in New Guinea (Gardner 2007, 1963). Without discipline and hierarchy to provide cohesion and concentrated fire, however, it could prove inconclusive and unduly risky.

Lanchester's mathematical proofs are altogether too neat to capture the entire reality of conflict between groups of humans, chimpanzees, or ants. The ideal type of conflict suggested by the square law is an abstraction because there will always be some impediment to bringing to bear the concentrated fighting power of all against one. But it nonetheless points to a hardy perennial of strategic affairs: where something like this can be done, the advantages will be disproportionate.

Persistent Warfare Leads to Cooperation and Scale

For Lanchester's law to work efficiently as a force shaping human evolution toward ever-greater cooperation, war would have had to be frequent and deadly. This is what an increasingly robust consensus in the literature suggests. From Keeley to Azar Gat, Steven Pinker, and Max Roser, accumulated data drawn from the archaeological and ethnographic record suggest that intergroup conflict was widespread, persistent, and deadly across a broad sweep of prehistory and among many diverse cultures in different parts of the globe (Keeley 1996; Gat 2006; Pinker 2012; Roser 2016).

In his short *Science* paper, Samuel Bowles articulates the linkage between war and enhanced cooperation, asking whether, if there were significant martial benefits to cooperation, there is enough warfare in the historical record to account mathematically for the persistence of nonkinship cooperation against the benefits obtainable from free-riding (Bowles 2009). He argues that there is—though this finding, as the product of modeling, should be treated cautiously. The available data set of prehistoric warfare is patchy, and the assumptions of his model (about population size, for example) are considerable. Mathematical modeling aside, however, the argument is intuitively plausible: if cooperation is very important for generating fighting power in warfare, and if warfare is persistent and defeat has profound consequences, then cooperation should survive free-riding, even though the incentive to shirk danger may be considerable.

Moreover, as Lanchester's square law suggests, the cost of cooperation in combat may not have been particularly onerous in all-against-all fighting anyway. If that law is operative, not only does lethality rise disproportionately with scale; casualties fall in similarly nonlinear fashion. It's safer to be part of a swarm of fighters finishing off an isolated combatant.

Bowles does not mention Lanchester. But the mutual logic is compelling and reinforcing: war favors both cooperation and scale. Johnson and MacKay do note the effects of Lanchester's law in promoting social cohesion, and cite Bowles's paper in support. The effects of Lanchester's law would, they note, have been operating on human psychology as we evolved. We can see it at play in the offensive, especially in strategies to generate local power imbalances via raid and ambush. And we can see it at play in the defensive, too, especially in the use of terrain and the construction of fortifications to ward off powerful adversaries and prevent them turning battle into a free-flowing melee of all-against-all. Both of these approaches require strategy: foresight, creativity, and imagination. And both require language to articulate and communicate strategy and tactics. With war so persistent, we can say that it would, at the very least, have encouraged the expansion of the group and cooperation within it—even if it were not the sole responsible factor.

We might venture to suggest even more than this, tentatively arguing that war prompted the sort of cultural flexibility that gave rise to civilizations. The incentive to form large groups far beyond the constraints suggested by Dunbar's number would have required considerable cognitive flexibility to create new shared identities, using culture as a badge of membership. Humans would have to trust people they had never met without any way of reliably gauging their reliability other than knowing that they subscribed to similar cultural norms. This is a dramatic departure from the sort of localism that governs the lives of other primates.

Where weapons technologies were fairly even, the chief advantages in fighting power would have derived from scale and moral cohesion—and both of these depended on the ability to cooperate flexibly with nonkin. In addition, however, these larger cultural groups of über-cooperators could also have worked to improve weapons technologies, drawing on their resources and on scope for specialization. In short, warfare shaped the evolution of human cognitive processes and human society alike.

This analysis chimes with Peter Turchin's grand historical theory of human sociability (Turchin 2015). Like Bowles, Turchin argues the case for larger, more intensely cooperative groups—although at some point he notes the tendency for these to shift from the essentially egalitarian world of the hunter-gatherer to one that is dominated by tyrants able to compel obedience. This is a step-change he associates with the "Axial age" of sometime between the eighth and third centuries BC, when human societies began employing agriculture to make significant inroads against pastoralists and foraging societies. Napoleon Chagnon finds that tyranny has its origins at a smaller scale: in order for a Yanomamö village to expand much beyond Dunbar's number, a particularly brutal headman is required to compel obedience.

Two final observations are worth noting here. First, that there must be considerable residual uncertainty about the processes being identified here, because the archaeological record is so patchy and because we must make many inferences about the evolution of cognitive psychology. This is why the debate about mankind's bellicosity remains, the weight of evidence compiled by Roser notwithstanding. The patchiness of the record, however, is equally a problem for those who argue contrarily that early human life was largely pacific. Moreover, they need a compelling alternative to explain such things as flexible social identities, nonkinship cooperation, and consciousness.

Second, the neatness of the argument belies the complexity of the processes at work. The patterns Turchin identifies in his grand theorizing about the rise of cooperating egalitarians, then large tyrannies, then eventually more representative governments finds echoes in macro-theories by Francis Fukuyama, Jared Diamond, and many others. But these grand narratives typically become ever more intricate to account for myriad local variations. Consider the cultures of classical Greece: small city-states coexisting in an epoch alongside the vast Persian empire, with each city-state being a unique balance between oligarchical and representative government. Variation, as much as trend, is clearly a feature of cultural evolution.

Implications for Strategy

This short consideration of warfare in early human history provides several enduring themes to take forward into the following chapters. Warfare seems to have been a major aspect of our evolutionary history, and it seems at least plausible to suppose that we have evolved psychologically to help us meet the challenge. These psychological adaptations are perhaps more significant than the physical ones—the fists to punch with, the shoulders to throw with. But the dichotomy is false: the mind is part of the body and intimately connected to it, as Wrangham's argument about cooking and the evolution of the human brain makes plain. Among other psychological changes, we have become adept at cooperating in larger groups and coordinating our activities for mutual gain. We instinctively recognize the signals of physical dominance in other individuals, an ancient evolutionary skill, but we are also aware of skills and other signs of prestige or status. We are able to communicate abstract ideas, including about the goals and values that bind the group together, and to imagine and articulate shared futures.

Strategy is (relatively) easy when you can create the sort of local size imbalances that Lanchester's laws suggest will be decisive in combat. The trick is to generate mass and concentrate force in time and space. For the weak, however, alternative strategies must be found. Thankfully for them, and for reasons that will become plain, the defense is often stronger than the attack, psychologically, if not physically. Maneuver, deception, and surprise, meanwhile, can prevent an enemy from concentrating; so, too, can discipline. And technologies can offset the advantages of mass. In all these cases, however, evolved human psychological tendencies still play an important role. The next chapter considers some in more detail, starting with the balance between conscious and unconscious decisions.

This view of evolutionary psychology and strategy starts from the premise that our social world has shaped our cognitive processes (Lieberman 2015; Fiske 2008). As humans became an intensely social species, the social group as much as the physical environment began to constitute the arena within which genes competed for selection. Because violence and competition is an inescapable part of that social world, we have evolved particularly strategic minds. These minds allow humans to make good judgments about which behaviors, especially social ones, are best to adopt in any given context. (By good judgment, evolutionary psychologists mean "good enough," on average, such that over time the cognitive disposition in question becomes a feature of human nature.)

Much is uncertain about all these developments because the archaeological record is sparse and does not capture nonfossilized abilities like those needed for sophisticated language. Hence there is, and will likely remain, considerable debate about when such things arose in human history. Modern genetic sequencing research is beginning to unravel some of the history. For example, it can provide more robust evidence for the date in which human populations migrated from Africa and establish when some parts of the human diaspora interbred with other strains of *Homo*, including Neanderthals; or it can identify the gene FOXP2 that is implicated in brain systems involved in the comprehension and construction of language (Harris 2015). Evidence from the campsites of *Homo erectus* suggests that cooking and the biological changes it permitted are evolutionarily very old, further back than a million years (Berna et al. 2012). Yet ivory and bone flutes, the oldest musical instruments yet found that are indicative of sophisticated culture and shared grooming, are far more recent, at some forty thousand years old (Higham et al. 2012).

The cognitive revolution that has contributed to our species' strategic repertoire seems to have been built on evolutionarily ancient developments that permitted large, social brains but which may itself have more recent origins. Soberingly, perhaps, it seems that for a very long time our strategic advantages do not seem to have been much greater than those of chimpanzees.

CHAPTER 3

Strategic Heuristics and Biases

THE PSYCHOLOGICAL FOUNDATIONS OF STRATEGY EVOLVED IN HUMANS because they needed to organize larger groups to prevail in conflict against other humans. Conscious reflection, I suggest, is an important human ability that differentiates our approach to strategy from other animals, including chimpanzees. Now we turn to focus on the unconscious influences that shape our strategic decision-making, consciousness notwithstanding. These unconscious "heuristics" or routines aid rapid decision-making in ways that have proved evolutionarily "good enough," including in judging who is in our group and how to behave toward them and others.

Choice: Free Will versus Determinism

Strategy is ultimately a question of choice, but the notion of unconscious heuristics acting on "our" behalf complicates this idea somewhat. Consciousness implies a degree of free will—certainly most people would instinctively perceive themselves as deliberative agents. The issue is larger than unconscious heuristics: there is much debate in philosophy about whether we can ever have free will in a "deterministic" universe, where everything (in theory) is already set in motion (Dennett 1993; Baggini 2015). It is worth exploring some of this debate since choice is so integral to my definition of strategy—but, *caveat lector*, the philosophical conundrum of determinism is not about to be solved. Rather, my intention is to sketch the debate for newcomers from strategic studies who may simply take as read that humans are agents, in the sense of autonomous, freely choosing actors.

The issue certainly relates to consciousness. However, even if we allow that much is decided outside the narrow band of conscious deliberation, we can still defend the notion that this is *us* doing the deciding. Our social world and previous life experiences lead to conditioned responses in our unconscious mind, but even so it is still our mind, unconscious or not. So part of the free will question devolves to the issue of what constitutes "us"—is it the narrow band of consciousness or is it the entirety of our embodied, encultured brain? My view is the latter: the brain is a complex, crowded marketplace of cognitions, each suggesting what we should think and how we should behave. Consciousness plays a part in deciding, but only a part.

It is the second strand of the argument that has really seized the attention of philosophers of mind: the notion that whatever we "decide" has already been determined by previous processes. This is known as determinism. At the atomic level, we understand from Newtonian physics that forces act on matter in predictable ways. As thoroughgoing materialists we should believe that the mind, and cognition, is generated from physical matter—there is no ephemeral, supernatural spirit animating our thoughts. Suppose, then, the thought experiment runs, that we could map every particle in the universe at time T=0 and also the forces acting on those particles. If so, then we could predict the position of those particles at T=1; indeed, for all subsequent positions as T=n. Where is free will if we can predict in this manner how things will unfold?

There are a few "get out of jail free" cards in this scenario, and those who accept them are known as compatibilists. One escape is via complexity: we simply can't map those things and their multitudinous possible interactions for every second that passes. There are some eighty billion neurons in the human brain and over one hundred *trillion* synaptic connections. Vast networks of neurons interacting in real-time pulse-like electrical storms across the brain; this is the stuff of chaos theory. A related argument from complexity is that we can't map the forces acting on the matter, even if we know where the matter is right now: the pattern of atoms we observe at T=0 could have arisen from two or more very different universes and be heading off in wildly different directions thereafter. A further get-out comes via a "phase transition"—the qualitatively different sensation of the conscious mind that emerges somehow from the interaction of physical matter, which is poorly understood by modern science. We cannot yet account for the first-person subjective experience of consciousness, even if we can (crudely) describe some of the physical processes involved in generating it.

A final escape may be possible by casting doubt on the Newtonian properties of brain cells—what we could call the quantum solution (Hameroff and Penrose 1996). Allowing that subatomic particles behave in random and unpredictable ways offers an intuitively plausible escape from determinism. But this struggles to be credible because 1) we haven't seen how these quantum movements might map in neural terms—not least since the firing of neurons is explicable by conventional physics (perhaps, though, the quantum nature of free will applies only on the other side of the phase change from neural patterns to subjective, experienced consciousness); and 2) the mechanism through which randomness of some kind happening in conscious experience might result in free will is poorly specified. By definition free will must be something different from random choice, and the quantum solution does not specify how.

So there is no easy answer here for defenders of free will, as readers of Sam Harris and other free will skeptics know (Harris 2012). Space for free will can be preserved by adherence to either one or some combination of all three approaches. (My personal inclination is the complexity and phase transition, with phase transition really just being another aspect of complexity.) Our predictive powers operate so poorly in complex systems, even in those that are far simpler than the human brain. The swirling patterns of complex interacting matter that generate cognition and action are essentially unpredictable. Moreover, if we allow the possibility of recursive feedback loops in cognition, complexity only increases. If some of that recursive looping comes from one side of a phase transition into another, there is yet more complexity, as cause and effect are endlessly repackaged and densely interwoven.

One interesting addendum to the philosophical debate is to see conscious free will as an impeder of behaviors that might otherwise happen. Certainly this is how Daniel Kahneman sees it: when we engage our slower, more narrow-band deliberative cognition, we can curb our more instinctive instincts (Kahneman 2011). Roy Baumeister's view of willpower as a function of conscious deliberation that can be depleted by fatigue and hunger also chimes (Baumeister 2012). From this view, "free won't," perhaps, rather than free will shapes our actions.

So when we say that strategy entails choice we are on treacherous ground, philosophically speaking. Yet the human mind is an agent and the repository of processes that seek to orient the organism in its environment in the most effective way. Moreover, it is a farsighted agent able to reflect on some far distant situation and weigh the relative importance of many various cognitive processes. This is sufficient evidence to talk meaningfully of choice and autonomy. That's as far into the knotty philosophical thicket of free will as we shall penetrate until the later discussion of AI and the possibility of intrinsic motivation in machines.

Heuristics and Biases

People are conscious strategists, certainly, but we should not neglect the extent to which unconscious biases and heuristics continue to shape strategy—both in design and execution. There's little danger of that nowadays—at least in popular writing on decision-making. Modern psychological literature is replete with examples of automated thinking. Malcolm Gladwell refers to "Blink" decisions, or the instantaneous judgments that might prove better than more deliberate reasoning (Gladwell 2005). That contrasts with much current political psychology, which stresses the errors brought about by such automated thinking. Elsewhere, Robert Cialdini talks about "click-whirr" responses to particular situations and focuses on how these are often related to social context (Cialdini 2014). In his *Art of Thinking Clearly*, Rolf Dobelli compiles ninety-nine common cognitive biases, while the Cognitive Bias Codex poster from Design Hacks artfully arranges biases in categories (Dobelli 2014; Manoogian 2016).

The history of heuristics in psychology extends back even farther. Daniel Kahneman, the doyen of the field, contrasts what he terms "Type 1" automated, instinctive decision-making with a more deliberative, conscious "Type 2" mode of thinking. In the 1980s, with Amos Tversky, Kahneman explored whether mental models could simplify a great deal of the complex, noisy clutter of the environment in which the decision-maker acts (Kahneman, Slovic, and Tversky 1982). Farther back still lies Freudian psychoanalysis. Indeed, the notion that the unconscious mind shapes behavior predates modern psychology altogether. Robert Louis Stevenson, in my favorite account, describes his writing process in which his stories were created wholesale while he dreamed (Broks 2003; Stevenson 2012).

Many experiments have sought to establish the link between these subconscious processes and our decision-making and behavior. The genre is sometimes known by the term "priming," whereby subtle experimental stimuli work to steer the unconscious mind into certain choices. The deliberative, conscious mind might not be aware of why it chose to act the way it did, even after the fact and even if it is rather adept at devising justifications afterward to account for a behavior. The concept underpins much research in the emerging discipline of behavioral economics (Thaler 2009; Ariely 2009).

The replication crisis in experimental psychology of recent years has challenged some famous findings, including some that involve priming—as with one that suggests clamping a pen between your teeth might move the face into a smile shape and thus subtly trigger better moods (Strack, Martin, and Stepper 1988; Wagenmakers et al. 2016), and another that suggests that adopting "power poses" acts to instill confidence (Ranehill et al. 2015; Carney, Cuddy, and Yap 2010). Replication is a serious issue for psychology, and science more broadly. Yet the general phenomenon that unconscious brain processes do much of our deliberating for us is so robustly established in both experimental psychology and cognitive neuroscience that we can accept the broad premise while at the same time still questioning the circumstances in which it is most influential.

Instinctive decision-making of this sort is an energy-saving device: our resource-intensive attention might be needed elsewhere. It also saves time. In some instances it is better to react first and worry about why at a later date, when you are some distance from any danger. We need not even be aware of why we have responded in certain circumstances—and here again is the notion of the conscious mind coming in after the fact to supply a plausible and satisfying account for behavior, ideally a rationale that preserves our sense of being a purposeful, skillful agent (Gazzaniga 2011).

Strategic Heuristics

Which heuristics from this plethora are most relevant to strategy? Given the distinct advantages of social scale and cohesion in generating fighting power, we might expect heuristics that work to favor these dynamics to be adaptive. And indeed, this is true for a wide range of heuristics. Two familiar caveats should be stated: some linkages between heuristics and social identity are rather less obvious than others, and there is always the ever-present danger of the "just so" story, where we project an evolutionary rationale backward onto a particular cognitive tendency without any robust means of demonstrating a causal link.

First, and most obviously, consider biases that favor our own group over others. The concept of "social proof" applies, where we more readily accept information that originates within our social milieu than that from outsiders. After all, this is one of the most powerful rationales for the extended group culture: it acts as a shortcut for trust. This is an aspect of "confirmation bias," in which we accept more readily information that coheres with our existing theories of the world as opposed to information that challenges it. Related to this social rationale is a suite of biases that makes us disposed to act favorably toward our group (as opposed to outsiders), and to match our behavior to conform with group norms (especially, but not exclusively, if we feel observed by the group), or even just to favorably stereotype our group and denigrate others on the basis of a limited range of indicators.

Another set of strategically useful biases clusters around our sense of agency. We believe ourselves autonomous agents, and even those of us disabused of the notion by the study of social psychology and unconscious decision-making cannot shake fully the powerful illusion of determining our own fate through conscious acts of will. Related is an "optimism bias," familiar to academic publishers waiting on an author's promised manuscript, where we systematically overrate our attributes and abilities (Sharot 2012; Weinstein 1980). There are plenty of other ways biases shape our decision-making. Some relate to the goals we seek through strategy. Later, for example, we will see Clausewitz argue that we have a tendency to fight harder for what we possess—similar to what modern psychologists have variously called an "endowment" effect or the fallacy of "sunk costs" (Kahneman, Knetsch, and Thaler 1990; Thaler 1980).

Still another way heuristics might shape strategy is in judgment of risk. We have a tendency to exaggerate the likelihood of low probability events and of vivid events, both of which help explain the disproportionate spending on the safety of rail over road, and perhaps also disproportionately high spending on counterterrorism. Weighing risk is clearly integral to strategizing, even if sensitivity to risk varies between cultures (Coker 2009). But heuristic thinking is not rigorously probabilistic. In particular, Kahneman, Paul Slovic, and others note the tendency of emotions to skew our judgment of risk such that, for example, anger makes us more certain (Slovic 2010; Kahneman 2011).

An Emotional Heuristic?

In fact, we can see emotions themselves as heuristics, as do Antonio Damasio and others (Panksepp 1998; Slovic et al. 2007; Damasio 2006). Emotions are integral to cognition, conscious or otherwise—both in prioritizing information and suggesting behavioral responses. Recall Damasio's clinical finding, that emotion plays an important role in bounding and ordering the overall range of possible decisions in a given situation (Damasio 2006). Without emotion to guide us, he argues, we can be exceptionally poor decision-makers. This should be unsurprising since emotions evolved precisely to produce timely, good enough decisions in dangerous and ambiguous situations. The perception remains that emotional cognition is somehow inferior. Yet not only is it adaptive but, in healthy brains at least, it is also inevitable. One complication: some emotions may be consciously felt by self-aware minds; indeed, Damasio describes consciousness in largely emotional terms, but even those emotions that do not cross this threshold will still be shaping our decisions.

In the subfield of political psychology, recent years have seen the beginnings of research aimed at incorporating emotions into theories about politics and strategic decisions. Thus Jonathan Mercer explores the utility of emotion in international affairs, while David Houghton considers the emotional dimension to analogical reasoning, and I explore it in the context of decision-making about the Vietnam War (Mercer 2005; Houghton 2009; Payne 2015c).

We can readily see how "basic" emotions—fear, anxiety, and anger, especially—work to orient an organism within its environment (Panksepp 1998; LeDoux 1999; Ekman and Cordaro 2011). Humans additionally possess a rich panoply of social emotions that help navigate the dense and meaning-rich social networks of everyday life: envy, schadenfreude, embarrassment, and many more. Social relationships, especially those affecting the esteem within which we are held by the group, are of critical evolutionary importance, and we might expect them to play a part in strategic affairs, especially in the dynamics of policymaking groups or in responses to adversary behavior. Social emotions play a part in sympathy or antipathy felt toward others, including adversaries.

Ralph White, a pioneering affective political psychologist, distinguishes empathy from sympathy by noting that the former is more of a cognitive act, while the latter involves shared feeling (White 1984). This seems like an overly binary distinction since emotions are probably implicated in both, with warm feelings of sympathy (only sometimes) flowing from our instinctive fellow feeling for others. Mercer, meanwhile, notes the difficulty for adversaries to gain a favorable reputation with us, in part because of our emotional response to their behavior (Mercer 1996). To me this likely reflects the localized and fragile nature of our empathetic abilities, especially when someone isn't either present or part of our group. There may indeed be an "expanding circle" of empathy in the modern world, as the ethicist Peter Singer contends (P. Singer 2011). We are certainly capable both of empathy and sympathy with strangers, even though it sometimes requires a personal connection or some token of belonging to a shared culture. Indeed, these warm social emotions underpin the expansion of the group beyond the kinship band into altogether more plastic identities. Yet our social emotions and empathy evolve in the context of small, close-knit groups. Without that basis of fellow feeling, antipathy comes to mind more readily than sympathy, especially since, as Mercer notes, we are likely to over-ascribe hostile intent to outsiders' behaviors. Groups are easily formed and have a powerful emotional basis. And strategy is intimately bound up with how we instinctively feel about others both inside and outside our own group. So, while there are groups with conflicting agendas, emotions are likely to act as a heuristic that shapes our strategic decision-making.

Emotions and Consciousness

Emotions in their basic sense might not call for a particularly well-developed consciousness. "Basic" emotions—fear, rage, and anxiety—involve evolutionarily ancient parts of the brain that have counterparts in other animals (Panksepp 1998; LeDoux 1999). Contra Descartes, who suspected that feelings were a uniquely human attribute, there is plenty of neuroscientific evidence of emotional cognition in animals, even among neurologically simple species that are unlikely to experience rich consciousness. Additionally, there may be emotional states that we humans experience that do not reach the level of conscious awareness or that, if they do, are misattributed by the conscious mind. These emotional states and the attendant bodily responses need not require conscious self-awareness.

But consciousness and emotion are connected—especially where the emotions involved are social. This is hardly surprising, given the argument earlier about a social rationale for consciousness. For Damasio, consciousness is an inherently emotional experience (Damasio 1999). There is no conscious "self" that is separable from the feelings associated with being embodied and of being in the world. (Here is another important argument for my later discussion of the strategic implications of general AI, particularly in asking whether it might develop something akin to consciousness.)

It is likely that consciousness has borrowed and adapted existing cognitive systems. For example, as LeDoux describes, there are two channels of experiencing fear in response to a stimulus: a direct route, straight from the sensory cortices to the amygdala, and a more circuitous and slower route, in which the stimulus is appraised by the neocortex (the parts of the brain associated with deliberate, rational thought, and implicated in consciousness). As for our social emotions—envy, pride, schadenfreude, and so on—it may make more sense to talk of emotional blends rather than discrete neural systems. As with fear traveling by its slower, neocortical appraisal route, these social emotions will engage networks in the neocortex that weigh meaning in its social context. For humans, meaning has at least two dimensions: one is categorical, linking and integrating concepts with one another, as with the global workspace; the other is emotional, as with the indelibly emotional hue to conscious experience—the feeling of what happens, as Damasio aptly puts it.

Emotions like these are an important guide to the social world of dense meanings and complex interrelationships. Indeed, Damasio's research shows that damage to the ventromedial prefrontal cortex, a part of the brain implicated in many emotional experiences, can result in poor decision-making among afflicted individuals (Damasio 2006). In place of emotional judgments, these people seemingly engage instead in laborious, slow, and sometimes inconclusive rational cost-benefit analyses.

The social rationale for the evolution of consciousness in humans is even stronger when considering the role of emotion in orienting individuals and in prioritizing cognitions from among the many parallel unconscious processes in the brain. Alongside the "thick time" dimension of its recursive, looping quality and the sense of a continually unfolding narrative stream, this emotionality is surely among the most commonly remarked-on aspect of conscious experience. The link back to war and strategy is worth reiterating here. War heavily favors large, cooperative groups united by shared meanings or cultures. There is, accordingly, an evolutionary rationale for a consciousness that can reflect on those complex meanings and be guided by social emotions.

Adaptive "Glitches"

Some of our many cognitive heuristics might seem of dubious worth, at least on the account offered here. They produce distortions in what might otherwise be the rational act of seeking our collective and individual goals. They can lead to behaviors that are not optimal in the modern world—for example, groupthink that closes down consideration of alternatives; or the emotional surge produced by piqued esteem that fuels escalatory retaliation (of special import in an era with hugely destructive weaponry); or the stereotyping of outgroups leading to mass, industrialized atrocity (Sémelin 2007; McCullough 2008; Janis 1982). Or consider the heavy time discounting that favors a bird in the hand over two in the bush: this is an evolutionarily advantageous state given the perils of early human life, but it is also a serious impediment to considered long-term thinking in general and especially in strategy among democracies where the clamorous demands of the present can drown out deliberations about the long run (Soman et al. 2005). Much of the literature in political psychology focuses on the possibility for these "glitches" in human cognition to produce errors in policy that a more calculating, abstractly rational mind might avoid (Khong 1992; Houghton 2001). But this notion of a "rational" mind more rigorously appraising the various options for strategy is both implausible and of dubious merit.

This logic of maladaptation to modernity is also the thrust of much evolutionary psychology. As we evolved over a period of millions of years, reaching back to before our common ancestry with the chimpanzee and other great apes some five to six million years ago, the architecture of our brains was honed to best fit the prevailing environment of the time, not that of the post-Enlightenment West. This is an argument one encounters routinely in respect of our unhealthy addiction to sugar and salt: once scarce commodities, they are now available in superabundance.

An alternative approach is to ask how we have come so far, if evolved heuristics are so maladaptive or produce systematic errors in decision-making. As a supplementary question, what can be done to address the more egregious errors in modern strategizing that arise nonetheless? To answer the first, consider the case for heuristics being maladaptive. Remember that the Paleolithic man's world was more violent than today. If we consider our cognitive biases as having been so well suited to that epoch but not today, how do we explain that the modern world is a far better place for most people, with vastly greater populations living comparatively long, peaceful, and prosperous lives in dense and extended social networks?

Heuristics evolved precisely because they work to a greater good for the individual, or rather for their genes. On average, the benefits should outweigh the damage that might ensue through distortions in individual episodes. Most important, heuristics do this by saving time and cognitive load, especially conscious effort, which might be better dedicated to more important matters elsewhere. One famous psychology experiment showed that people whose conscious attention was absorbed in a memory task made poorer food choices by choosing high-energy foods over healthier salads (Shiv and Fedorikhin 1999). This looks like damning evidence from the perspective of the modern calorie-rich world but is a highly adaptive autopilot mechanism in resource-scarce hunter-gatherer communities.

Often the greater good served by heuristics was social. Conscious attention could be dedicated to particularly important challenges, perhaps those that involve long-range planning or careful, deliberate reasoning. Meanwhile, unconscious heuristics could leverage the power of the group. So we might instinctively favor the in-group over outsiders and seek to establish and promote our place within it. The automation of these cognitions may sometimes impose a cost—as, for example, when we conform to social norms that do us harm. For an extreme example of that, consider the ultimate social cost of cult group suicide (Reiterman 2008).

But set those disadvantages against the marked advantages that accrue to an individual who is a member of a cohesive, secure social group—particularly the strategic advantages. As should be very familiar by this stage, the logic of cohesive and increasingly large groups able to generate fighting power was strong in prehistory because intergroup conflict was commonplace. So the instinctive tendencies to favor the group, to conform to it and punish transgressors, are readily explicable. When we outsource the cognitive heavy lifting to the group, whatever we risk in decision-making accuracy is usually more than compensated for by benefits received from group membership.

A similar argument can be mounted in favor of emotional decision-making: it may be adaptive in the aggregate even if it is suboptimal in particular cases. And many emotions offer a shortcut to socially effective decisions. For example, the burning indignation experienced upon learning that the conventions of the group are being thwarted motivates people to conform and to police the norm. If that instinctive indignation comes at a cost to the punisher—so-called altruistic punishment—then it is subject to the same logic as altruism itself: on average the good accruing to the individual through membership in a cohesive group must outweigh the personal cost of altruism (Crockett et al. 2010). Again, the selective pressure of war suggests this is true.

Heuristics, social or otherwise, are about making sense of complexity and having to cope with too much information, too much uncertainty, or both. That's a problem today, with huge volumes of information, multiple possible social identities, and vast social groups. It is certainly possible that heuristics may produce maladaptive decisions, because our world is so very different from the resource-scarce, violent, and competitive world of the hunter-gatherer. Yet it is also evident that heuristics take up much of the strain of decision-making on our behalf, in contrast with the view of ourselves as rational agents. There is an inevitability to heuristic decision-making, and that's not all bad.

Ameliorating Heuristic Errors

With some forethought, however, we can introduce structures to ameliorate the maladaptive effects of heuristics on decision-making. "Red-teaming" to combat the effects of groupthink, for example, attempts to institutionalize dissent within the decision-making process and is a staple of intelligence analysis. Institutional solutions like this are fallible, as the Butler Review found when assessing the performance of the intelligence agencies ahead of the Iraq invasion in 2003. The "sofa-style" informal decision-making process favored by Prime Minister Tony Blair served to undermine the Chinese walls that should have separated the rigorous analysis of intelligence from its political employment (Butler of Brockwell 2004).

Ad hoc processes may also work to ameliorate the effects of emotion. For example, US president Richard Nixon's risky approach to brinkmanship and his brittle personality so alarmed his senior decision-makers that they would interpose themselves as "firebreaks" between his orders and action. Melvin Laird, his defense secretary, apparently did so when Nixon decided to raise the nuclear alert in response to developments in Vietnam, ostensibly so as to convince his adversaries of the dangers of escalating against a "madman"; Henry Kissinger did so more regularly, giving his boss a chance to cool off before seeing if an order still stood (Kissinger 1979; Burr 2015). This cooling-off period is similar to the extended process of decision-making about the "surge" of troops into Afghanistan that President Barack Obama considered at length in 2009—taking fully three months to weigh his options, at the risk of being considered an indecisive micromanager by opponents (Baker 2009). Obama inserted a time lag into the decision-making process in much the same way that Nixon's advisers had done.

Thus heuristics, like the affect heuristic, can produce flaws, which we can seek to ameliorate through institutional structures or personal decision-making styles. Heuristic glitches (and there are enough to suggest that the "blink" thesis of superior instant and unconscious decision-making advanced by Gladwell is at best debatable) are to some extent amenable to resolution. But there are limits. Even with the best systems and most rigorous attempts at deliberation, complexity will inevitably remain.

Heuristics and Satisficing

Rather than being unidimensional utility maximizers, humans are satisficers across a range of issue areas, and we may not even be aware of some of the goals we are trying to achieve (Simon 1957). Heuristics play a part in arbitrating among various, sometimes incompatible goals. A crisis may dominate the thinking of a policymaking group, but it is rarely the only issue in play. Kissinger's memoirs of his time in the White House ably attest to this question, with the Middle East vying for attention with the Vietnam War and European politics. Add in the domestic issues competing for presidential attention, and it's little wonder that policymakers make extensive use of simplifying assumptions.

Recent research on multitasking has established the conscious brain's limited capacity to switch rapidly between tasks without considerable loss of efficiency (Carrier et al. 2015). Findings like this suggest that the modern world of the strategist, with its glut of rapidly shifting information, multiple issues, and limited time, is one in which heuristics will be used extensively to reach decisions. Whether we view those decisions as necessarily suboptimal depends on a subjective judgment about the extent to which more deliberate, systematic consideration of all available information produces qualitatively better outcomes. Kahneman argues that it can, particularly in situations that call for statistical evidence. This more rigorous deliberation contrasts with our inherent propensity to personalize and analogize on the basis of personal experience. Philip Tetlock and Dan Gardner find something similar, with their idea of "superforecasters," who avoid the systematic, heuristic errors made by many when making predictions (Tetlock and Gardner 2016). There is always scope for the strategist to improve knowledge and even to promote more deliberative decision-making.

Perhaps, then, Clausewitz was overstating it when he asserted that action could never be based on anything firmer than instinct. But this idea at least captures something of the way in which we actually reach decisions, including on strategy—particularly the limits of our capacity for conscious deliberation, the way in which we actively construct an internal version of reality, and the extent to which our decisions are based on heuristics.

Conclusion: Strategy as Evolved Psychology

Strategy is a function of human groups and draws on repertoires of behaviors that have proved evolutionarily adaptive. We may flatter ourselves that we know the goals of our strategy and that we proceed logically to determine the best way to realize them. But this is somewhat illusory.

The goals that we seek through strategy are a case in point. Rather than clearly established *ex ante bellum*, they are sometimes revealed to us through our decisions. Sometimes we may be pursuing goals that do not even meet this low bar, having found conscious justifications (including to ourselves) for behaviors that are otherwise motivated. We might in theory articulate goals that a future self would be happy with; but equally we might be pursuing goals that currently fixate us now but that would be less compelling to a future self (Payne 2015c). We assume that what makes us angry today is what will make us angry tomorrow, even though, when that future comes, we tend to rationalize away setbacks of the past (Gilbert 2006). We have a tendency to invest in emotionally engaging sunk costs far beyond what any rational actor would pursue. We are unlikely to possess consistent and neatly ordered (transitive, in the jargon) preferences, instead satisficing between a range of sometimes conflicting goals, the priority among which may be in flux.

In sum, we are not rational actors, at least in the sense supposed by rational actor theories. But there is an altogether more human rationality underlying our strategizing. No matter how elliptical it sometimes seems, we can connect our use of collective violence to the evolutionary imperative to advance our individual genes. We do so socially and in groups where prestige counts, though that which confers prestige may vary considerably from group to group. To maximize our reproductive chances we need both status within the group and for the group to prosper against others—often in conditions of pervasive conflict. This requires scale, which in turn selects for ability to cooperate with nonkin. Reputation and standing are thus important proxy goals for human strategies.

Much of this is instinctive and the product of heuristics bubbling away beneath the surface of our awareness, even though we might consciously rationalize our behaviors after the fact. Still, consciousness serves an important strategic purpose, beyond safeguarding our sense of agency. It has allowed us to reflect in more depth than other species on the beliefs of others, endowing us with a rich, though certainly imperfect, theory of mind. We can also reflect on our own future minds. All told, this gives us a powerful package of conscious abilities—including imagination, creativity, understanding of others, and communication.

The human brain is a massively parallel processor with very limited conscious capacity to deliberate "rationally" on all the varied information it receives. We seek to satisfy our motivations, but these motivations are multiple, they may be in tension, and they may remain obscure to our conscious mind. The decisions that emerge from the collective deliberations of human groups are more complex still. It is little wonder that our ability to predict behaviors in complex social settings is so limited, as Tetlock argues (Tetlock 2005). And little wonder that there is, as Lawrence Freedman avers, an inevitably improvised, contingent dimension to strategy that is often made up on the fly as circumstances unfold (Freedman 2013).

Yet, when reflecting on the limitations of consciousness and the systematic errors of heuristic thinking, we should really pause to marvel at the whole cognitive architecture. Fast and flexible human thinkers have proved to be strategically adept and able to adjust to many environmental niches and to overcome the threat of other megafauna, including, quite possibly, other branches of our genus. Ours is an evolved psychology that has been shaped by violence and a need to cooperate in groups to meet threats communally.

PART II

Culture Meets Evolved Strategy

CHAPTER **4**

The Pen and the Sword in Ancient Greece

It is not possible to meaningfully compress more than twelve thousand years of history into a few pages. Human culture reaches much farther back into prehistory anyway. Accordingly, the objective here is far more modest: to identify a handful of major themes that can withstand scrutiny without being banal. My overarching point is to explore the effect of culture on the evolved strategic behavior and strategic psychology described earlier. Amid all the tremendous diversity of human experimentation in cultural life, what can be said about the way in which humans have thought about war? The answer, perhaps surprisingly, is that the tremendous cultural variation, including the development of new weapons technologies, do little to alter its fundamental underlying principles.

Readers will rightly deduce that this is not a sweeping overview of human civilization of the sort that animates Yuval Hariri's popular *Sapiens*, Steven Pinker's *The Better Angels of Our Nature*, or Jared Diamond's *Guns, Germs, and Steel* (Hariri 2015; Pinker 2012; Diamond 2005). These works and others like them seek macro-themes that reach through human history to account for some of the rich diversity in culture around the world and the way in which it has developed or culturally evolved. My goal is comparatively much simpler: to understand whether, despite the manifest great variety of human cultures, including in their approaches to war, there are some common themes in strategy.

The evidence suggests there are. No matter how long and elastic the tether that connects a culture to its evolutionary past, the link remains. Most fundamentally, human evolution has led to greater cooperation because of the importance of scale in warfare, as illustrated by Lanchester's square law. The ability for large-scale human societies to exist at all is an important function of our capacity for culture itself. Culture provides a badge of belonging and is a powerful indicator, often instinctively felt, of who can be trusted. The scale and flexibility of our groups facilitates specialization so that skills can be exchanged within a group on the basis of comparative advantage. Technology, the product of that specialization and cultural learning, enters the strategic calculus, with the potential to transform the fighting power of the group. Status within and between groups is measured by prestige and is sometimes derived from skill and knowledge, as well as by dominance. The remainder of strategy falls out of this. Much of this might be characterized, perhaps unfairly, as the strategy of the weak—featuring the canny use of surprise, maneuver, and deception. Strong groups can practice all these too, of course, but the imperative to do so is less pronounced.

Strategy in modern, encultured groups still has a psychological essence: in making decisions using evolved heuristics; in the importance of immaterial factors like morale and shock in determining outcomes; and in constituting the identity and interests of the group. These are the essential ingredients in human strategy, and they persist regardless of culture, a persistence that allows the best theorists—like Thomas Schelling and Carl von Clausewitz—to make enduring observations rooted in psychology.

There is no inevitability to this process of greater cooperation via the pressure of war. That would imply a direction, even a destination, to history in the fashion of Hegel or Marx. Francis Fukuyama's *End of History* is only the most prominent recent example of this sort of teleology (Fukuyama 1992). Certainly, biological evolution has created a powerful logic in humans that promotes greater cooperation and requires empathy and a flexible conception of the group and its culture. But this logic isn't fate. With the tremendous firepower at the disposal of modern civilizations there can be no certainty that the trend will continue indefinitely toward the era of Hegel and Fukuyama's idealized "Last Man." It will take only one such burst to bring any general trend to an abrupt halt.

The evolution of human psychology has created repertoires of possible behaviors that to a considerable degree are animated by context. It produces tendencies rather than determines outcomes. Azar Gat, exploring the cultural implications of this, stresses the broadly Hobbesian nature of prehistory; this is certainly visible in violent and unstable intergroup relations (Gat 2006). In an earlier book, by contrast, I emphasize instead the evolution of cooperation and argue that this is the logic that has driven the macro-trend of reduced intergroup conflict (Payne 2015a). Both were inevitably features of prehistoric life, and both persist into the cultural epoch. Still, humans are capable of great violence and destructiveness and have exterminated whole peoples and species—including perhaps all other species of our genus.

Three Illustrations of Culture and Strategy

To illustrate the argument that strategy is inherently connected to our evolved psychology, regardless of the particulars of society, epoch, or technology, I consider three admittedly well-thumbed examples. This means that the broad historical picture, at least, may be familiar to many readers of strategic studies, allowing us to zero in on specific themes. Briefly stated, those themes are:

- Technology can shift the balance between scale and violence that is suggested by Lanchester's laws;
- Ideas about how to assemble and use force are important—technologies are one such concept, but not all ideas must involve technology, as Napoleonic armies amply demonstrated;
- Technologies both shape societies and are shaped by them. The debate between scholars about whether hoplite warfare caused or reflected the rise of a democratic middle class is illustrative;
- Writing is a technology that can lay most claim to being strategically revolutionary, insofar as it alters our cognitive approach to warfare. It outsources knowledge as an external device for storing memories. Cognition, including conscious cognition, is embodied, but writing is a first step to externalizing this cognition (Rowlands 1999);
- Still, writing is simply a development of our evolved capacity for abstract reasoning. At heart, encultured strategy continues to reflect evolved psychology and pits strength against guile; and, finally,
- Even the most advanced and destructive weapons technology—thermonuclear weapons—leave intact the bases of evolved human strategy. Emotional heuristics, attempts to gauge the intentions of other minds, and the will to sacrifice on behalf of the group all remain inescapably part of strategy.

I illustrate these themes with three cultural examples, starting with a focus on the classical world of ancient Greece—mostly the Peloponnesian War. Thucydides's timeless account of that war exemplifies humanity's transition to the historic era, as oral histories gave way to a world of literate philosophers and historians. Themes to note here include the increasing importance of specialization, hierarchy, and technology (notably writing itself, but also the weapons package associated with hoplite warfare).

Next, I focus on Clausewitz's writings. It is a giant leap from late antiquity to the French Revolution, and perhaps somewhat cavalier to claim that not much

happened in strategic affairs, because of course plenty did—with cultural variations of tremendous variety. There were hugely destructive wars of religion and
repeated encounters between starkly different cultural milieus, often entailing
tremendous violence. Societies existed at greatly different scales: some empires
endured for many centuries, while other empires blossomed and quickly fell away.
There were tiny city-states in patchwork Italy, powerful continental dynasties, feudal agricultural societies dominated by landed elites who fought on horseback,
and swaths of the world where preagricultural life continued in clans of nomads
and hunter-gatherers.

Similarly, there was great experimentation in ways of warfare and in associated
technologies—for example, in the development of pike, stirrup, longbow, heavy
armor, and maritime navigation. Warfare took on a corresponding variety, from
the stylized dueling of single combatants or the clash of elite horsemen to the
wholesale destruction of communities by rampaging warriors. Sometimes weapon
technologies are described as revolutionary, suggesting a dramatic shift in warfare
or more profoundly in the relationship between war and the societies that produced it. The term is subjective, but my inclination is to set the bar high: societies
and their armed forces may have changed dramatically in response to new technological developments without such change constituting a truly radical shift in
the essentials of strategy.

Amid this kaleidoscope of human cultural evolution, Clausewitz produced a
timeless theory of warfare that, while inconsistent, identified some enduring themes
in strategic affairs. He did so primarily by recourse to psychological themes—
notably, the role of chance, the inevitable uncertainty of warfare, and the instinctive
decision-making of the commander. He also argued repeatedly that defense is the
stronger force in warfare, and in so doing he made an important evolutionary point.

Last, I jump ahead again, this time to the era of nuclear weapons in the mid-
twentieth century. Here is another technology that seemed to have fundamentally
transformed the nature of warfare and strategy but that was—from the perspective of evolutionary psychology, at least—rather more conservative. Radical and
potent technology notwithstanding, the psychological basis of strategy remained
intact. Tolerance for risk and brinkmanship may have arguably diminished in
the nuclear era, given the apocalyptic consequences of nuclear exchange. But the
judgment of risk, via our evolved cognition, remained integral to strategy. Mid-
century efforts to imbue strategy with mathematical rigor ultimately failed and,
when nuclear crises emerged (thankfully rarely), the evidence suggests that policymaking owes more to human psychology than any abstract notions of rational
behavior of the sort common in the social sciences of the day.

Cultural Caveats

An important caveat: in reaching for points of cross-cultural commonality, many undeniably important differences will be glossed over, perhaps too many. Some of this might relate to psychological processes—for example, the propensity to cooperate for the common good, or conversely to value individual well-being over that of the group. Most experimental psychology has been conducted on a narrow spectrum of humanity: modern, mostly Western, affluent, and mostly young (often subjects are students at university, responding to psychology department ads). The degree of cultural difference is an active research field in psychology.

Similarly, it is simply impossible to capture the mind-set of those in preliterate societies who left a few physical artifacts but very little scope for psychological insight. We ought to be wary about the extent to which we assume commonality in societies that are far removed from our own, even where they have produced their own documented histories. There is plenty alien about other cultural practices in warfare, such as the treatment of prisoners or sacrificial rites. There are also differences at a more profound level, as with views about the role of chance or fate and hence about the scope for free will; or alternatively about the capacity to bend fate through moral judgment or virtue. In arguing that the essence of psychology remains common to *Homo sapiens* regardless of epoch, there is a danger of overlooking these and other significant cultural differences.

Still, notwithstanding its overall sampling bias, there are some cross-cultural comparisons in modern experimental psychology. Some of these suggest significant differences in social attitudes between individuals of different groups, including the appropriate balance between individual and collective rights, the degree of fairness owed to other individuals within a society, and attitudes about corruption (an indicator of how much trust to afford others) (Greene 2014). In the "dictator game," for example, two players divide a lump sum of money, with Player 1 dictating the amount that Player 2 is given, and Player 2 then having the right to reject the offer, meaning both sides get nothing. Clearly there is an incentive for Player 1 to pitch the offer within the culturally expected norm, or risk punishment by Player 2. In their study of fifteen different small-scale societies, Joseph Henrich and colleagues found significant cultural differences among the sample, which suggests that societies vary in their shared view on what is fair (Henrich et al. 2001).

Similar differences seem plausible between modern and prehistoric societies that differ along many dimensions, including in strategic affairs. Evidently there are culturally acquired differences in the human propensity to cooperate—the central, evolved disposition that underpins strategy. These differences might themselves vary through time within a given society, including under the pressure of warfare. This scope for dynamism complicates notions of "strategic culture," which typically sees culture as a slow-moving independent variable that can help explain how groups conceive of strategy.

The degree of cooperation in a society may be a function of many cultural, historical, and geographical factors—the degree of predatory threat, for example, or the sort of farming and fishing commonly practiced. Yet, regardless of this considerable variation, the basic evolutionary point stands: culture everywhere rests on reciprocal altruism and the reciprocal punishment (costly to those doing so) of norm violators.

Writing Transforms Strategy

With that caveat in mind, let us turn first to the ancient Greeks, a human society that first developed techniques of writing and of historical inquiry. Other societies had invented writing prior to the classical era, of course, including societies in ancient Greece. But it is the combination of writing technique with research method that makes Thucydides's work so interesting. Thucydides explicitly applied to warfare the emerging tradition of rational, evidence-based inquiry, making him the first rounded strategic studies scholar. In time this development would have truly revolutionary implications for strategy, including, to gaze far ahead, enabling the information-processing abilities of artificial intelligence. But the transformations wrought over the nearer term were highly significant too, and partly in the psychological dimension of strategy.

Writing allowed greater specialization (including for specialists in the history and theory of strategy) and greater technological sophistication. It catalyzed the already remarkable ability of humans to express abstract ideas and to form cultural groups based on them. Writing supported large bureaucracies—indeed, bureaucratic accounting was the main purpose of earlier forms of cuneiform writing in Sumeria (Postgate 2014). The effects were not solely to promote "rational" cognition. Writing also allowed the construction of enduring myths and narratives of the group, extending the existing oral process of mythology and storytelling through time and across geographical space. The transition of the *Iliad* from oral to written poetry illustrates the point powerfully (Gottschall 2013). Evidently, performers of oral poetry can accurately memorize large volumes of information and reproduce it with tremendous consistency on separate occasions: studies of oral poets in the Balkans and Scotland testify as much. Moreover, as Milman Parry famously showed, oral poets can work by assembling the verse from a tool kit of parts, following a set narrative structure and using stock phrases to fit the rhythm of the poem (Parry 1987).

Writing, however, democratizes that process of information production and dissemination. While still an elite activity that requires education and access to costly writing materials, writing transforms the nature of collective discourse, expands vocabularies, and possibly even promotes empathy (especially in creative writing)—all of which deepen the sense of cultural belonging (Mar, Oatley, and Peterson 2009; Bal and Veltkamp 2013).

Scarcity of access and production meant that other information media remained important for many centuries. For the Greeks, theater plays carried important cultural and political messages to knowledgeable audiences, as with the satirization of Pericles, Alcibiades, and other notable politicians (Sidwell 2009). New technologies and modes of conveying information can supplant older ones without entirely eliminating them, as vinyl enthusiasts and fans of performance poetry know in our own times. Yet by the fifth century BCE writing had begun to supplant the oral tradition—if not yet completely replace it (Yunis 2003). This corpus of writing may not have emerged readymade as part of a program of rational inquiry; there is perhaps a danger of projecting our view of a Greek "enlightenment" backward onto an altogether more organic process (Steiner 2015). Nonetheless, the effect was certainly beneficial for that rationalism; the epistemological contrast between Thucydides and his predecessor Herodotus is illustrative.

The origins of classical Greek writing are obscure, lying in the Archaic period some five hundred years before Thucydides and the events of the Peloponnesian War. This is perhaps the same time as the emergence of hoplites—the other technology considered here as a shaper of strategy—and, perhaps, the same time as the composition of Homer's great epics (there is considerable speculation about the origins of both hoplites and Homer). The effect on strategy was dramatic but not so much as to redefine its fundamentals.

Rational Inquiry and Strategy

Three of the landmark texts about warfare in classical Greece track the transformation of writing from the oral tradition, dominated by mythology and legend, to one that is, at least ostensibly, about objective inquiry into strategy. Where we do have insight into preliterate historic communities, we sometimes find evidence of our common humanity in common psychological responses, including to war. Homer's *Iliad* is one such window (Homer 1991). The *Iliad* has resonated down the ages because of the echoes in our own lives—it depicts the human condition in war. We and many other societies before us can relate to the motives of the pre-historic Acheans: the romantic jealousy that started the conflict, or the searing rage of Achilles in his desire to revenge the death of his friend Patrolocus. We can find in its verses the dehumanization and desecration of enemies, the striving for honor and acclaim, the bonds of mutual recognition between warriors of similar status on opposing sides. It's a good starting point to consider the cultural impact on strategy.

Adam Nicolson argues that the *Iliad* represents the collision of a freewheel-ing pastoralist society with the settled agricultural city-state, or the horsemen of the steppe arrayed against urban opulence (Nicolson 2014). That is more sug-gestive of an earlier composition than the conventional dating of ninth century BCE. But it certainly captures something of the strategic situation: the nomadic Greeks camped on the beaches across a plain from the walled city.

There are glimpses of strategy in the *Iliad* that encompass siege warfare and bat-tle in open country between armored infantry and charioteers. There is shock ac-tion, maneuver, attrition, and deception. We should be cautious, though: a myth, however beautiful, can tell only a limited amount about strategy as enacted by its protagonists. The action is more a vehicle to demonstrate the valor of mythologized heroes than any great exposition of strategic insight. Insofar as it does demonstrate that valor, there is some suggestion that it typifies a style of war that is aristocratic and rooted in individualistic combat. Yet it also foreshadows the roots of hoplite warfare as the hallmark of classical Greek combat. Consider this passage:

> Hearing the king's command the ranks pulled closer,
> Tight as a mason packs a good stone wall,
> Blocks of granite blocks for a storied house
> That fights the ripping winds—crammed so close
> The crested helmets, the war-shields bulging, jutting,
> Buckler-to-buckler, helm-to-helm, man-to-man, massed tight
> And the horsehair crests on glittering helmet horns brushed
> As they tossed their heads, the battalions bulked so dense. (Homer 1991,
>   16:250–57)

The Greek warrior Ajax, meanwhile, spurs his men on by telling them to "dread what comrades say of you here in bloody combat! When men dread that, more men come through alive. When soldiers break and run, goodbye glory, goodbye all defenses!" (Homer 1991, 15:652–55). Modern studies of combat cohesion can add relatively little to that. Courage in combat comes in large part from fear of disgrace in front of comrades. Such is the logic of altruistic cooperation in human society: the importance of reputation and the fear of disgrace.

Many strategic questions are left unanswered though, not least how the Greeks are sustained, year on year, in their exposed beachhead. How is command exercised in battle? Is it just a matter of federated gangs operating under the direction of a "big man," as with primitive warfare? Much of the savage combat is a confused and unrelenting (not to say unrealistic) blur of carnage as heroes cut through opponent after opponent. Even the deception that ultimately annihilates Troy is more convincing as an allegory than as a real tactic, with the triumph of horsemen pastoralists symbolized by their hollow horse. At best the *Iliad* might tell us something about the sort of warfare practiced in preliterate Greek society: it was a confused melee of warriors fighting largely as individuals, using throwing spears, ornate shields, and chariots.

But the *Iliad* does serve a purpose in thinking about strategy and culture. Later accounts of the barbarians beyond the pale of civilization come to us secondhand from historians of the literate world. The depictions of battle along the Roman frontier by Caesar and Tacitus, for instance, provide a contrast between the ordered, disciplined "us" and the wildly unruly "them." In *The Annals*, Tacitus has the Roman commander Germanicus describing the tribal enemy to his assembled army: "Physically they look formidable, and are quite good for a short rush. But they cannot stand being hurt." He explains that the Germans wear no breastplates or helmets and that their shields are not reinforced with iron but are just wickerwork. Later, with the battle under way, Tacitus describes how the Germans, hemmed in by terrain, cannot charge freely as was their wont but must fight the ordered ranks of Romans at close quarters. The Romans, "with shields close to their chests and sword hilts firmly grasped, rained blows on the enemy's huge forms and exposed faces, and forced murderous passage" (Tacitus 2003, 83–86). As a review of the strengths of discipline and close formation in battle, it is compelling, especially when a concentrating force against easily isolated individual warriors. We do learn something of the motivations of the *barberoi* indirectly from this and other early histories—but via a filter of ingrained cultural stereotypes whose sometime pejorative tone can obscure the real motivations of the preliterate.

In the *Iliad*, by contrast, readers are among the barbarians, and we find them altogether familiar. They are concerned with honor and prestige, and they negotiate leadership between rival big men with differing objectives. It might be epic poetry, as opposed to strategic analysis, but it is an authentic expression of the social world of the oral poets and their audience. It is also a bridge that connects the modern historic world of conflict with the preliterate wars of early humans, and indeed with other primates.

The other thing Homer has in spades, of course, is the gods. Magic is invoked routinely to explain the course of events as well as tragedy and the role of fate in shaping destiny. This world—with the Oracle at Delphi and routine offerings made to the gods to placate or win favor—was still very much the world of classical Greece during the Peloponnesian War.

Thucydides Invents Strategic Studies

By the time Thucydides wrote his landmark *History of the Peloponnesian War* in the late fifth century BCE, much had changed about Greek warfare and culture since the Homeric age (Thucydides 2008). Weapons and tactics had changed, and so had Greek society itself. There is considerable academic debate, largely unresolved, about the relationship between these two.

The protracted war provides a first opportunity to explore the ramifications of culture for strategy, and it does so because of Thucydides himself—and his combination of writing and rational inquiry. He made use of the new technology in a radically new way. Reflecting wider intellectual trends in Greek (especially Athenian) society, Thucydides made a rational inquiry—in his case into the causes of the war. In so doing he produced the first thoroughgoing work of strategic studies. This was a new approach to history. Herodotus, a near contemporary, may have conducted his own investigations and travels to inform his writing about earlier eras, but they came with a heavy dose of the supernatural (Herodotus 1996). Thucydides, by contrast, was committed to the secular idea that human causes underpin warfare and the notion that these causes can be examined through inquiry. As an attempt to use evidence and establish causal relations, the work succeeds—perhaps overly so, as it has become the received wisdom on key events in the war, which perhaps speaks to the scarcity of alternative accounts rather than to the objectivity of Thucydides as historian.

Thucydides explicitly sought to produce a work that would endure, "a possession for all time," as he boldly wrote at the outset. Its claim to immortality lay in two principal features: an aspiration to describe the underlying human nature that brought about and sustained the conflict, and its method. Thucydides was the first strategist to recognizably adopt modern methodologies, including the use of primary sources (which in his case was access to the key personalities and events of the time).

Consider this small example from Herodotus as illustrative of the contrast. Herodotus was writing of events that had taken place many decades before, during the Persian invasion of 480 BCE when he himself would have been a young child. He mentions one Scyllias of Scione, who deserts from the Persians to the Greeks:

> I cannot say for certain how it was that he managed to reach the Greeks, and I am amazed if what is said is true; for, according to this, he dived under the water at Aphetae and did not come up until he reached Artemisium—a distance of about ten miles. (Herodotus 1996, 453)

A "tall tale," as Herodotus puts it, adding his personal view that Scyllias probably traveled by boat. Probably. The episode certainly appeals to me as an open-water swimmer, but more pertinently it captures both the social reality of the day and Herodotus's method. This is a world where a ten-mile underwater swim might be given serious credence. But it is also a world where the historian conducts research, weighs the evidence, and adjudicates on its plausibility. Herodotus acts as a bridge between the straightforward legend of Homer and the more careful parsing of evidence by Thucydides (Baragwanath and Bakker 2012).

By contrast to both Herodotus and Homer, the supernatural features only passingly in Thucydides's writing—and when it does, that is because it featured in the lives of his protagonists rather than being invoked as an explanatory factor itself. For example, Thucydides relates that the Spartans sent a delegation to Delphi to consult the Oracle about whether to go to war; they were promised victory if they fought with all their might. Indeed, it is possible that religion features too little relative to its actual presence in everyday life—which has led to scholarly speculation that Thucydides himself was agnostic at best (Jordan 1986; Hornblower 1992).

Instead, Thucydides offers a very human account of strategy, which is perhaps why his work has proved so durable and enjoys the reputation it does within modern strategic studies. We can find a sophisticated treatment in his work of the sorts of human motivations that animate strategy (and where we do, they are rather familiar psychological factors that run throughout: fear, hate, greed, and so forth). We also can find rich detail about the particular character of warfare in his era: the weapons, generalship, and even the financial underpinnings of strategy.

Thucydides's history is, however, rather less than an objective account of the war. Indeed, while he offers some intriguing and highly plausible psychological insights into the strategic machinations of the protagonists, there remains an important and indissoluble subjectivity and partiality to his account. Thucydides is a storyteller, just like his antecedents. As Ned Lebow argues, he was self-consciously so, given his understanding of the way convention and identity shape behavior (Lebow 2001). He was engaged in an act of constructivism, not least by forging a new way of using research and writing to uncover the truth, but also by dint of the argument he constructed, which may, as Donald Kagan argues, have been contrary to the perceived wisdom of the day (Kagan 2009).

As part of his method, Thucydides presents as verbatim extensive speeches from leading protagonists. This certainly stretches credulity—though he was a key player in some of the events he narrates, as an Athenian general exiled for battlefield failure and acquainted with other important players on all sides of the conflict, he quotes from speeches he did not attend and which would have required prodigious feats of notetaking even if he had. Some important speeches in key debates are not included or are glossed over, as Thucydides exercises editorial judgment. The speeches are devices to aid his narrative and strengthen his argument, which may be less objective than appears on first viewing. Thucydides is the staunch advocate of Pericles, Athens's leading strategist in the early years of the war, and he is chary of the Athenian mob, whose passions could be aroused by demagogues. He had personal experience of that, having been stripped of military command and exiled after being deemed negligent in his duties when the Spartans took the Athenian colony at Amphipolis.

Perhaps we shouldn't be too critical. If Thucydides writes advocacy rather than an objective account of events, as Kagan alleges, he presages many later historians, whose endless cycles of revision and counterrevision often reflect as much the authorial present as the events they ostensibly describe.

What about his strategic insights? Are they as timeless as he hoped? Thucydides is often described as a realist—and the long-standing tropes of realism are evident in his concern with power dynamics and alliances. His hero is Pericles, whose defensive realism and conservative strategy led him to establish the Athenians' long walls, which so irritated his more aggressive peers. He also connects fighting power to economics—not least in this example of Pericles's patience in the face of the Spartan invasion of Attica. Culture enabled a more long-sighted approach to strategy, marshaling resources over time. Kagan suggests that Thucydides was one-eyed in his measure of Pericles's grasp of the financial implications of his strategy of passive resistance—another example of his bias; on the other hand, Victor Davis Hanson argues that the Spartans would have found that ravaging the deserted Attican countryside was harder than it might at first appear (Hanson 1998). Revision begets revision. The important point here is that culture enlarges the scope for strategy: beyond battle into campaigns that extend over time and space.

Lebow, having earlier cast Thucydides as a proto-constructivist, also sees in him a classical realism that preserves space for agency and reflects a pessimistic take on human nature (Lebow 2003). There is a harsh amorality in Athens's attitude to its imperial subjects and neutrals—and which is especially evident in the famed Melian dialogue. Power, this episode demonstrates, is as much a matter of perception and reputation as material superiority. When the Melians chose to go down to annihilation, it also demonstrates that identity and a sense of honor can win out even against an objective assessment of the odds. The episode, in short, does much to substantiate the evolutionary account of strategy in which social identity is an important motivation. Thucydides recognized as much in his timeless observation, that honor as well as material gain motivate conflict (Lebow 2006).

This connection between political action and underlying human nature is why Thucydides is relevant to my study. His account of human nature is certainly insightful enough to resonate two millennia later. The work is both profound and flawed. But, regardless of the accuracy of his view of human nature or the objectivity of his narrative of the war, most important is what Thucydides represents: the first attempt to systematically and rationally consider organized violence. From the perspective of evolutionary psychology, writing had opened the scope for a new mode of cognition. First, it produced a means to account for the bureaucracy of larger groups, a handy aid to empire. Second, it established a way of communicating ideas, including ideology, about the identity of the group. Third, it served as a way of developing a specialized epistemic community of strategic thinkers. Much of that specialized literature, like that of the Roman Vegetius, would concentrate on battle tactics; others produced political tracts offering "mirror books" as a guide to statesmanship (Vegetius 1993). Slow to start, inaccessible to many, and of widely varying quality, the systematic study of war and strategy was nonetheless under way.

War, Writing, and Rationality

Writing was a radical invention—or, rather, inventions, since it was rediscovered several times over—with profound implications for war that would gather pace in the millennia to follow. We can understand war, as recent scholars like Stephen Rosen and Thomas Schelling have done, as an exchange of information, not least about the will and cohesion of adversaries and their fighting power (Schelling 2008; Rosen 2005). Writing is part of that information exchange and a means itself of creating fighting power. In a sense, writing is the first step toward an "artificial intelligence" that augments our natural, evolved abilities.

What difference did writing really make to the essence of strategy? The character of the wars of classical Greece are certainly far different from the wars of the modern world. Equally, they might not look too far removed from the wars of nonliterate Greece a few centuries earlier. Indeed, there is some risk of making too much of the contrast in strategy and war between the prehistoric and historical eras, as I have just done with the contrast between Homer and Thucydides.

Yet, for Christopher Coker, there is a clear contrast: war as an institution becomes meaningful with the onset of history, when it becomes a matter for philosophical speculation, as with Thucydides (Coker 2010). For Martin van Creveld, meanwhile, there is something distinctly emotional and existential about primordial violence, in contrast to the more reasoned, instrumental approach to strategy by modern societies (van Creveld 1991). The former he terms nontrinitarian warfare, to contrast it with the logic set out by Clausewitz, who had balanced rationality with passion and chance in a "remarkable trinity" that underpinned the way states thought about war. For both van Creveld and Coker, then, there is something different between modern and primitive warfare. But van Creveld's view does a disservice to the instrumental logic that sometimes underpins primitive warfare, just as it does for "civilized" states.

Coker's argument about civilization and rationality is more profound. Literacy is key: writing creates the possibility for reflection about war, which changes its essence. Most particularly, it enlarges the scope for peace. This chimes with Jared Diamond's view of war in hunter-gatherer societies, where war is an ever-present threat partly because there is so much scope for misinterpretation and misperception about what has been agreed to at the end of hostilities (Diamond 2013). War was, as Napoleon Chagnon argued of his Yanomamö subjects, a chronic and endemic problem. The causes of war are altogether more slippery when they cannot be held up to objective scrutiny, and blame apportioned accordingly. Writing by no means solves this issue, of course, but at least it enhances the possibility of peace by promoting rational consideration of the cause and purpose of fighting. There may never have been a social contract in the form that Hobbes speculated about, wherein men compacted to the Leviathan, exchanging absolute freedom for security; but at the very least the scope for a written contract was an aid to rational deliberation about the benefits and costs of war. Michael Howard has argued that liberals "invented" peace through the Enlightenment emphasis on rationality and the attendant notion of equality (Howard 2002). Of course, there had been plenty of *actual* peace before this time, but the essence of liberalism—laissez faire, so long as you were not thereby harming others, to paraphrase John Stuart Mill—meant that for the first time there was a logic of peace to set against the logic of war.

Howard was right about liberalism, but Coker is right too: the roots of modern liberal rationality lie in the earlier Enlightenment of classical Greece and the use of writing as a tool for reasoning about war and peace.

Rationality entails the capacity to reflect about our own cognition and the cognition of others as well as the ability to carefully examine evidence and reason about cause and effect. It was already there in our evolved ability to think abstractly and to recombine cognitive images with dazzling speed and flexibility. But literacy certainly enhanced this evolved ability; it outsourced our somewhat limited capacity for explicit memory and allowed information to be more faithfully scrutinized and shared between individuals.

Writing was initially scarce, requiring expensive materials and laborious reproduction and education, which perhaps explains the slow initial progress of strategic thought that Beatrice Heuser remarks on (Heuser 2010). The more immediate impact of writing lies less in thinking about strategy itself and more in the creation of new technologies through which to wage war. Additionally, it fostered debate about how one ought to behave in warfare, as exemplified in the Christian doctrine on just war. The accumulation of information through human history was very gradual at first, and not linear thereafter. But the specialized knowledge that writing permitted has borne spectacular fruit over the longer term. Incremental cumulative gains in knowledge eventually accelerated, becoming by our time a relentless torrent of information. Modern estimates for the growth of information are staggering and almost incomprehensible for minds that had evolved in an environment of slow, linear change. No one can know for sure whether the rate of information growth is really exponential, as some claim, since reliable metrics are hard to come by. Nonetheless, the general acceleration of information production and exchange has given rise to the notion of a "technological singularity" in which machine intelligence harnesses and accelerates the generation of information still further, perhaps leading to the eventual emergence of an artificial "superintelligence" that supplants humanity (Vinge 1993; Kurzweil 2006). Writing was the first step in that process and, as such, was the most dramatic strategic development during our evolution as a distinct species.

Passionate Statesmen and Rational Bands

Contra van Creveld, existential and passionate motivations for violence are usually mixed up with instrumental, material motivations, regardless of who is making strategy. War entails passion for modern states and hunter-gatherers alike.

Organization—of governance or militaries—may mitigate the whims of passionate decision-making, but it can never eliminate it. This is as true of nonstate warfare before the historical era as it is with modern nonstate groups, including those waging terroristic war today. When John Mackinlay argues, in *The Insurgent Archipelago*, that today's violent Islamists are a new type of threat because they fight for existential reasons, he does a disservice to their altogether political motives and their sincere attempt to use violence instrumentally, even to the point of developing their own strategic theories (Mackinlay 2009; Payne 2011).

The same is true from the other end of the spectrum. Statesmen may pride themselves on their rational deliberations, but there is usually more to their deliberations than that—a reality of which Thucydides was keenly aware. When he argued that wars were fought for reasons of fear, honor, and interest, the first two, at least, pointed to psychological rationales for conflict. Even the third allowed for considerable psychological interpretation and subjectivity. This trinity of causal factors appeals to modern writers too—Colin Gray routinely makes regular reference to it, and it can also be found in Ned Lebow's *Cultural Theory* (Lebow 2008; Gray 2016). And for good reason: it is a concise distillation of the evolved motivations for conflict. In a work that has become beloved of "realist" scholars interested in timeless and objective realities of interstate relations, Thucydides's "remarkable trinity" (to borrow a term from Clausewitz) is double-edged: on the one hand he alights on timeless factors underpinning conflict, and on the other he suggests that the particulars can vary widely: *What*, exactly, is considered honorable or of interest? It varies, and is often a matter for interpretation. So, broadly, there may be concern for security and the relative power of other states, but there is also scope for agency and for a rich array of motivations—the somewhat anarchical structure of the international system seldom, if ever, entirely determines outcomes. That is, in part, because the outside world is always interpreted; power is perceived rather than ontologically given, and security is often subjective and a matter of personal perception.

Thucydides suggests that strategy retains some common features across eras. Then as now it is animated and sustained by the search for status as well as more directly by the desire to possess material resources. Powerful evolved psychological motivations shape the conduct of the action too—as with the tendency for moral cohesion to be built around the values of the in-group, while the out-group is stereotyped and dehumanized.

And yet war in the era of "cultural evolution" seems qualitatively different from the wars of hunter-gatherer communities, notwithstanding the huge variety of cultural practices. Perhaps Coker is right and literate societies create the space for reason and peace. A related claim is that agriculture reined in our bellicose tendencies. In its most recent guise we find Azar Gat and Steven Pinker as the most prominent to suggest that agriculture and the social changes that accompanied it brought about a dramatic reduction in levels of societal violence (Pinker 2012; Gat 2006). Larger social groups geographically settled and based around ethnic and linguistic identities led to the rise of proto-states and empires.

The idea that agriculture is revolutionary is commonplace. Alvin Toffler argued that the agricultural revolution was one of three such revolutions in human affairs; the others being the industrial and then information revolutions (Toffler 1980). But the meaning of that "revolution" for war is contested. For example, Reinhold Niebuhr, one of the great realist scholars of IR theory, argues contra Pinker and Gat that agriculture actually *enhanced* the bellicosity of mankind by upending the egalitarianism of hunter-gatherers (Niebuhr 1932). In this he mirrors the Rousseau-like anthropological mood music of the time, which stressed the corrupting influence of civilization on essentially pacific natives.

Gat and Pinker seem to me to have the more robust evidence about a decline in violence. And they also marshal a plausible logic to account for the decline in violence. Pinker attributes this to two large factors: a spreading of empathy, so that more people are deemed worthy of humane and fair treatment, and the onset of rational argument. On empathy, it is difficult to see what could have changed so rapidly, in evolutionary terms. Empathy remains fragile and our instinctive sympathies are local and personal, although it is evidently possible to feel instinctive empathy for people quite different from you. The physical capacity to empathize with strangers, even those quite different from ourselves, must have long been there, with something making its expression more pronounced in recent times. And that is where the other logic kicks in: the rational part to Pinker's argument is the most persuasive. This rationalism is the product of our evolved conscious capacity for reflection combined with the tool of writing that catalyzes it. It is this capacity for rational reflection that enables empathy with far distant and unfamiliar people. Enter Coker, with his argument about literate society and war. Writing allows for larger groups, deeper cultural connections, and specialized epistemic communities, including those engaged in war. It intensifies the rational and enlarges the scope of strategy across space and time. Toffler was right about an information revolution but a little off on the timing: the information revolution got started with writing and the rational method of Thucydides and his peers.

The Hoplite Revolution:
Warriors, Weapons, and Society

Another technology from classical Greece is worth considering briefly. This is the "hoplite panoply"—a weapon system consisting of heavy body armor, spears, and large round shields fixed to the arm rather than gripped only in the hand. The panoply can tell us something about the relationship between culture, weapons, and our evolved psychology.

Key to the success of the hoplite was the phalanx, a close formation of warriors with adjacent shields who could form a wall, with each protecting not only himself but the man to his left. This characteristic feature of warfare in the time of Thucydides entailed lines of spearmen, perhaps as many as eight ranks deep across the battlefield. The clash of arms as the two opposing phalanxes met would be tremendously jarring; if the line should break, individual warriors would be exposed to the thrusting spears and short swords of their adversaries. Among the limiting factors were terrain (a flat plain worked best) and the cost of the armor (which dictated who could serve in the phalanx).

Hoplite warfare makes several useful contributions to my argument. First, it shows how technology complicates the abstract mathematical relationship between scale and fighting power that Lanchester identified—in this case, constraining the geometric correlation by forcing combat back toward the linear law. The armor, when used by disciplined, well-organized infantry, prevents the effective concentration of force of all against all—blunting, thereby, the impact of scale. Small societies, as the Spartans famously demonstrated at Thermopylae, might hold off far larger ones.

Additionally, the hoplite panoply illustrates the scope for specialization in culturally sophisticated societies in which not everyone does the fighting, unlike in hunter-gatherer communities. Societies are both specialized and stratified, with people performing different roles that confer different amounts of prestige. Fighting is a form of comparative advantage traded within the society according to the principle of reciprocal altruism. It certainly confers status and prestige and is prized in many societies more than many other skills. Specialism as a warrior went only so far in Greece since it was typically combined with other roles. The scholarly debate concerns the role of middle-class farmers, who might fight as hoplites when called on but who would not be full-time warriors. Command, too, would be performed by multitaskers—the *strategos* who combined politics, business, and military command in one person. This degree of specialization contrasts with the egalitarian world of the hunter-gatherer, where almost all males would be warriors when needed and where leadership would be achieved through the charismatic example of a strong man. Now warriors could come in different guises, from irregular skirmishers to aristocratic horsemen. Even the hoplites would be of different status, with the best quality warriors traditionally found to the right of the line (the objective being to fold the adversary's line backward in a counterclockwise fashion).

There would be many local variations but only one clear-cut example of a professional warrior caste. In Sparta's unique social structure, all able male citizens were trained from birth to be warriors, which among other things created a reliance on a slave underclass of *helot* farmers and limited the size of available armed forces (thereby increasing reliance on allied states) (Cartledge 2003). Elsewhere, however, broader sections of society would have engaged in hoplite warfare, though there is still much debate about how extensive the hoplite class was (Kagan and Viggiano 2013). Let us consider this issue now, briefly, not least because it sheds light on a dynamic that will return in the discussion on AI and the relationship between society, technology, and strategy (McNeill 2008).

Technology and Society

Hoplite warfare may initially have been the preserve of better-off members of society, not least since armor was prohibitively expensive for many but also because of the time required to train. While it may have started as the preserve of the elites, by Thucydides's time hoplite warfare engaged a broader social strata and included a middle class of landowners, not just the narrowly drawn elite. In many early agricultural societies, mounted warfare played a similar role to hoplite warfare for the Greeks. This continued through history and not only in feudal Europe. Often, only landed elites could maintain a stable, acquire armor, and afford the leisure time to hone cavalry skills.

In classical Greece, however, the hoplite foot soldier was the *acme* of warriorhood, and a close association arose between the phalanx and the civil life of the polis. There were still cavalry, which could play an important part in flanking and in routing disorganized infantry, but the nobleman and the middle classes of many cities met in the *phalanx*, where even the *strategos* himself was vulnerable to the clash of arms. Hoplite warfare was doubtless expensive, but it was still within reach of a broad section of Greek society. The pace at which this expansion of the hoplite class occurred, however, is a matter for considerable debate among scholars, as is the direction of causality. Which came first: middle-class farmers or hoplite warriors? And when?

On one hand, an orthodox view suggests that a military-technical revolution occurring in the Archaic period of Greek history, sometime around the seventh century BCE, gave rise to hoplite warfare and in consequence produced societal changes by empowering the new warriors relative to the existing aristocratic elite. The necessary virtues of discipline and order on the battlefield transformed the freewheeling, existential valor of the heroic warrior of Homeric legend into a citizen-soldier. Perhaps the aristocrats in traditional, pre-hoplite society of the sort found in Homer were the first able to afford the new mode of fighting, but the clear advantages of scale in a phalanx would very rapidly have necessitated an extension of the hoplite group to a more inclusive basis. Larger phalanxes would outmuscle smaller ones or outflank them with a longer front. Expanding the hoplites would in turn encourage new structures in society, as the "middle class" warriors demanded a say in governance. The close association between the rise of the hoplite and the middle-class farmer is most strongly associated with the writing of Victor Davis Hanson (Hanson 1999).

Perhaps this expanded hoplite class would lend its support to tyranny, as the more broadly constituted middle classes backed one strong leader to offset exploitation by the better-off elites. In this way hoplite societies prefigured one of the dominant tensions underpinning the Peloponnesian War: between a narrow oligarchy of leading aristocratic citizens and a more powerful populism that might be broadly democratic or be exploited by an adroit tyrant.

On the other hand, a gradualist school suggests that the change to hoplite warfare took place over a far longer period. Moreover, the causal direction need not be as straightforward as the orthodox account suggests, with revolutionary hoplite warfare driving social change. Perhaps instead changes in society brought about by other factors fed into the adoption of hoplite ways of fighting, which emerged piecemeal and at an uneven pace. Among the contenders would be an increasing population density and the adoption of more intensive farming techniques that enabled that increase. Small farmers may or may not have played a part in this evolution. It may also be that hoplite warfare was an evolution of existing mass combat, albeit perhaps of a more freewheeling variety, rather than a rapid break with aristocratic, heroic dueling. If mass combat already existed, then the social changes ensuing from hoplite warfare might be rather less pronounced.

This remains a debating point because of a paucity of documentary or archaeological evidence that could settle the argument definitively. There is bronze armor from ancient Greece, and hoplites feature on pottery dating to the seventh century BCE. The lines in Homer are strongly suggestive of contemporary hoplite warfare, but this is hardly conclusive. There is also a passage from Aristotle linking hoplites to the emergence of the middle classes far back in Greek history. The Spartan phalanx and hoplite panoply saw off the Persian invaders in 490 BCE, well before the Peloponnesian War. And Sparta evidently enjoyed a formidable reputation in hoplite warfare from the sixth century BCE. The question of what warfare was like before that era, however, is rather less settled. So, too, is the extent to which Sparta should be considered an outlier in the degree to which its social structures reflected the dominance of the hoplite (Trundle 2001).

And so the debate rumbles on, somewhat inconclusively—both as to the timing and speed of hoplite warfare's rise to prominence and the causal relationship between warriors and their societies. The debate is important for us because it illustrates themes that extend much more broadly than ancient Greece. For example, a good deal of similarity between otherwise different cultures can be found in the relationship between warrior elites (often mounted) and peasant infantry. The relationship echoes into the modern era. In more than a century since cavalry was last a factor on the battlefield, the cavalry regiments of the British Army remain the preserve of the well to do, often with a long family tradition of service in the same regiment. And the British Army retains hundreds of horses for ceremonial purposes—more, even, than main battle tanks. Truly this is a demonstration of the lingering power of class and tradition, even when set against the exigencies of battle.

The questions raised in the particulars of hoplite debate are also useful in contextualizing a more general relationship between society, technology, and strategy. Technology shapes the possibilities for strategy—for example, in the extent to which massed fighting power can be offset by organized defenses. It may also shape the structure of societies that do the fighting. In reality, though, it may be impossible to separate out the range of factors shaping warfare and society into discrete, ordered causal and dependent variables. It seems more plausible, for example, to see the emergence of hoplite warfare as resulting from the interrelationship among many factors, some narrowly technological, including technologies related to combat, and others more broadly sociological.

Other Forms of Warfare Persist

The debates about hoplite warfare should not obscure another interesting point about technology and society: that the pace and extent of adoption of the full "package" may have varied across societies within the Greek world, depending on local conditions. While hoplite battle may have emerged as the acme of Greek warfare, with its cultural impact assured in literature and art of the time, other modes of fighting continued. There were slingers, archers, horsemen, and light infantry skirmishers in the Peloponnesian War—and different regions had reputations for expertise in each. Even where a particular society extols glory for one mode of fighting, other modes nevertheless persist, and they might even make more of a contribution to strategy than the culturally dominant mode.

Nowadays we talk about "combined arms" warfare, where fighting power is enhanced through the combination of weapons systems, each adding to martial effectiveness more than the sum of their individual contributions. We also talk of asymmetric warfare, where one side seeks to structure combat to suit its comparative advantage in a particular mode of fighting. Neither concept is particularly novel, and the Peloponnesian War illustrates both to compelling effect, as Hanson has noted (Hanson 2005). It also demonstrates that modes of conflict evolve during warfare. Most obviously, that war had a large naval dimension, offering—initially at least—an asymmetric advantage to coastal Athens rather than landlocked Sparta. Its huge navy was manned by freemen as well as slaves, though the balance between them likely changed as the war persisted, which created manpower constraints. The crews of triremes, the large fast-moving vessels powered principally by oarsmen, would engage in hand-to-hand combat as marines once their ships had battered against one another. The navy was central to Athens's expedition to Sicily and its regular forays to the islands of its empire. Later, in acknowledgment of the centrality of maritime warfare to the overall campaign, the Spartans bolstered their own navy, funded by the opportunistic Persians. At the battle of Aegospotami in 405, Lysander's Spartan fleet annihilated the Athenians so comprehensively as to end the war.

A similar cultural evolution was under way on land. Hoplites might be celebrated as the epitome of martial prowess, and there were indeed some spectacular set piece battles, some of which proved influential in shaping the course of the war. One such was at Mantinea in 418 BCE, when some sixteen thousand hoplites clashed and gave Sparta and its allies a decisive victory. Yet much of the action in the war did not involve pitched battle between heavy infantry arrayed in a shield wall. For example, even the vaunted Spartan hoplites on the island of Spachtria were undone when surrounded by the combined arms assault of light infantry, archers, and slingers. These more mobile fighters were able to move rapidly—seizing the high ground and surprising the enemy in his rear. Overwhelmed, the surviving Spartans capitulated and became war hostages. Similarly, in their doomed expedition to Syracuse, the Athenian hoplites were eventually exposed by the absence of cavalry with which to protect their vulnerable flanks from the more mobile enemy. In that campaign as elsewhere, siege warfare—notably the engineering of walls and counterwalls, played a prominent part in determining victory. So, too, did those lighter, more mobile forces, including skirmishers and irregulars.

The heavy infantryman in line abreast remained the acme of Greek warfare: a culturally distinct mode of war that distinguished the Greek polis from the barbarian world without. And the ideal type of the hoplite was the Spartan marching rhythmically onto the battle plain in chilling, ordered silence. But the mythologized ideal, as so often happens, was rather distinct from the actuality of internecine Greek warfare. Even the Spartans, who experienced a precipitous decline in manpower as the war went on, seem to have broadened the franchise to include the lower classes from within their highly stratified society, including the *helot* underclass (Cawkwell 1983).

Some Lessons from Greece for Lanchester

We can recognize the densely packed ranks of the phalanx as a way of subverting the logic of Lanchester's square law, which underpinned the evolution of strategic intelligence. The classic hoplite formation limits the ability of an attacker to concentrate force and so prevents combat becoming a struggle of all-against-all. If the hoplite shield wall holds, combat becomes many parallel one-on-one encounters. Not in the sense of the isolated duels that pepper the *Iliad*, perhaps, but as a consequence of the limitations of space in which to fight. The cohesion of the infantry and the protection of their large, double-gripped shields stopped attackers from isolating defenders and destroying them in detail. Of course, if the ranks should break—perhaps as a result of the shocking impact of colliding with their antagonists—then the resultant gaps could be exploited and the defenders defeated.

There was a clear logic for adopting hoplite warfare once its superiority in pitched battle became apparent: it was a way of offsetting the advantages of charioteers and of skilled warriors fighting as individuals in a more freewheeling battle. Fighting as a phalanx provides a way of mitigating adversary strength in numbers—ideal for relatively small city-states that can muster only a few thousand hoplites, even for their largest battles.

Yet size would still count in hoplite-on-hoplite warfare: other things being equal, a large hoplite force should possess more fighting power than a smaller one even if the mathematical relationship is linear and not square. A large force could extend the line of battle and deepen the front, adding to the weight of its shock effect. So, even if the hoplite "revolution" started with aristocratic warriors who could afford the panoply and the time to dedicate to training, the pressure to extend the ranks would likely have been considerable. This logic itself might bring pressures to agglomerate—whether through alliances, as those that litter the *Iliad* and Thucydides's *History*, or through societal changes that would extend the hoplite mode of fighting to a larger social group, perhaps even the middle-class farmer of Hanson's account.

Still, even a culturally dominant weapons technology like the hoplite panoply plays only a part in warfare. The phalanx may have blunted the ability of attacking forces to concentrate, but other modes of fighting remained viable and sometimes decisive. The spread of smallholders by the classical period *may* have been nudged by hoplite technology and the cultural significance of the phalanx. But fortification, maritime power, and light skirmishers suggest that there were alternative ways to attain victory.

We can recognize here the familiar interplay of offensive and defensive countermeasures: the interrelationship between speed and maneuver on the one hand and the weight of fire and protection on the other. Related to this, the specialization of weapons and the advantages of combined arms brought a new problem for strategists to wrestle with: concentrating force in battle would be problematic, given command-and-control difficulties, demanding discipline, training, and communication amid the chaos of battle. The hoplite battles of the day were comparatively simple affairs, perhaps another advantage of the panoply, as two opposing ranks advanced into each other. But where there were combined arms, or even where there were hoplites of differing abilities, culture presents another challenge for Lanchester's laws: fighters possessed different attributes that would need to be combined at the appropriate moment. Thus strategy, once sophisticated culture enters the scene, becomes infinitely richer in possibilities, and not just tactically. The Spartans deliberated on maritime strategy, the Athenians on whether to sail for Sicily. Earlier, both sides weighed the economic balance of Sparta laying waste to Attica while the Athenians refused battle behind their long walls.

The broad parameters of Lanchester's logic could still be discerned, however, even though technology and combined arms had transformed the crude mathematical logic of attaining local dominance, especially through raid and ambush. Scale might not factor geometrically in fighting power, per the model, but it still evidently mattered. Pericles's patient strategy of waiting out the Spartans came undone in the plague that devastated crowded Athens and in the huge manpower losses in Sicily. And Sparta's eventual eclipse in the fourth century BCE is commonly attributed to manpower issues. The strategies of the weak remain similar, too: avoid pitched battle, as the Athenians did before the crack Spartan hoplites;

use terrain and fortification to prevent the enemy from concentrating force, as the Athenians did in Attica; or use maneuver and surprise to outflank stronger enemy forces, as they did against the isolated Spartan contingent on Sphacteria.

This sketch of Greek warfare also fits with the idea that the prevalence of warfare acts as a key driver for enhanced cooperation within human societies. Regardless of the speed with which the hoplite phalanx spread and the effect it might have had on the structure of Greek society, it is unarguable that it required organized cooperation from large bodies of men. The pressure of war had produced warriors who would fight in organized, disciplined formations—held in place by a sense of belonging and civic convention as much as by compulsion. Chimpanzees do not fight in phalanxes—it takes culture to design specialized weapons and to produce the economic surpluses that can finance sustained campaigns. And it takes either compulsion or a sense of obligation to hold the soldier in place amid terror. For many Greeks, certainly, it was the honor that made the difference: a positive sense of belonging and a negative fear of shame or worse, just as Ajax declared.

To see the effect of war on cooperation and free-riding we need look no further than the intensely introspective world of classical Athenian politics. Athenian *strategoi*, routinely summoned before the assembly to account for their decisions, faced strict censure for any failings, as Thucydides knew well from his own prolonged exile. The hard-pressed Athenian *strategos* Nicias, weighing withdrawal from Syracuse, knew it too, as did the inconstant Alcibiades, who fled to Sparta ahead of his recall to Athens. On the battlefield, if the shield line broke, defeat could result in many deaths. For survivors it could lead to death or enslavement, as happened on Sicily and elsewhere. Cohesion and cooperation were vital for survival.

Conclusion: Technology Complicates Strategy

While we may speak in shorthand of a "hoplite revolution" and debate the origins and implications of this technology, when it comes to strategy and society more broadly, to do so masks considerable variation among contrasting societies with different traditions—albeit still forming a coherent and overarching Greek culture. Yet this debate about hoplite technology is important to the wider discussion here because it touches on issues far broader than the admittedly fascinating social changes in classical Greece. Specifically, it allows us to sketch some enduring themes in the relationship between technology, society, and strategy.

The same is true of writing. The particulars are fascinating, and the histories of Herodotus and Thucydides make compelling reading. But my purpose here is to make a more abstract point: once humans start using tools, there is scope for complex dynamic interrelationships between war, society, and technology. This aspect of strategy is perhaps underplayed in the classical literature because, as Heuser contends, the pace of technological change was relatively slow, at least when compared to the modern era (Heuser 2010). Aristotle, however, spotted the connection between weapons and society precisely on this question of hoplite warfare—outlining an early version of the modern orthodoxy that connects ranks of shield-men to the political structure of their society. This is his famous observation:

> The earliest constitution (after the kingships) among the Greeks was in fact composed of warriors of the cavalry in the first place, because it was in them that strength and superiority in war were to be found (for without organized formations a hoplite force is useless, and the ancients had no fund of experience of such things and no tactical procedures for them). . . . Then when states became larger and those with [hoplite] arms became stronger, the number of sharers in the constitution became larger. (Aristotle 2000, 275)

This perspective, of course, does not settle the debate about timing or even the direction of causation in the evolution of war and society. But at least it points to a connection between society and armed force. The best strategic studies scholarship has been careful in its treatment of this complex relationship—seeing technology in a rounded way as both a product of societies and a factor shaping them. Technology is both encultured and an influence on that culture, so that both coevolve.

With war-relevant technologies there is a third factor to weigh: war itself. War is a relationship between contending societies; their violent interaction catalyzes the development of new technologies and new modes of employing existing technologies. Additionally, the relationship between belligerents allows for cultural exchange, as the most effective technologies and practices are imitated. Culture has a degree of fluidity, always, and the exigencies of war may prompt rapid adjustment. In the Peloponnesian War the adoption of a maritime strategy by Sparta is illustrative, and the relationship holds more broadly. Philip Bobbit, for example, makes a connection between military technology and societal structure in Machiavelli's era, arguing that profound cultural change was intimately related to the development of mobile bronze cannon capable of breaching existing fortifications (Bobbitt 2013). As the balance swung dramatically away from the defensive, new forms of constitutional arrangement were called for on the Italian peninsula—small city-states employing mercenary warfare became vulnerable to outside predation by larger forces.

The complex interactions between these three groups of factors—war, society, and technology—make deriving any concrete relationships problematic. They undoubtedly enlarge the scope of possible strategic behaviors. Yet the psychological basis of strategy remains intact. We are still motivated, as Thucydides himself observed, by the need to gain prestige—to excel within the bounds of the normative framework of our group. And we decide strategy on the basis of our evolved cognitive heuristics and our capacity to rationalize consciously. We think emotionally—a susceptibility that, Thucydides claims, played a part in the doomed Athenian expedition to Sicily after the impassioned interventions of demagogic leaders. The same expedition demonstrates yet more evolved strategic thinking, including our over-attachment to existing commitments and, related to that, our resolve to fight hardest for existing possessions rather than acquisitions. I return to this idea in the next chapter.

These heuristics, and others, too, originate in our relationship with our social group. The development of rich cultures, a process that began to accelerate only very recently in human history, has radically changed the context within which strategic decision-making occurs. Technology, especially weapons technologies, complicate the simple relationship between scale and martial effectiveness. Manifestly, small-scale societies can persist and even prosper—sometimes inflicting defeat on larger adversaries, as, for example, the Greeks proved against the larger Persian fleet at Salamis. But strategy, for all that cultural change, retains its essential psychological basis, which is hardly surprising since groups of humans were still attempting to use force purposively against other groups.

CHAPTER 5

Clausewitz Explores the Psychology of Strategy

CARL VON CLAUSEWITZ, RATHER THAN THUCYDIDES, IS THOUGHT OF NOW-adays as the doyen of strategic studies. I jump forward more than two millennia and across a large period of strategic and cultural history to Clausewitz's writing for several reasons. First, even though that distance looks a long way from our perspective, it really isn't, in the context of evolutionary time, which saw the first *Homo erectus* campfire dating back nearly a million years. It is not long even in human evolutionary time, which extends back perhaps three hundred thousand years to our earliest human ancestors and the acceleration of the "cognitive revolution" discussed earlier.

Second, doing so reveals a second important point about evolution and strategy: culture distorts but does not entirely obviate the relationship between our evolved psychology and warfare. The neat relationship between fighting power and group size abstractly set out in Lanchester's square law is complicated by the ability of sophisticated cultures to produce technologies that enhance fighting power. Two technological breakthroughs came during the era of Thucydides—hoplite warfare and writing. There were no comparable developments in Clausewitz's time. Yet the character of war nonetheless changed dramatically—which illustrates another important theme: that cultural ideas or concepts about how to generate and employ force also matter. Here, nationalism and the Enlightenment combined to give a particular character to Napoleonic warfare, and these are reflected in Clausewitz's own writing. Romanticism, an additional intellectual theme, also infused his writing with a distinctly rich understanding of rationality.

The third reason to alight on Clausewitz is that his writing is explicitly psychological—indeed, he offers some insights that have stood up rather well to the later advances in experimental psychology, which did not exist as a separate, more rigorously scientific discipline until much later in the century. This didn't stop Clausewitz from making important contributions to strategic studies and psychology alike, not least about the role of the unconscious mind in weighing decisions. I focus here on two large and related ideas from among his many enduring psychological insights: first, that war is typically limited, even if in the abstract it might tend to the total; second, that defense is stronger than the attack. Both ideas are important to my overall thesis about psychology and strategy. Notably, if the defense is stronger than the attack, then we have an inbuilt break on Lanchester-type logic, where scale delivers disproportionate gains in fighting power.

Napoleonic warfare certainly lent itself to Clausewitz's early observations about total war. Large armies clashed and the imperial French forces were especially able to take advantage of the powerful sentiments unleashed by nationalism after the French Revolution. Unsurprisingly, Clausewitz was struck by that driving force, and much of his writing reflected that tendency toward ever more intense and consuming warfare, once the passions of the belligerents were unleashed. There is some powerful psychological support for this notion—when angered, for example, we become more certain in our judgments and less prone to aversion in judging risk (Payne 2015c).

But two constraints against ever more intense and destructive war appeal to me. The first is group size. We have certainly far exceeded the biological constraints of the sort suggested by Dunbar's number, such that vast armies numbering in tens of thousands were able to meet in Clausewitz's own era. Our highly flexible social identities allow us to form meaningful groups with and fight for many millions of anonymous others. Yet there are practical limits that shape how best to coordinate the actions of such large bodies of fighters. Clausewitz stressed the constraints imposed by "friction"—the innumerable difficulties that arose when trying to coordinate the activities of large bodies of men in uncertain times. Certainly, what we call today "command and control" was hugely difficult in his era; logistics, which Clausewitz neglected somewhat, were equally challenging. Technology has ameliorated the problem, though not eliminated it.

A second and more profound constraint on total war is the psychological dynamic between groups of antagonists. Clausewitz was again right on the mark with his notion of the culminating point of the attack, which can be neatly juxtaposed with his insistence that the defense is the stronger force in war. As the attack unfolds, its energy dissipates, while the resolve of the defender redoubles. The attacker needs to apply more effort to realize its goals, and eventually the imbalance becomes too great to continue. Together, the relative strength of the defense and the culmination of the attack suggest that achieving scale is not the end of the matter in strategy; and both concepts rather neatly fit with Napoleon's doomed invasion of Russia in 1812.

Before exploring these themes, two last reasons to alight on Clausewitz should be mentioned. First, he sets the scene for the analysis still to come about nuclear weapons. Clausewitz's repeated emphasis on battle contrasts with strategy in the nuclear age, which is, rather, about the *threat* to use force. Second, his work and his epoch will be very familiar to strategic studies scholars, which, as with Thucydides, both aids the reader's comprehension and raises the bar to make an original contribution.

The Enlightenment Meets the Romantic Mind

A tremendous cultural variation in warfare took place between the Peloponnesian War and the time Clausewitz was drafting *On War*. Weapons systems had changed the balance between attack and defense, with implications for the structure of society. In Europe, feudal horsemen had given way to new phalanxes of pike-men and archers. Later, elaborate fortifications had been outmoded by the invention of powerful mobile artillery, giving rise to a whole new wave of fortification building. The particulars of strategy had, in other words, shifted dramatically as cultures invented technologies and new modes of social governance in response to the competitive pressures of warfare. Cycles of innovation and emulation and round after round of the security dilemma ensued. For Clausewitz the richness of this history posed a problem: how best to identify enduring patterns of strategic behavior when so much of history seemed detailed and particular to its time? The tension was between theory and historicism. This was a concern for strategists more broadly—and two alternative approaches suggested themselves: first, to draw on classical scholarship, which enjoyed an elevated reputation, and second, to look to the natural sciences for inspiration in order to derive universal laws for social behavior that might mirror those found in the natural world. Clausewitz, broadly speaking, was inclined toward the particulars of history and made a close study of military campaigns, especially those of Frederick the Great and Napoleon. Moreover, he was skeptical about universal laws—deriding especially his more mathematically minded contemporaries and suggesting that strategic theory lent principle to art rather than laws to science.

Still, Clausewitz's enduring value rests not on his historical insights or his acute understanding of the societal changes under way in his era. Rather, it lies in his landmark psychological observations about war and strategy. He arrived at those by drawing on the ideas swirling in philosophy at the time, especially in the Romantic reaction to the Enlightenment.

The psychological dimension to Clausewitz's work is central to the understanding offered by his greatest modern-day interpreter, Peter Paret, who adroitly connects Clausewitz's ideas to the intellectual currents of his time (Paret 2007). Psychology was not then a separate academic discipline in the modern sense, which employs the experimental tradition from the natural sciences. Indeed, Clausewitz himself conceded that it was still something of a dark art. But the study of the mind was certainly a key part of the Enlightenment project, as were connected debates about the part that an immaterial soul played in cognition (Makari 2015).

Clausewitz arrived on the scene sufficiently late in the Enlightenment that philosophical ideas about an immortal soul had advanced somewhat beyond Descartian dualism. This idea held that the soul existed separately from the empirically observable material of the brain. This artful construct had preserved important theological space from the claims of scientific materialism, whose adherents held that the mind was simply an embodied product of sensory experience (Cunning 2014). Empirical philosophers thereafter continued to preserve space for a human soul, but they afforded it progressively less weight in explaining human behavior—John Locke's notion of the mind as a "blank slate" open to the molding effects of experience via sensation, in particular, challenged the idea of an immortal soul that was the seat of personality (Locke 2008).

By the time Clausewitz was writing there was still plenty of mystery about the machinations of the human mind. Religiosity, however, had diminished in influence, in both philosophy and politics, partly as a legacy of the devastating religious conflagrations of seventeenth-century Europe. The cultural pressure to invoke the divine to explain human affairs was less pressing, though plenty of philosophers still did so. But by the early nineteenth century, generations of materialists, especially in the English empiricist tradition, had argued that minds and their deliberations were faithful reflections of outside influences acquired by sensation. This happy distinction between a rational, instrumental mind and an eternal soul preserved space both for the divine and for Enlightenment materialism.

By the late eighteenth century, however, the rational Enlightenment had prompted a broad cultural countermovement. Romanticism, as it has become known, was especially prominent in Clausewitz's native Prussia, and his work reflects some of the broad themes associated with that movement. The term covers a broad range of intellectual activity rather than being a coherent philosophical program—more unified, perhaps, by what it stood against than what united it.

Immanuel Kant, perhaps the most prominent exemplar of the tradition, argued for an internal representation of reality that was neither readily open to introspection nor shaped by the senses—there was, in his view, an immutable internal reality, a moral law within (Kant 2007). Actually, this idea echoes in the modern sense of an evolved mind possessed of some innate concepts separate from the acquisition of sensory experience. Since the 1970s at least, the pendulum in modern brain research has swung away from the notion of mind as "blank slate," entirely malleable by experience. Some cognitive functions are evidently preloaded. For example, the notion of cause and effect is logically related to our sense of time: time progresses forward, and cause precedes effect. Another example: our evolved propensity to make sense of visual input by assuming that light is shining from above, per the sun in the natural world. Or perhaps Noam Chomsky's notion of a hardwired universal grammar, though there is considerable debate about the mechanisms through which this might work (Chomsky 2015). As a bare minimum, however, language relates to our evolved cognitive capacity to organize mental imagery, including words, into meaningful concepts—again, preloaded.

Modernity allows us to see these innate cognitive functions as a product of evolution, but Kant and his fellow Romantics lacked that intellectual framework. For them the mind or the soul (the distinction between the two varying depending on the philosopher's religious inclination) was unfathomable by the sort of armchair introspection beloved of metaphysical philosophy, and it was no less amenable to the empirical research of the day, via medical dissection. Some things were just mysterious. The spirit of the times—and *geist* was an apposite word—favored the nonrational and mysterious over the Enlightenment's determined assault on ignorance.

Johann Fichte tapped into the zeitgeist with his notion that rather than being a passive receptacle for sensation, the mind is an active constructor of its own reality. As with Kant, there are echoes of this in modern psychology, which demonstrates the extent to which perception is a combined product of sensory input and top-down modeling. Fichte also offered another far-sighted idea: that self-consciousness is a product of man's social relations with other similarly sentient individuals (Fichte 2000). This idea chimes with recent ideas about the evolution of consciousness as a means of orienting the (social) animal's relations with others, especially via a sophisticated "theory of mind". Clausewitz, soldier-scholar, was caught in the philosophical cross currents of his times. He was certainly, as Paret relates, familiar with Fichte's writing, and was even in correspondence with him. The philosopher's influence can perhaps be seen in Clausewitz's concern with what we might now call the unconscious mind and with the role that instinct plays in shaping decisions.

Clausewitz emphatically rejected a mechanical understanding of strategy, of the sort that appealed to contemporaries more enamored with Newtonian mechanics. At the crudest level, strategic theorists could describe warfare as the predetermined product of a clockwork universe, resolvable via intricate geometric calculation. Dietrich von Bülow, a contemporary, earned Clausewitz's scorn by doing just that (Gat 2001). Measuring the interior lines of communication was one particular favorite of the geometrically minded strategists. It was a small imaginative leap from the snowflake-like proportions of contemporary fortifications—revetments and outposts carefully placed to provide interlocking fields of fire against assaulting forces—or the patterns of infantry arranged in column, line, and square, to the structure of a campaign in toto. Equally anathema to Clausewitz was the reduction of strategy to aphorism—a series of general principles that might be universally applied to any strategic situation. In this he again reflected the currents of the Romantic period, with its historicist insistence on the particularities of each instance. Clausewitz urged practitioners to be guided by their own experiences, by a diligent reading of military history, and only lastly by precepts of theory.

Yet Clausewitz himself was engaged in theorizing, and his work is replete with abstract principles—that the defense is stronger than the attack; that the passionate hatred of populations will sustain conflict; that war might tend toward the total; or, most famously, that war is the continuation of politics. There were many others besides. Clausewitz squared this circle by grounding his theorizing not in the particulars of an era but instead in his understanding of psychology (though he used historical examples extensively to illustrate his points). This tactic provided a more stable anchor around which to theorize. His core ideas—the genius of the commander, the fog of war (not his phrase), and the passionate hatred of the belligerents—are all inherently psychological and, more than that, originate in affective and heuristic psychology rather than coolly logical reasoning. Some were astute insights—as with the role of unconscious, instinctive reasoning in shaping decision-making amid complexity, or the role of chance. Despite his emphasis on mass, which so appealed to later generations of military officers, he also stressed the importance of will in deciding on victory—another immaterial, psychological factor.

The intellectual tensions between the Enlightenment and the Romantic period are reflected in the relationship Clausewitz explored between material, objective phenomena and the psychological, subjective experience of reality. This theme recurs in the writings of Thomas Schelling and John Boyd, both of whom are featured later, and it is an important observation when thinking about artificial as well as human minds. For Clausewitz, the judgment of the commander can be tuned by experience so that decision-making becomes more instinctive—another parallel with modern concepts of unconscious, conditioned learning. Still, the concepts Clausewitz develops, while profound, are somewhat limited: What, exactly, *is* genius, beyond the idea that one possesses it innately and can use it to impress oneself on reality?

Azar Gat, meanwhile, observes that Clausewitz was not alone in his Romantic interpretation of warfare (Gat 2001). Clausewitz's historicism, for example, owes much to his mentor Gerhard von Scharnhorst, and his observations about psychology were preceded by Georg von Berenhorst, whose *Reflections on the Art of Strategy* foreshadow Clausewitz's concern with the mind, especially with emotions and moral forces. Clausewitz, however, is the theorist we remember today—even if that wasn't the case in the immediate aftermath of the Napoleonic wars, when his great rival Antoine-Henri Jomini enjoyed a lasting prominence. Perhaps this has something to do with the unsystematic jumble in which Clausewitz's ideas are presented in *On War*. In Britain and America, at least, something as prosaic as poor translation may have played a part in the work's reception. Those looking for more practical, digestible advice on strategy, especially on the tactical dimension to warfare, could turn instead to Jomini, particularly his comparatively simple principles of war that are still widely cited in staff colleges. Jomini made as a major theme the need to concentrate fighting power at the decisive point in combat; his tactical principles, drawing on mathematics and geometry, reflected that concern (Jomini 1992). This of course chimes with Lanchester's logic—and has often proved sound enough in practice—provided, that is, one can identify *ex ante* what the decisive point was. On that question Jomini kept his focus on battles and tactics.

Yet Clausewitz, immersed in the philosophical arguments of the day, was the more profound thinker. Some among the array of strategic ideas he produced relate directly to the argument being made here. First, while mass is often critical in warfare, per Lanchester, Jomini and Clausewitz himself, there are limits to the ever-more intense total warfare. Second, per his argument that defense is stronger than attack, a psychological motivation, must be set against the logic of numbers. Both these ideas add to our understanding of psychology and strategy. Clausewitz's writing, above all, demonstrates that ideas, as much as mass or technology, are important in the construction of fighting power.

Passionate Hatred and Mass

Consider the first main psychological insight I take from Clausewitz: war is limited. Or, in the terms of our discussion, that the logics of Lanchester and Jomini go only so far. This is perhaps not how it immediately appeared on a continent at war for over a decade, with huge armies regularly meeting in colossal set-piece battles. Indeed, Clausewitz was initially rather taken with the idea that war would tend toward the total, following the two motivations that drove it onward: emotional hatred between competing societies and the advantages of mass and concentration in battle.

Napoleonic forces gained from scale—not necessarily by being larger in any particular battle but rather by being able to replenish their ranks in between times. In contrast to the hoplite revolution of classical Greece, there were no major technological developments in this era that increased fighting power to the benefit of societies able to master it. That is, while technologies associated with war continued to develop, the pace of change was slow. Moreover, there was no game-changing technology that imperial French forces possessed which their enemies lacked. Napoleon's infantry was equipped with smooth bore muskets developed in the 1770s, inaccurate even at close range and able to fire three rounds per minute at best effort. His artillery, like that of his antagonists, consisted of bronze cannon in a variety of bore sizes, again, developed in the middle of the eighteenth century. Imperial artillery was, however, distinguished from that of other countries by its lighter weight and greater mobility, allowing the emperor to deploy it skillfully on the battlefield close to enemy lines. At sea, meanwhile, the Royal Navy was quantitatively and qualitatively superior and able to enforce an effective blockade of the French coast. Clearly, Napoleon's tremendous battlefield successes derived from something other than a marked advantage in weaponry (Chandler 1993).

This lack of material advantage was further compounded by the quality of the imperial forces; certainly, Napoleon possessed many seasoned troops and elite units of guards and cavalry. But the imperial forces were again not markedly superior man-for-man: indeed, some conscripted units were decidedly inferior to their professional adversaries. Moreover, the overall quality of infantry diminished as the campaigns wore on and the armies expanded, with more experienced soldiers being replaced by increasing numbers of raw recruits. Lastly, Napoleonic armies did not always outnumber their opposition on the battlefield. Indeed, at the Battle of Jena in 1806, Prussian forces outnumbered their antagonists but suffered a calamitous defeat, allowing the emperor to occupy Berlin.

Perhaps the French edge owed something to the élan of its marshals, particularly their ability to act with relative autonomy. But there were more fundamental strengths as well. French armies were motivated, at least initially, by the nationalistic fervor unleashed by the revolution and then later by the glory of the emperor and his grand vision of conquest. What revolutionary armies lacked in tactical sophistication they made up for with nationalistic fervor, attacking in a mob of skirmishers who were followed with columns of less-well-trained infantry, which more easily maneuvered over uneven ground than did lines of troops but which were capable of bringing to bear comparatively less firepower, across a much narrower front. To be sure, this fervor might wilt in the chaos of combat and require some impetus from more experienced troops behind. But as a nation, postrevolutionary France proved able to make good its manpower losses over many years of conflict, even into the last years of empire, when the inexperience of recruits at last began to tell.

Napoleon continued the revolutionary reliance on columns over lines, although his preference was for advance in mixed order, "*l'orde mixte*," which flexibly combined the benefits of both formations (Nosworthy 1995). This tactic typically consisted of a patchwork of battalion-sized columns that were themselves organized into a larger, often brigade-sized, formation. The overall order of battle would consist of huge lines or columns, each made from the constituent battalion columns. Each constituent battalion might then reorganize across a wider frontage to deliver more firepower as it closed with the enemy lines. Where implemented successfully, this tactic proved to be a hugely successful model of combined arms warfare.

In addition to its undoubted benefits in shock action, the column was less easily outflanked than a line by enemy cavalry, against which it could rapidly form a closed square; it might then—if the troops were sufficiently disciplined—redeploy into lines upon reaching musket range of the enemy. This battlefield equation was further complicated by artillery, with mobile cannon attempting to suppress or break up enemy lines as the French column approached. Similarly, screens of skirmishers operating ahead of the advancing infantry column would pick off opposing infantry while exploiting available cover. The last piece in the jigsaw was the cavalry, which would seek to attack enemy infantry while they were exposed in lines or while they were operating out in the open as isolated skirmishers. If the initial cavalry charges of a battle could force the enemy into a defensive square, so much the better for the approaching columns of infantry, because the square could lay down less fire than a line. Then, once a formation broke, the same cavalry could rout the stragglers.

We cannot easily apply the simple algebraic logic of Lanchester's square law to this sort of complex battle, given the functional differentiation in fighting units. But the general thrust holds: concentrating mass at the appropriate place is critical. Deploying riflemen in a line or as a screen of skirmishers allowed them to concentrate withering, if haphazard, fire. The massed column, meanwhile, could deliver shock action on a concentrated front, including with the bayonet. Artillery would also be concentrated in an effort to force a breach in enemy lines. The offensive, then, was all about concentrating fire and mass. On the other side, defense through denial was possible through the use of square formations, favorable terrain (especially by concealing soldiers on reverse slopes), and interlocking fields of fire, all of which worked to offset the advantages of mass and concentration.

Coordinating the increasing scale of Napoleonic warfare was a severe challenge, but it provided Clausewitz with two of his core concepts: the fog-like qualities of battle, where uncertainty abounded, and the "genius" of the commander, who might make decisions on the basis of imperfect information. Sensibly, the emperor relied on delegated command. Finally, for this sketch of Napoleon's approach to warfare, one must also consider logistics. Clausewitz himself did not dwell much on the matter, but we might add logistics to the list of French advantages: in addition to replenishing depleted ranks over time, the emperor's armies also traveled light, taking only three days of rations, and otherwise lived off the land. It was, altogether, a formidable military package. There is the usual retrospective debate about which ingredients were most significant, but it is hard to separate out the strands in what was always a cohesive and constantly evolving whole (Muir 2000; McConachy 2001).

The Imperial Army represents the apotheosis of conventional warfare: a large society able to sustain huge and complex armies. Strategy was manifestly more complex than what was found in hunter-gatherer societies. Yet there were many psychological connections—not least in the emotional dimension to warfare— that allowed France to generate those massed forces.

For Clausewitz and his mentor, Scharnhorst, the challenge was to emulate the strengths of this approach without unleashing the revolutionary social changes that begat it (Paret 2009). It was an impossible challenge, notwithstanding their efforts to reform the curriculum of the Prussian War College and raise the standards of professionalism among the officer corps. In the end, of course, Napoleon over-reached; for all his battlefield triumphs and undoubted ability to inspire and motivate large armies, his overall strategic aim was uncertain. The invasion of Russia in 1812 revealed the limits of scale and passion, as the Grande Armée was depleted and harassed on its way to and from Moscow. It also showed the fundamental flaw in making battle the central feature of war. The Tsarist armies, retreating from Moscow, traded space for time, thereby conserving their strength while depleting the imperial forces. Even capturing the enemy's city proved insufficient for victory. The abstract mathematics of combat neglected the impact of numerous real-world contingencies, including the exploitation of terrain and logistics—the latter being vital in sustaining such large forces when they could not live off the land through which they maneuvered. The Russians had employed a classic strategy of the weak: using depth as a passive impediment to stop the stronger force bringing to bear its concentrated fighting power. This is classic defense through denial. Their success inspired further revisionist thinking in Clausewitz, who was serving with the Tsarist army, and contributed to his key idea about the strength of the defense.

Napoleon recovered and restored the devastated Imperial Army and won further battles—a testament to the power of nationalistic fervor as well as his own personal reputation, the two perhaps indissoluble. Still, when the grand coalition of the Continental and British armies inflicted the ultimate defeat at Waterloo in 1815, they enjoyed a large advantage in manpower. Agglomeration had ultimately solved Clausewitz's conundrum, avoiding the need for thoroughgoing, perhaps even revolutionary, societal reform in Prussia. Still, even then the battle was, by Wellington's admission, a close-run thing.

To summarize: scale mattered for effective strategy, most obviously on the battlefield. There the Napoleonic system was brilliant at concentrating force in the right place, even if, as the fate of the Grande Armée in Russia showed, scale in battle was not always strategically decisive. But scale was also important in the round—the product of a society's ability to generate and sustain mass over the long term. And here again, Napoleonic France was exemplary.

The Limits of Warfare

Perhaps, then, mass still mattered. Napoleonic battles were huge, and the passions unleashed in societies waging them were equally monumental. They were a radical departure from the more constrained affairs of previous eras, and unsurprisingly this scale seized Clausewitz's imagination. There is plenty of emphasis in his writing on the importance of mass and on the enemy's army as the most relevant "center of gravity." Fighting and battle, he stressed, were the signature elements of warfare, a contrast to the earlier era that had prized maneuver and clever stratagems as ways of attaining victory without risking the verdict of battle. There is enough of this sort of thing in *On War* to lend credence to Basil Liddell Hart's later critique of Clausewitz as the "Mahdi of Mass": a man obsessed with the clash of main force units in battles of annihilation (Heuser 2002).

Yet Clausewitz is much more sophisticated than this caricature allows. Rather late in life he set about redrafting large parts of the manuscript that became *On War*—and the heavily revised chapters presented a rather different vision. Having argued that an idealized version of warfare might tend toward the total, Clausewitz now made a significant concession: real-world wars rarely tended to the total, as he had earlier thought. He ascribed the limitations to "friction," a broad and somewhat amorphous category of factors that might intercede between the commander's intentions and actual behaviors.

Our interest here is less in the material factors that contribute to friction—the inevitable difficulties of coordinating large bodies of men—and more in the psychological factors that limit the intensity of war. Clausewitz makes a decent start on that, too. First, while warfare would be sustained by the "passionate hatreds" of the belligerents involved, there might, in the real world, be limits to those hatreds. He balanced them against logic, and though he associated that logic mostly with the government of the state, it was not its exclusive purview. Notwithstanding our innate chauvinism and tendency to denigrate out-groups, especially when our own culture is under threat, we have a rational ability to weigh ends against likely costs, and this acts as a counterweight to passion. Heuristics, especially emotional ones, are a powerful cognitive force; but the reflective and inhibitory capacity for reason is one of the principal strategic advantages we humans enjoy over our near relative, the chimpanzee. Passions may run away with us, but not always. So, while wars are often fought with greater tenacity than the original stakes might warrant, there are limits.

There's a related point: only a part of society is recruited to participate in the wars of states, even if the devastating violence they unleash is sometimes inflicted on civilians too. In Clausewitz's era the growth of mass armies, presaging industrial warfare, made for a close association between society and those doing the fighting on its behalf. This was perhaps less true of the period immediately prior to the French Revolution, and it is certainly not true in the modern era of liberal warfare (Payne 2015a). And even in Clausewitz's day not everyone would be involved in war—certainly not the entirety of society, as was the case for small hunter-gatherer bands in conflict with their neighbors. If society at large is rather dissociated from the fighting of a war, then the passions that push it toward the total might be attenuated. Large social groups typically suffer proportionately less destruction in war than do small ones. Even the hugely destructive wars of Napoleon left most people in Europe unmolested. The intensity of the destruction wrought by larger groups equipped with modern weapons, like Napoleon's bronze cannon artillery, was manifestly larger than in ancient Greece, still let alone in hunter-gatherer communities. Yet the trend for progressively more destructive weapons systems broadly parallels the decline in mortality *rates* in conflict.

Why? As Gat notes, a large group enlarges the internal space for peaceful relations within society, pushing war, for most people, to the periphery (Gat 2006).

This, after all, is the essential logic of Hobbes's Leviathan. Meanwhile, the global population had begun to rise rapidly—further diminishing the aggregate deaths as a proportion of the total. Max Roser's compendium of statistics on violence are again revealing. In the nineteenth century, which included the later Franco-Prussian War as well as Napoleonic warfare, France suffered deaths in war of seventy per hundred thousand per year. That's lower than all but three of the thirty ethnographic studies of nonstate societies Roser lists, and much lower than most. With smaller communities, war is both more pervasive and proportionately more destructive. Lawrence Keeley, in his review of prestate warfare, describes it as "total war" in the sense that it can entirely consume the societies involved. Genocidal wars between state groups, by contrast, are extremely rare.

Evidently, while modern states have the capacity to inflict greater violence, *in general* their wars embroil a proportionately smaller section of society as combatants or affected civilians. Even with unprecedented defense spending and the mobilization of entire economies for "total" warfare, the Great War and the Second World War produced proportionately fewer deaths than those of many prehistoric and ethnographic communities embroiled in violence—and those two wars are themselves outliers among modern conflicts.

In sum, as Clausewitz realized, war in the real world is limited: among other factors, by the available technologies, the causes that animate violence, and the size of the groups fighting.

Defense Is Stronger Than the Attack

In his failed 1812 invasion of Russia, Napoleon found that while mass could count in pitched battle, it was not synonymous with strategy. The Russians traded space for time, refusing pitched battle while constantly harassing the Imperial Army. They even abandoned Moscow to the invaders, who occupied it briefly before beating a retreat, exhausted after losing four-fifths of their strength over the campaign. If neither defeat in battle nor possession of territory could assure victory, then other forces must have been at work in arbitrating conflict.

One of Clausewitz's core concepts provides an answer. At first blush his repeated assertion that defense is the stronger force in war appears somewhat cryptic. There are evidently times when the reverse is true and the offense dominates. In his own time, Napoleon amply demonstrated the battlefield advantages of the bold offensive, sending huge formations of motivated, patriotic Frenchmen against lines of defenders, and breaking them. On a larger strategic canvass, too,

Napoleon's lightning advances through Europe seemed to demonstrate the gains to be had from decisive and dynamic campaigning. There are historic examples aplenty of bold operational art attaining success through attack—consider the lightning surprise attack of the Japanese at Pearl Harbor and in Malaya in 1941, or the dramatic breakthrough by German panzer divisions at Sedan in 1940 before their charge across northern France to the channel ports.

By the same token, however, we can plunder the historical record to find many examples of the defense winning out in battle or campaigns, sometimes against great odds. Herodotus's famous description of the three hundred Spartans at Thermopylae and the epic British defense of Rorke's Drift against Zulu impi provide compelling illustrations that heavily outnumbered defenders can thwart determined assault. Many factors, it seems, can play a part in shaping the balance. Some of these are technical, having to do with the relative power of weapons, and some are psychological (Quester 1977). With so much variation, how is it possible to generalize about the relative balance? The germ of an answer lies in Clausewitz's writing about the psychology of defense.

A related idea of his is that there is a culminating point to the attack beyond which the shrewd commander should not persist in the offensive. Part of the "genius" of command lies in knowing exactly when that point had been attained. As Clausewitz averred, this was about being an astute judge of risk. He wrote: "It is quite clear how greatly the objective nature of war makes it a matter of assessing probabilities" (Clausewitz 1993, 96).

The quote is revealing: strategy is about choice, and Clausewitz understands that this places strategy largely within the psychological domain. There are simply too many unknowns for any precise rendering of the odds; some measure of experience must be applied to the task. Again, his metaphor of war as being most like a game of cards is apposite. As he noted, "In the whole range of human activities, war most closely resembles a game of cards" (Clausewitz 1993, 97).

This business of probability and uncertainty comes to the fore in thinking about the balance of defense and attack. Clausewitz comes close (but not quite all the way) to scooping Daniel Kahneman and Amos Tversky's revelations about risk and framing, which they shared in perhaps their most famous contribution to psychology: prospect theory. The two psychologists identified a striking relationship between the way in which a situation is "framed," or expressed, and the amount of risk that individuals are willing to accept (Kahneman and Tversky 1979). Specifically, given the choice between accepting a guaranteed loss or gambling on the small possibility of avoiding a still-larger loss, people are more inclined to gamble on the possibility because they *might* thereby avoid *any* loss. More inclined, that is, relative to behaviors with the same payoffs and odds when they are expressed as a gain—the choice between a sure gain and the small possibility of an even larger gain. Here people typically are comparatively risk-averse, settling for the sure thing. In the most telling financial experiment that the two researchers conducted, the payoffs and probabilities in either the "gain" or "loss" scenarios were *exactly* the same, with the only change being language in which the options were described. This was done by having the participants imagine themselves, in the loss scenario, being given a sum of money that they might then lose some of—thereby finding themselves in a "domain of losses" below their initial imaginary starting point. In the other scenario, the possible payoffs were expressed simply as a gain from their existing coffers.

In a nutshell, prospect theory suggests that we are loss-averse and relatively risk-acceptant when we are in that so-called domain of losses. This domain is psychological, and judged relative to some anchor point that we use as a benchmark for calculating risk. The mental benchmark or anchor helps to frame the payoffs.

Prospect theory is another example of a heuristic—the mental shortcuts we use to make decisions efficiently. As with many heuristics, there's a plausible evolutionary logic: it chimes with what we know of the evolutionary landscape and war among primates and hunter-gatherers. Gambling to acquire new resources, including territory, food, and sexual partners, comes with uncertain odds and the possibility of grave consequences. Losing resources in marginal environments may similarly prove decisive in the struggle for survival. Proverbially, of course, a bird in the hand truly seems worth two in the bush, and discretion really is the better part of valor.

In essence, we have an aversion to losing possessions and are prepared to risk more to keep what we hold. The notion is similar to that of the endowment theory, where we inflate the value of our possessions simply by dint of owning them (Thaler 1980). This also makes sense in an evolutionary setting, especially if it involves life-threatening violence. With the most primitive medicine, even minor injuries can prove fatal—so it is little wonder that pitched battle is comparatively rare, while raid and ambush, utilizing deception, surprise, and the rapid concentration of force, are staples of human strategy and commonplace in intergroup conflict.

Clausewitz's psychological thinking on the strength of the defense was not particularly advanced, relative to his discussions elsewhere, especially his theorizing on instinct versus reason in commanders. He offered some largely plausible practical explanations for the dominance of the defense, including shorter internal lines of communication for the defender, the capacity to wait and choose when and where to offer battle, and the ability to shape one's disposition ahead of any invasion. All these had worked for the Russians. But there was also more than a hint in his writing about the psychological advantage of defense. It required a degree of passivity—waiting for the attacker to take the initiative—that might be psychologically debilitating, at least relative to the dynamism of going on the offensive with movement, élan, and purpose. Yet that downside might be offset by the advantages accruing once the assault was under way. First and foremost was the moral and practical support offered by one's own population. Clausewitz wrote that "the collective influence of the country's inhabitants is far from negligible," and added that the sort of passions exhibited by the Spanish population in their popular war against the Napoleonic forces were a "genuine new source of power" (Clausewitz, Howard, et al. 1993, 446–47). Elsewhere he had noted the passionate hatred of the people as an essential force in war, which was a part of his "remarkable trinity." While he did not expand much on these ideas, preferring instead to concentrate on the more material aspects of defense, they seem to me to be key to understanding his contention that defense is the stronger of the two forces.

Related to this was his concept of the culminating point in the attack, or the point at which the gains from the offensive are maximized. After this, diminishing returns set in, and the overly bold commander who pursues the offensive too far risks a counterattack as the defense swings over onto the attack. Again, there are obvious material reasons for the diminution in offensive power—longer lines of communication being foremost; also fatigue and unfamiliar territory.

There is a puzzle here: How did the general principle weigh against the many particularities of military history? This again raises the question of historicism versus theory. Obviously there were times when the offensive did dominate, as Napoleon demonstrated time and again in dispatching adversaries with bold offensive action. With so many other factors in the mix, how could one hold things constant to allow the sort of general condition to be established? Certainly later admirers of Clausewitz didn't let his injunction about defense prevent them from following bold strategies of offensive dynamism. This is the lesson of the Franco-Prussian War of 1870, which itself was a spur to French emphasis on the inculcation of offensive spirit, whose deficiency, it was assumed, had been responsible for the failures at Sedan and later Paris. Moreover, the historical record could be plundered as readily for times when bold offensive had triumphed as for when a doughty defense had seen off the assault. Return for a moment to the variation in account Thucydides provides of the Peloponnesian War: the long walls outside Athens thwarting the Spartan heavy infantry or the fast and light Athenian skirmishers routing the Spartans on Sphacteria. Morale, terrain, even just plain luck—all could interfere with the balance between attack and defense.

The answer perhaps lies in seeing the defensive not as a physical activity per se, at least certainly not at the tactical level but rather as a general state of mind with an ingrained sense of loss aversion and territoriality. Or even as a collective state of mind, as Clausewitz alluded to when referring to the guerrilla warfare on the Spanish peninsula. In applications of prospect theory to international relations, Ned Lebow, Jack Levy, Rose McDermott, and others have sought to illustrate the effects of risk aversion on state behavior (Lebow 2010; Levy 1997; McDermott 2001). The problems for such accounts are formidable because the messy complex world outside the psychology laboratory does not so readily permit experimentation of the sort that establishes the effect for Kahneman and Tversky. In particular, it is almost impossible to know with any certainty the benchmark, or anchor, against which risk is judged. One candidate for approximating this anchor is the status quo prior to any conflict. Indeed, Clausewitz himself offered this as a point around which onlooking members of international society will make their decisions about whether to intervene in a dispute. That's certainly possible—and indeed this sort of "offshore balancing" was the basis of British continental policy for a long while, not least during the Napoleonic wars.

But this need not be the anchor point, even for conservative states interested in preserving the status quo. Even diligent offshore balancers might tolerate a revanchist state if their risk aversion is too acute, as was the case for 1930s appeasement Britain. Aims in war are often revealed as events unfold, and we may only discover how far we are prepared to fight for something once put to the test. Misunderstandings can result. In one famous example, Secretary of State Dean Acheson gave a speech listing US commitments in the Asia Pacific region, failing to include the defense of South Korea. Whether or not this error gave Stalin and Kim il Sung false confidence that an invasion of the south would be allowed to stand is moot; by neglecting to mention the country that soon thereafter became the scene of bitter and protracted US ground warfare, Acheson demonstrated the point that the value attached to goals can shift, and rapidly, depending on events. South Korea may have been within the US perimeter all along, but it wasn't pressing on Acheson's mind, which was much more focused on the potential flashpoint of Taiwan.

Clausewitz knew this, too. It is evident in his argument that war itself can shape the politics that ostensibly governs it. If the anchor point or the mental break-even value suggested by prospect theory is subjectively experienced and flexible, it becomes an impossible task to calculate the relative appetite for risk on either side.

Prospect theory, the glum conclusion of this analysis suggests, joins the legion of other failed attempts to articulate quantifiable, robust causal relationships in social science. This, however, would scarcely have surprised Clausewitz, considering his Romantic outlook on the myriad complexities of social life and his conservative take on the utility of theory. The difficulties of robustly establishing the dominance of the defense are a striking illustration of the broader problems of articulating general strategic principles. Still, for all that, Clausewitz was rather resolute about it—repeating the contention throughout his work. And in the end, at some level of abstraction, the notion is a useful way of thinking about strategy. The balance of offensive and defensive weapons systems, the relative fighting power of the forces arrayed against each other, and the myriad other factors that can weigh in the balance between intention, action, and outcome: these factors cannot be held constant. So defense dominates, but not everywhere. Sometimes élan, maneuver, and superior morale can bear fruit, and the offense triumphs, of course.

If we accept, however, the broad principle from prospect theory—that people are more acceptant of risk when they perceive themselves to be losing something—we can see the merit of Clausewitz's interpretation. It is as simple as saying that people will fight harder to hold what is being taken away. Moreover, we might add in other complementary ideas from psychology. From social identity theory, for example, comes the notion of referent identities, which can be made more salient depending on the situation. Attacking a group may be sufficient to make it set aside, if only temporarily, other competing identities (Tajfel 2010). The same theme emerges from terror management theory, in its contention that the contemplation of death makes people more aware of their cultural identity and more partial toward it (Pyszczynski, Greenberg, and Solomon 2003). In the end, few things seem more likely to enhance cohesion and encourage in-group cooperation than an attack on the group.

Conclusion

There were no dramatic technological transformations in warfare during Clausewitz's era. Earlier, the scientific advances of the Enlightenment had already brought more destructive firepower to the battlefield, especially in portable artillery. In a counterbalancing fashion, the science of defensive fortification had also advanced rapidly. Major technological developments were fast approaching, in the industrialization of warfare via telegraph, the steam engine, the railroad, and the development of steel hulls and submarines at sea. Rifled barrels and automatic weapons would soon transform battle decisively in the direction of the tactical defensive—which made the coming cult of the offensive spectacularly ill-timed.

But the key strategic developments of Clausewitz's era were ideas about society itself, not ideas about technology and weaponry. This perhaps explains why Clausewitz's ideas have proved so enduring and profound. There was an intimate connection between society and the forces employed on its behalf—which, as Paret notes, constituted a cognitive challenge for Clausewitz and others (Paret 2009). Nationalism was central to this, along with Enlightenment ideas about rationalism and egalitarianism.

Still, this new era of mass armies fighting for a modern state did little to amend the fundamental tenets of strategy in its most abstract sense. Scale clearly mattered, and as Jomini knew, the side that could concentrate its firepower decisively in battle ought to carry the day. Of course, as Clausewitz averred, the particular problems of strategy were unique to each era. In his time, scale meant that coordination was a particular problem for commanders. So, too, were logistics, and although Clausewitz did not dwell on the matter, logistics were intimately connected to professionalism and broadly based societal participation in warfare. Morale was also vital in war, not least because it underpinned the scale of armies and enhanced their fighting power by bolstering cohesion. The moral dimension of war was not a new idea, but it was recast by the French Revolution and the *levée en masse*. At the level of grand strategy, defense was clearly the stronger force in war when it entailed defense of the motherland and the shared values that constitute it. All members of society could feel a stake in the action.

Yet, these particulars notwithstanding, Clausewitz triumphantly succeeded in theorizing about war more broadly. He could do so because the psychological tenets of strategy had not fundamentally changed. It really *was* possible to theorize about war and avoid banality. The essential tenets of strategy still existed, even if they were sometimes in tension. On one hand were scale, cooperation, and concentration of the attacker; on the other were the psychological advantages of defense: cohesion, solidarity, will, and the tendency to fight that much harder for what is already possessed. Cultural variety is almost infinite, and societal change can be rapid and dramatic. Technologies and the emerging modern state changed warfare, as did new relationships between citizens and elites. Logistics, engineering, and efficient staff work were increasingly central to good strategy. But underneath the maelstrom of change, Clausewitz had discerned and articulated the enduring and evolved psychological basis of strategy.

CHAPTER 6

Nuclear Weapons Are Not Psychologically Revolutionary

As a weapons technology, nuclear weapons are profoundly disruptive and have brought about some innovative thinking about how to use force. But my argument here is that nuclear weapons are not as revolutionary for strategy as is sometimes thought. This is because they ultimately left intact the evolved psychological basis of strategic decision-making, a marked contrast with the prospect of artificially intelligent weapons that will make decisions autonomously, on the basis of wholly nonhuman processes.

Two aspects of psychology are of particular interest when thinking about nuclear weapons: the need to gauge the intent of others, via a theory of mind, and the ability to engage careful, rational, and conscious deliberation when making strategy, as opposed to the instinctive heuristic processes that do much of our cognitive heavy lifting. Both, we will see, played an important part in the Cuban Missile Crisis—justly famous and intensely studied.

One thing nuclear weapons did do was decisively undermine the relationship between scale and fighting power. Lanchester's law should be not be taken literally as either a guide to the relationship between social scale and combat power. Nor should scale be read, as the law does, as being solely the preserve of fighting units on the battlefield. To do that is to see strategy in overly mechanical terms largely entailing the concentration of force in battle at the decisive point.

Lanchester fails to account properly for modern warfare partly because of the possibility of dramatic variations in fighting power between individual units. Machine guns, for example, shatter the mathematical logic because one gunner can devastate large numbers of enemy fighters lacking equivalent weapons. The law makes more sense as an abstract guide rather than a rule to be followed dogmatically. Size matters, and it motivated our cognitive evolution at a time when weapons technology was more basic. Prehistoric man could certainly use projectile weapons—sling, bow, spear, and blowpipe—but more modern technology greatly complicates the issue of combat strength, as the Spartan phalanx and Napoleonic artillery demonstrate.

However, this logic only holds, even as an abstract principle, while the weapons remain within certain bounds. Modern states possess nuclear arsenals that can devastate entire enemy societies out of all proportion to any numerical input—whether that's counting combatants or more broadly those in the kill-chain: scientists, engineers, factory technicians, and so forth. At the extreme, nuclear weapons render the logic of Lanchester's laws nonsensical. The *Enola Gay*, the B-29 Superfortress bomber that dropped the first atomic weapon, could cause as much damage to Hiroshima with its crew of nine as could hundreds of conventionally armed bombers. Soon, intercontinental missiles with multiple warheads could destroy entire cities with a single warhead. These weapons require very few people to deploy. So, the argument that scale on the battlefield is necessary to increase fighting power has become progressively more dubious as weapons systems become more powerful.

Scale does still shape fighting power, even in modern, technologically sophisticated societies. But now it is often related to the attributes of a society rather than simply the aggregate number of its fighting forces. The Manhattan Project that developed the first atomic bombs employed tens of thousands of people and cost billions of dollars. It required a large, advanced, and wealthy society able to sustain the necessary research and development. Thus Lanchester's law needs careful treatment on two counts: weapons vary, with combined arms a staple of modern warfare, and technology extends the scope of strategy, allowing sustained campaigns and demanding considerable resources.

Nuclear weapons produced unsurpassed fighting power. In this sense, at least, they seem revolutionary. They allow states that possess them to threaten disproportionate destruction regardless of the scale of conventional force that any adversary can muster. This logic has contributed to the acquisition of nuclear weapons by smaller states facing conventionally powerful adversaries or perceiving themselves vulnerable to conventional attack. Israel and Pakistan (both of which lack the depth), North Korea, and Iran—all have been able to offset conventional vulnerabilities with atomic weapons. They are evidently a powerful defensive weapon. The question, though, is whether nuclear weapons are sufficiently powerful as to constitute a departure from the evolved psychological foundations of strategy that preceded their invention. My answer is no.

A Nuclear Revolution?

If any technology were able to radically transform the essence of strategy, the nuclear weapon would surely be it. From the outset, nuclear bombs, and later warheads, were so powerful that they challenged the essential utility of force in attaining political goals. One problem was of a disconnect between the scale of violence unleashed by nuclear weapons and the many plausible strategic goals that attended them. The threat of nuclear attack was simply incredible in relation to minor provocations. Wars might, as Clausewitz contends, be susceptible to escalation toward the total, especially once the passions of belligerent societies are fully engaged. But, as he also realized, many wars do not end up as all-out, total warfare. Instead, they are constrained not just by the technologies on offer to belligerents but also by the goals being sought.

This was essentially the problem with early US approaches to the weapon via the Eisenhower administration's strategy of massive retaliation. This strategy broadly fit the US approach to industrial warfare—what Weigley and others have termed an "American way of war," in which the focus is on the annihilation of enemy forces through the concentrated application of industrial firepower (Weigley 1973). That approach would handily allow the thrifty Eisenhower administration to save on the expense of conventional forces, and it might also help avoid protracted and bloody stalemates in marginal theaters like Korea, where the Eisenhower administration threatened nuclear escalation (Gaddis 1982). But it risked undermining the ability of the government to credibly respond to challenges that were less than vital.

A second strategic dilemma for those wielding nuclear weapons arose because of the threat of a nuclear counterattack, at least once both sides in the increasingly antagonistic Cold War possessed such weapons (Brodie 1959). One state could threaten an adversary with the use of such weapons, but such a threat would be somewhat empty if the enemy had a similar ability to strike back. With this "second strike" increasingly unavoidable, at least once the Soviets had actually generated comparable numbers of bombs, warheads, and missiles in the 1960s, there was no way to use nuclear weapons without risking mutual destruction. It was a terrifying prospect—one that Albert Wohlstetter described as the "delicate balance of terror." In fact, the balance proved robust despite several close calls (Wohlstetter 1959). With nuclear weapons on both sides, rather than strategy being the employment of *actual* force to coerce the enemy, nuclear strategy shifted the focus to the use of *potential* force as a bargaining tool.

For Robert Jervis, this distinction makes nuclear weapons a revolutionary technology that is transformative of strategy (Jervis 1989). Previously, the defense would work to *deny* the attacker their objectives; but with nuclear arsenals on both sides, the threat of *punishment* rather than denial was the cornerstone of defense. Moreover, once both sides acquire a secure second-strike capability, there might be a stable balance between them, with each threatening mutually catastrophic retaliation. Much strategic effort in the Cold War went into assuring this capability, through the proliferation of warheads, missiles, and aircraft and through passive concealment and hardening. Eventually the submarine provided a robust second-strike capability.

The advent of nuclear weapons did not signal the end of conventional strategic thinking—but as an academic discipline it understandably became dominated by the superpower nuclear standoff (Freedman 2003; Gaddis 2007). There were debates about what to target—enemy forces or civilians? Debates also arose about whether it would be possible to "win" a nuclear conflict, most likely by forcing the enemy to capitulate through the threat of further escalation. No one could know for sure what course a superpower conflict would take, whether extended deterrence of America's European allies would be honored, at what point a conventional confrontation would cross the nuclear threshold, or at what point "battlefield" nuclear weapons would give way to the destruction of cities.

Herman Kahn, the model for Stanley Kubrick's Dr. Strangelove, posited a hugely complex "ladder" of escalation through which war might pass (Kahn 1960). The challenge was to achieve "escalation dominance" in order to intimidate the adversary. Here Kahn fell into the rationalist trap. His concepts for escalation within a conflict were an advance on the idea that massive retaliation would deter most probes. But his elaborate ladders lent a false sense of order to an essentially hazy and undefined reality. Perhaps an enemy might read your intentions correctly, if you deployed battlefield or counterforce nuclear weapons against a particular target; perhaps it would understand the signal that you were trying to deliver. But there was no certainty to that. Anger or fear might prompt an unexpected response instead, or the adversary might feel the need to defend its reputation and credibility by matching your provocation. Who, in the end, knew how an enemy might respond to an attack whose meaning was obscure, whose means were uncertain, and whose stake and resolve one could only dimly perceive?

Jervis called approaches like this "conventionalist": the idea was that nuclear weapons might be used in the same way as other weapons technologies in order to coerce through force rather than deter through threat of punishment. This conventionalism certainly appealed to many military officers, but as Kahn showed, it wasn't solely the preserve of uniformed men frustrated by not being given sufficient latitude to "win" America's wars through force. Still, the nuclear era was remarkable for the growth in civilian defense expertise and in the adoption of methods from the social sciences to model conflict and force structures (Kaplan 1991).

Nuclear weapons strategy increasingly focused on the management of risk and on the threat of force rather than its employment. This resulted in a peculiar through-the-looking-glass quality to some aspects of nuclear strategy. Protecting a target through missile defense, for example, could be destabilizing and dangerous because it undercut the ability of the enemy to reliably get its retaliation in, which might make a surprise "first strike" more likely. Stability came through assured mutual vulnerability: if one side perceived that its retaliatory attack might not get through newly assembled defenses, a preventive strike, before the enemy could complete its shield, might result. In this way defensive systems were actually offensive. A treaty limiting the deployment of antiballistic missile technologies ensued. If civil defense programs had been at all promising, they, too, might have shifted the strategic balance and allowed the side in possession of an effective defensive system to be more sanguine about the prospects of national survival and thus more ready to engage in coercion. Similarly, technologies that threatened the survivability of one's own retaliatory capacity—a new antisubmarine technology or the capacity to penetrate hardened silos—would be similarly destabilizing of existing balances. It was an unusual strategy that deliberately cultivated vulnerability. In this strange, unfamiliar world in which effective defenses could be offensive, there seemed to be an opening for a new sort of strategic thinking.

Rationality versus Psychology

Robert Jervis was right: nuclear weapons did change some aspects of strategy because of the scale of destruction they made possible and the consequent emphasis on defense via deterrence. Punishment was not new—it had been a feature of conventional warfare, along with bluff and brinkmanship, two other key components of a nuclear strategy. For example, preemptive warfare was a way of achieving security through anticipatory punishment. And the threat of preemption, as well as the threat of retaliation, amounted to defense through punishment. It was, as Thucydides claimed, the fear of Athens's rising power that prompted the Spartan invasion of Attica. The Spartans got their retaliation in first, at least if we credit the logic of Thucydides. And in the nuclear era there was still an element of old-fashioned defense through denial below the nuclear threshold, as with US-led forces battling to repel the communist invasion of South Korea.

But nuclear weapons certainly shifted the balance dramatically between deterrence and coercion and between denial and punishment. Additionally, another new element had to be considered too: with mutual retaliation, the challenge was to somehow make credible the threat to commit national suicide. Credibility rested on possessing both the capability to survive a first strike and the intention to retaliate, even though it would be hugely counterproductive to actually do so. Here, the landmark concept came from Thomas Schelling, who in so doing underscored that strategy in the real world is a matter of human psychology, not abstract rationality (Schelling 2008).

American strategists, especially those working at RAND Corporation, had drawn extensively on mathematical simulation to understand how nuclear confrontation might play out. In doing so they were reflecting a broader current of positivism in American social sciences, especially economics, which borrowed ideas from mathematics to model human behavior. They were also building on the tradition of operational research developed during the Second World War in a bid to quantify the effects of strategy—notably in understanding the impact of the USAAF bombing campaign in Europe. Prominent among the approaches adopted were ideas from the exciting new field of "game theory," which seemed particularly appropriate for strategists insofar as it modeled dynamic adversarial relations among two or more players. That looked like strategy. And there could be clear benefits from using this sort of theorizing, as when operational researchers at RAND called into question the vulnerability of Strategic Air Command's nuclear basing and readiness to respond. But there were dangerous limitations too—and Schelling's analysis brought them starkly into focus.

Among the assumptions of much mathematical modeling were that actors were rational—that is, they possessed "perfect" knowledge of the options available to them and had fixed, ordered preferences that they were seeking to realize. This is, of course, not the way in which people actually make decisions in the real world, a conundrum economists evade by imposing a logic of market efficiency: real-world actors, if there are enough of them, arbitrage against one another so that their behaviors more closely approximate the "rational." The problem is that this abstraction does not really apply to international relations, with fewer states interacting than participants in a financial market and with sui generis peculiarities in each crisis situation. It does not account for the way in which preferences are sometimes "revealed" to actors themselves in the course of events, as when the United States discovered a profound interest in defending South Korea once it had been invaded by communist North Korea (Samuelson 1938). Nor does it account for the ways in which real, as opposed to rational, individuals "satisfice" between a broad range of sometimes conflicting goals, often aiming for "good enough" rather than optimal solutions. Lastly, it does not account for imperfect knowledge: for example, with asymmetric information that opens the prospect of bluffing and brinkmanship, or for what the payoffs of a particular strategy might be if it is successfully employed. Rational-actor models do not really work in economics, either, but they have proved remarkably resilient nonetheless.

Schelling's idea, presented in a chapter titled "A Reorientation of Game Theory," posed a direct challenge to rational-actor approaches. The problem was clear: rational behaviors make sense on the mathematical grid of the prisoner's dilemma, but was it truly conceivable that a "rational" statesman in the real world would either instigate or respond to a provocation when the outcome, in all probability, would be the mutual destruction of all parties, including himself? Where was the rationality in that?

Schelling acknowledged as much with his famous depiction of the challenge facing statesmen. How can they persuade a skeptical onlooker, especially an adversary, that their threat to retaliate is credible, even if doing so would ensure their own destruction? The enemy would need to believe that attack would not pay off; they would have to believe that retaliation, no matter how suicidal, would follow. In short, they would have to believe that the rational actor would choose *irrationality*. Schelling's solution was the analogy of two men, chained together, on a cliff, and one starts dancing close to the edge. The act of dancing takes away some element of control—it is deliberate and willed, but the outcome is difficult to control *ex ante*. Only by taking away the predictably rational self-preserving response can the statesman bring off his act of brinkmanship, persuading his adversary that he is serious. When it comes to jumping off the cliff, the task is to convince the other party that you can't quite help yourself and that if you go over the edge, he assuredly is coming too.

Rationality, in its theoretical game-theory sense, played a part in allowing civilians to shape nuclear weapons strategy. Unlike many in the military, they didn't just see the nuclear weapon as a bigger, more efficient bomb, and they were prepared to challenge many of the assumptions made in military planning. But Schelling's analysis points toward a more realistic understanding of rationality, informed by human psychology and taking account of emotional cognition and risk appraisal amid stress and uncertainty.

In another analogy, Schelling compares brinkmanship to a game of "chicken" played by two motorists—again, there is a need to persuade the other driver that you will not swerve, despite the suicidal nature of driving headlong toward him. The solution is to take the matter out of your hands—literally, by removing the steering wheel and demonstrating as much to the oncoming adversary before throwing it away. This analogy added additional elements missing from the rational actor model: statesmen, like everyone, could be driven by notions of status, and their decision-making inevitably entails emotional cognition.

In the early 1970s President Nixon borrowed from the logic of Kahn and Schelling with his "madman" theory of international relations: the supposed madman would, the logic went, deliberately promote a personal image of instability so that any adversary could not be sure whether he would overreact dramatically to any provocation (Dallek 2008; Kissinger 1979). As it happened, Nixon's persona was particularly well-suited to the task—his brittle insecurities meant that he frequently overreacted to perceived personal challenges. He apparently thought himself a cool, cerebral figure who used rash behavior as a front, but few of his subordinates would have concurred. In any event, nuclear strategy with Nixon certainly bore a strong resemblance to Schelling's game of chicken.

Earlier, as defense secretary to Presidents Kennedy and Johnson, Robert McNamara had brought to bear his managerial penchant for quantifiable processes, honed at the Ford Motor Company. As the Vietnam War intensified, McNamara was a leading advocate for the strategy that underpinned the bombing campaign against the North, Operation Rolling Thunder. The basic approach borrowed heavily from Kahn's idea about a ladder of escalation—in incremental steps the intensity of bombing was to be ratcheted upward (Clodfelter 1989; Pape 1996). Force would be employed less for the outright destruction it caused and more as a way of communicating American resolve to the enemy, alongside the prospect of more severe punishment to follow. It was straightforwardly a conventional application of escalation dominance. It failed, in part because American statesmen misunderstood the threshold of violence at which the North Vietnamese would capitulate. Had they understood correctly, it might have been deemed disproportionately costly or risky to apply so much force as to be out of kilter with the stakes that US leadership perceived to be involved in Vietnam (which again, they misunderstood).

The problem was simply that the enemy did not interpret the gradual escalation in the same way that the administration had anticipated. It was not that the reaction from Hanoi was somehow irrational, although it certainly departed from the sort of abstract mathematical rationality beloved of game theoreticians. Rather, the North defined its interests and stakes in ways different from the Americans, and this asymmetry of interest and commitment was reflected in North Vietnam's remarkable tenacity. Moreover, while they wanted to escalate until they met their objective of deterring further North Vietnamese incursions into the South, the Americans were anxious not to prompt a dramatic escalation of the conflict by drawing in the Soviet Union or China as active participants. They were keenly aware of the need to carefully calibrate any escalation, lest it do so. Lastly, the inevitably blunt instrument of air power proved a poor option against a society that possessed limited industrial capacity and whose armies required little logistical support and usually presented a fleeting target.

The result was abject failure for the US strategy—the conflict escalated, with each addition of US force being matched effectively by a deepening commitment from the Communists. As the Americans expanded the bombing target list and increased the number of sorties, so Communist infiltration of the South accelerated. The Americans increased ground forces concurrently, measuring the effectiveness of their commitment by the number of enemy combatants killed, which turned out to be a rather poor indicator of underlying enemy resolve. Expressed in terms that Jomini might recognize, there was no way the Americans could concentrate force on the battlefield at the decisive point.

In all, the application of graduated escalation in Vietnam provides a powerful illustration of the idea that strategy remains psychological and not reducible to calculus. Moreover, it showed that scale and technological dominance can be more than offset by resilience and moral cohesion (Payne 2015b). In fact, the conflict was a positively Clausewitzian demonstration that morale mattered at least as much as materiel and that defense is stronger than attack.

There was another important lesson from Operation Rolling Thunder and from Nixon's later application of the "madman" theory: conventional strategy is not, in many respects, all that different from nuclear strategy. The conflict demonstrated the importance of prestige and reputation in motivating escalation. It also highlighted the role of affective decision-making; the optimism bias, which leads statesmen to think they can achieve success despite manifest failures hitherto; the fundamental attribution bias, which involves reading unwarranted intentions into the ambiguous behaviors of enemies; and the role of the group in shaping decisions. With a wealth of available documentation, including that leaked by Daniel Ellsberg, himself a scholar of strategic decision-making, it is little wonder that the war has become one of the most studied from the perspective of political psychology (Ellsberg 2002). The binary distinction between nuclear and conventional strategy may have become more sharply drawn from a normative perspective, with an increasingly robust "nuclear taboo" (Tannenwald 1999). Yet, in practice US leaders were designing strategy without any certainty that it would not produce escalation beyond the nuclear threshold.

As Robert Jervis astutely identifies, the conventional utility of force had shifted with nuclear weapons. But insofar as strategy remained psychological decision-making, it was business as usual—and Jervis, a brilliant political psychologist himself, knew as much (Jervis 1976). In this respect, at least, nuclear weapons are rather less than revolutionary. Instead, one can see them as the most effective way that human society has yet found of offsetting force, blunting the logic of Lanchester by protecting most effectively against mass, concentration, and even surprise. Possession of nuclear weapons is a great equalizer for the weak—an implication not lost on regimes that have scrambled to obtain it or on those governments who have sought to bandwagon closely under the extended deterrence of nuclear powers.

Toward the Brink

There is no knowing if nuclear weapons might be useful in warfighting, because, thankfully, there has been no nuclear war since 1945. Similarly, there is no cast-iron way of knowing whether the threat of assured destruction of an enemy society will prove sufficient to deter aggression.

It is, of course, impossible to prove a negative—it may simply have been that the Soviets lacked the resolve to probe more aggressively than they did at the margins of the Cold War boundaries, in places that were of somewhat limited strategic importance to the United States. When they did, as in Korea, it may have been the result of miscalculation—perhaps prompted by the lack of explicit signaling from the Truman administration that Korea lay within its sphere of vital interest rather than from a steely and unrelenting commitment to expand the communist world.

The underlying assumption of much US strategy in the period was that nuclear weapons were defensive in character and a means of offsetting Soviet conventional superiority and an aggressively expansionist agenda. This supposed a reactive, defensive US posture in which the Soviets probed and the United States responded (Freedman 2003). There were, of course, more hawkish elements who argued for a dynamic, aggressive US approach aimed at rolling back Soviet gains. But on the whole the attitude was one of containment. There were a range of approaches to instrumentalizing containment as a grand strategy, not least between the overwhelming retaliation advocated by John Foster Dulles and the Eisenhower administration more broadly and the flexible response that replaced it. Overall, however, the sense was of being on the strategic defensive and the assumption was that a crisis would be brought about by some initial Soviet probing.

In truth, this picture did bear some semblance to the overbearing and provocative style of Nikita Khrushchev, who had been prepared to gamble with aggressive moves in Berlin and Cuba (Freedman 2000). But this view was less accurate as a picture of Stalin's inherent conservativism and caution. It perhaps said as much about the psychology of those in America as it did of the actual mind-set of the Soviets. Even the Berlin crisis of the early 1960s could be seen as more of an inevitable response to the unsustainable population losses that the Soviets and their East German ally faced rather than a calculated attempt to test the mettle of its capitalist adversary. For all the Soviet bluster, once the Berlin Wall went up, the crisis died away as superpower tensions moved elsewhere.

The same might be said of the "missile gap" of the late 1950s and the "bomber gap" that preceded it. In both cases, there was considerable American anxiety that the Soviets were developing technologies with sufficient quality and in sufficient quantities as to threaten the ability of the United States to assure the possibility of retaliatory action against Soviet aggression. It was a classic security dilemma that might have appealed to Thucydides: fear of an enemy's rising power prompting urgent rearmament amid fears of preemptive action. In fact, as eventually became clear when the Americans developed the capability to monitor Soviet production of missiles via satellite and U-2 reconnaissance flights, they discovered that there was no gap. Or, rather, that the gap heavily favored the Americans.

The problems of strategy in the nuclear age were once again largely psychological and involved a complex of factors. First was the difficulty of discerning enemy intentions from observable behavior. The tendency to over-attribute events to agency, as per the fundamental attribution bias, probably didn't help. Neither did the tendency to stereotype out-groups, making it extremely hard to earn trust. Second, there was one's own reputation and credibility and the need to signal resolve akin to Schelling's driver in the game of chicken. The logic here pointed toward ever-greater commitment, making it harder to back away from any crisis with face saved.

Part of the problem was a distinct bureaucratic interest in suspecting worst-case scenarios about enemy capabilities, which would mean the appropriation of more resources to counter the threat. In the 1950s, for US Strategic Air Command (SAC), this meant the development and large-scale acquisition of an intercontinental bomber, the B-52, which could diminish the vulnerability to surprise attack on regional bomber bases situated close to the Soviet Union. To close the supposed missile gap would have meant, of course, the acquisition of ever-greater numbers of ICBMs, which also were under the control of the air force. As Kaplan points out, when the submarine-launched ballistic missile came to maturity with the Polaris Program, the threat of losing its hitherto unassailable primacy in matters of nuclear strategy prompted some SAC leaders to change tack. They switched their advocacy away from the threat of massive retaliation against urban, civilian targets in the Soviet Union to instead favor some type of counterforce strategy aimed at the enemy's offensive nuclear capability (Kaplan 1991). The bureaucratic rationale for such a switch was clear: Polaris was incapable of the sort of precision needed for counterforce operations and was additionally unavailable in sufficient numbers.

There was an explicit, strategic rationale for counterforce too: that it was either a more effective way of deterring Soviet expansionism, especially while provocations remained conventional, or that it was a more humane and therefore more palatable response—it might avoid mass Soviet casualties and so, hopefully, mass American ones too, if the Soviets determined to respond at a similarly constrained level. But these strategic rationales were fuzzily arrived at. Having greater variety and volume of weapons in the arsenal might allow for a more flexible response to a greater variety of eventualities, even at the expense of "overkill"—possessing vastly more weapons than were needed to obliterate enemy society—yet ultimately it was all guesswork.

The nuclear threshold itself was a somewhat hazy line, the knowledge of which, like much else in deterrent theory, was impossible to determine before the event. And once the shooting was under way, the assumptions of counterforce too were impossible to verify before the fact. Would belligerents restrict themselves to counterforce attacks or not? Surely if an exchange left one side in a losing position—either with perilously little in the way of reserve nuclear forces or with a tattered capability to press home a conventional attack—there would be a strong incentive to escalate further in the hope of deterring further damaging assault.

The point at which an adversary would choose to capitulate in response to attack rather than escalate was simply unknowable. War could be seen in this way as a real-time exchange of information about resolve as much as about capacity. This would depend on any number of largely imponderable factors. One thing was clear to Cold War strategists: like so much about nuclear strategy, this would be impossible to calculate ahead of any exchange.

Cuba and Psychology

Other than the decision to escalate in Vietnam, the Cuban Missile Crisis of 1962 is perhaps the most prominent and well-studied example in the political psychology literature. The historiography of the crisis is large, and while new aspects continue to emerge, much is known of the detail—especially on the United States side, which was extensively documented. There is little point in rehashing the narrative here. Newcomers should start with Michael Dobbs's excellent historical account or Aleksandr Fursenko and Timothy Naftali's view from the Soviet side (Dobbs 2008; Fursenko and Naftali 2001). For more direct insight, readers could consult the recorded transcripts of the key meetings in the White House (May and Zelikow 1997). Robert Kennedy's vivid memoir captures some of the intense emotion of the situation among the close circle of Americans deliberating about what to do (Kennedy 1969). In short, we know as much about the crisis as we do for just about any other comparable foreign policy crisis.

For our purposes the episode serves to illustrate a few key points, principal among them being the enduring psychological basis of strategy. In particular, two points stand out. First, the crisis confirmed, if such a thing was needed, that strategy in the real world bears little relation to the abstract ideal of rational actor models. Most obviously, during the crisis there was imperfect information on both sides about the goals and will of the other, and decisions were being made amid intense emotion. Second, President Kennedy's signal achievement in solving the crisis was to engage in a deliberate effort to explore options and see things from his antagonist's perspective. The crisis abundantly demonstrates the sort of evolved psychology we've been considering to this point. Third, notwithstanding this, there was a tremendous amount of luck involved in producing a favorable outcome that was satisfactory to both sides, instead of risky escalation. The crisis was real—and there was a distinct possibility of escalation to nuclear exchange, either as a consequence of deliberate strategy by leaders, or, perhaps even more likely, as the result of local agents acting on their own initiative.

By the early 1960s, the United States had given some attention to the issue of vulnerability and taken measures to enhance the readiness of its strategic air forces to respond to Soviet counterforce attack. This made a second-strike capability more reliable; moreover, some hawkish American officers sensed that a first strike could overwhelm the abilities of the Soviets to counter. When the crisis came, several pressed for a robust military response: bombing of the Soviet missile sites on Cuba and even contemplating a mass invasion using marines and airborne infantry. On the other side, Fidel Castro was also convinced that the crisis would result in warfare and urged the Soviets to respond more forcefully to American provocations, like the repeated overflight of the island by reconnaissance aircraft. Happily, the two superpower leaders displayed a more circumspect response, at least once the crisis began to deepen.

The initial response of the Kennedy administration to the discovery of the missiles was emotional. Shocked incredulity, as Bobby Kennedy put it in his memoir (Kennedy 1969). There was anger at Khrushchev, who had earlier bullied Kennedy when the two met at a summit. There was a sense of personal challenge following the Bay of Pigs disaster, which had left the president looking weak and foolish, and the Soviet-backed East German clampdown in Berlin. Operation Mongoose, the covert attempt to oust Castro, had been under way for a year or more but with few discernable results, despite the energetic and belligerent involvement of Bobby Kennedy. Now the self-esteem of the president, and especially that of his emotional younger brother, were challenged by the failure to detect the missiles. Castro, a third-tier world leader, had been deliberately thumbing his nose at the Americans just by staying in power against their wishes. The arrival of the missiles, undetected, was further rubbing it in.

Strategically, the missiles were primarily a psychological challenge to America and its president. The deployment chimed with an underlying American perspective that the Soviets were aggressors, and there was an acute sense of being caught by surprise—the missiles, after all, had been discovered at the last moment when they were close to operational, despite a wealth of intelligence that pointed toward their presence on the island. In some respects it was reminiscent of the earlier surprise Japanese attack on Pearl Harbor, a formative experience in the life of all the administration figures.

Still, psychological or not, the weapons certainly shifted the balance of power in an objective sense, providing the Soviets with a more-diverse deterrent, and rendering any first strike attempt by the United States more complicated and less likely to obliterate all Soviet nuclear capabilities. This point was important, since, unlike the United States, the Soviets had few intercontinental missiles, some of which would take time to bring to launch readiness, and their second-strike capability could not be fully assured. So Robert McNamara was wrong to suppose, as he did, that a missile was just a missile—and that it didn't make much difference whether that missile was fired from Cuba or the Soviet Union. His was an analysis of the impact of a Soviet first strike, not the balance of deterrence, which the missiles greatly complicated.

The deployment was provocative and a direct challenge to the US sense of security in the Western Hemisphere, hitherto an inviolate part of America's regional sphere of influence. It was an indicator of a wider Soviet strategy of probing American resolve via provocative actions in important areas of geopolitical interest, where a response would risk further escalation. Moreover, it was a direct challenge to the Kennedy administration's twin ambitions to reclaim the initiative in the Cold War and rebuild the capacity to respond flexibly to just this kind of challenge. The administration's declared strategy of "flexible response" was being acutely tested and, it seemed, found wanting.

But Kennedy was also right to suppose that there was a large psychological element to the Soviet move. It is just this psychological dimension that makes the crisis so valuable to strategic studies scholarship. The episode demonstrates that even in the face of truly devastating weaponry, strategic decisions were made in a very human fashion.

Game Theory Meets Poker

If the Americans had used force to impose the removal or destruction of the missiles, they risked a nuclear exchange. The Soviet and Cuban forces defending the island were equipped with a range of tactical battlefield nuclear weapons: short-range rockets, cruise missiles, and venerable bombers capable of delivering Hiroshima-sized explosions against invading American troops. The Americans knew only some of this, and even then they could hardly be sure of the circumstances in which those weapons might be used, still less who might order such a step—would it be up to local commanders or to Khrushchev himself? The goals of the adversary and the means through which they might be sought were uncertain. Unlike in game theory knowledge was far from perfect. Even Clausewitz's preferred analogy of war being like a game of poker did scant justice to the complexity of the situation, in which neither player could objectively determine the value of the cards they held.

From the outset there were differences of opinion in how best to respond to the provocation. The initial reaction from the Kennedy brothers was to take the offensive—attacking the missiles from the air—but they quickly mellowed. The Joint Chiefs favored a full-scale invasion of the island, arguing that it would not prompt an escalatory response from the Soviets. Curtis LeMay in particular favored a dramatic military response, claiming that anything less would be construed as weakness and that the strategic balance anyway heavily favored the United States with its thousands of warheads.

But President Kennedy by now was wary: he could not be sure how the Soviets would react. And even if America had the wherewithal to destroy the Soviet Union, if it came to that, such a result—the destruction of an entire country and, presumably, significant damage to the United States itself—could hardly be counted as a great victory. The Joint Chiefs—gung ho, very aggressive, and schooled in the tradition of the offensive—were reluctant to back down from the challenge lest it bring on a more confident enemy. If the placement of the missiles were the first move in an impending conflict, it was better to avoid gradualism and shock the enemy into a rapid capitulation. The problem was that neither the hawkish generals nor the more circumspect Kennedys could determine with any degree of accuracy what the next step post-invasion would be.

In part it would depend on how hard Khrushchev wanted to fight for the stakes as he saw them. In fact, on that elemental strategic point, there was and remains (even after reams of analysis) a considerable degree of uncertainty over what, precisely, the Soviet leader and wider policymaking elite wanted. In the course of events Khrushchev's behavior revealed something about how he saw the stakes: he turned his ships away from the blockade and sent Kennedy a conciliatory and emotional message, talking about untying the knot of war before it was too late. He seems to have been genuinely afraid that matters could inadvertently spin out of control, with some justification, given local control of the weapons.

But the moment Khrushchev seemed to sense weakness in the American position, he went back to bargaining mode—calling publicly for a reciprocal removal of American short-range nuclear missiles from Turkey in addition to the pledge not to invade Cuba. The sense we get at this removed distance is of a leader with an acute sensitivity to the balance of power and a willingness to test it. But this was tempered by a degree of caution, given the incredible stakes. Unlike Castro, with his impassioned yet fragile sense of dignity and his willingness to embrace the idea of a final showdown with the Yankee enemy, Khrushchev, rather like Kennedy, seems to have been reluctant to pursue too far the idea of strategy via intimidation.

All this tells us just how highly the Soviet leader valued the stakes as the crisis unfolded. As for his initial objectives, we can still only speculate. Khrushchev seems to have felt a genuine fraternal bond with Castro, the romantic revolutionary, and we know from his previous behavior that he was committed to probing American geopolitical weaknesses. He also felt the basic inequity of the short-range American missiles stationed in Europe and saw the deployment of similar Soviet equipment in Cuba as a means of redressing that. Additionally, the crisis presented a chance to test the resolve of Kennedy, who he genuinely seems to have seen as weak, young, and inexperienced. Finally, it should be remembered that we are viewing the whole episode with hindsight bias: the missiles were discovered at the last moment, but had they not been, the Americans would have been presented with a fait accompli—a powerful deterrent in being, which the United States would have struggled to remove at an acceptable level of risk. It was a gamble that failed. Nevertheless, perhaps the margins were small enough to make it seem at the time not the monstrously risky episode that it looks with hindsight.

So much for the initial Soviet stakes, insofar as we can make them out. They are muddled, obscured in the historical record, and were likely even somewhat opaque to Khrushchev himself. As with much in strategy, it seems fair to describe them as a blend of ostensibly rational realpolitik—an attempt to shape the balance of power and secure a vulnerable ally against ongoing efforts to unseat him—and more existential strategic objectives; the status and prestige that Khrushchev himself vested in the policy is difficult to distinguish from the status and prestige of the country he led.

In truth, then, there were no purely objective stakes for either side on which to rest the foundations of strategic decision-making. Both leaders had instinct on which to predicate their subsequent behaviors, but little more. The missiles themselves were an objective reality, and their technical capabilities and likely impact were well understood. But their *meaning* depended on the interpretation placed on them by the various protagonists. Even so basic a question as their impact on the strategic balance was to a considerable degree a subjective matter. This would be true even had the US president possessed full knowledge of the number and variety of Soviet nuclear weapons on the island or the precise command-and-control arrangements that were in place to govern their use, which he did not.

Neither American nor Soviet leadership could be fully certain of the conditions under which their arsenals might be used, even though both sought to retain centralized control over them. For the Americans, there were safety measures designed to ensure that only authorized use of nuclear weapons could occur—authorized by the president, that is, who slept within seconds of a serviceman equipped with the necessary communications to set in train the vastly destructive Single Integrated Operations Plan for a nuclear strike against the Soviet Union. But there were gaps in the system. American aircraft equipped with nuclear missiles were flown by individual pilots, with no safety measures preventing them from deploying their missiles.

As for the Soviets, a formal letter from Khrushchev to the local Russian commander reiterated that control of the missiles lay with the Kremlin. But control of the scores of tactical nuclear weapons on the island, of which the Americans were apparently ignorant, lay with local commanders. Any American invasion or air strike might have prompted their use, with terrible consequences. Out at sea, the US decision late in the crisis to bring a Soviet submarine to the surface with depth charges almost precipitated the use of a tactical nuclear torpedo, which was under local command. Only a heated internal debate between the three ranking officers on board prevented the first use of a nuclear weapon (Dobbs 2008).

The steps that could be taken, should the conflict escalate, were therefore largely under the control of the leaders on both sides, but imperfectly so. This was true not just of the control of nuclear weapons but also the actions of subordinates in the conventional sphere too. Famously, the chief of naval operations clashed with Defense Secretary McNamara over the protocols to be followed during the naval blockade of the island. The navy had an established culture of "mission command" in which the commander would outline his intent, in this case to stop and search suspicious vessels heading for Cuba, but leave the management of that operation to more junior officers on the ships themselves, albeit operating within a set of protocols. This was far too risky for McNamara, who insisted on a direct line of communication with the officers on the spot.

A similar tension between policymakers and their subordinates emerged elsewhere. No one anticipated the acute danger caused when a U-2 surveillance flight mistakenly strayed off course while over the arctic and violated Soviet airspace, prompting the launch of interceptor fighter aircraft but fortunately no further retaliatory action. At the same time, ongoing CIA-sponsored subversive fighters were engaged in carrying out acts of sabotage on the Cuban mainland. These and other actions could very easily have resulted in a dramatic escalation of tension, regardless of the president's intentions. Collectively they indicate the limits on intentionality in strategy as a result of luck and complications arising from the need to delegate. This is the "agent-principal" dilemma, a staple of collective action familiar to many social scientists.

Right to the end, the American president faced splits within the ExComm, the ad hoc committee he assembled to tackle the crisis. Some advisers continued to advocate a military response, others were more dovish. Acutely conscious of the ambiguities and misunderstandings that could prompt war, not least and most famously from his own readings about the causes of the Great War, Kennedy displayed perhaps some very useful tendencies in thinking about strategy at moments of high crisis. He was cautious, even risk averse, despite the emotional challenge and shock at being placed in such a challenging position. He paused to consider options and invite alternative opinions. Perhaps most important, he sought to empathize with his adversary.

Heuristics and Conscious Reflection

Pausing is no guarantee of great strategy. There *is* no guarantee of great strategy—even the most astute strategist can go down to crushing and absolute defeat.

Strategy is dynamic and entails a sizable dose of luck, neither of which surrender readily to any sort of simple positivist analysis and both of which encourage analysts to retrospectively impose a too neat and plausible narrative on events.

Still, President Kennedy did two large and important things in the middle of the Cuban Missile Crisis: he deliberated carefully and exposed himself to contrasting views. Consider the earlier discussion about primates, which I suggested are capable of strategic thinking whereas ants are probably not. The "wars" of ants are effectively following a repertoire of evolved behaviors that have a degree of automaticity and that have been proved to be evolutionarily adaptive (Gordon 2011; Keller and Gordon 2009). But they are not suggestive of a degree of careful, abstracted deliberation. In contrast the "wars" of primates suggest a degree of greater forward planning. Chimpanzees and humans alike have the ability to stand back from a problem and work out the sequential steps they need to take to achieve their goals. They additionally possess, at least to some degree, a capacity for imagining what is going on in the minds of others.

Of course, this is all relative: like the chimpanzees and even ants, modern humans are in many respects instinctual decision-makers. Even if we are unable at this remove to understand precisely how subconscious processes would have shaped decision-making, we can offer some cautious suggestions. We might, for example, see the power of the unconscious at work in some other heuristics that the policymakers adopted to make sense of the world around them. The basic assumptions on the US side about the aggressive expansionist and monolithic communist world are revealed in the telltale vernacular name given to the Soviet troops on the island: they were referred to by the Americans as Sino-Soviets. These baseline assumptions often go unchallenged and feed into cognitive scripts that policymakers apply—a common theme in the political psychology literature (George 1969). Thus Ned Lebow's argument that the ExComm did not in fact consider *all* possible options, instead narrowing its discussion to those that would coerce the removal of the missiles (Lebow 1984). Why not leave them there? The same might be true of the other side: it seems strange to us that Khrushchev would be a true believer in a Marxist-Leninist worldview rather than a cynical practitioner of *realpolitik*, but perhaps his view of the United States was genuinely shaped by the view that its ostensible leaders were not actually in charge but merely reflecting the interests of powerful capitalists.

Other unconscious psychological tendencies are also conceivable. The crisis might readily be thought of as an example of prospect theory in action, and indeed scholars have already sought to describe it in those terms (Haas 2001). This theory, recall, suggests that individuals are more risk-seeking when they perceive themselves to be falling short of some imagined goal. For Kennedy that goal might well have been the *status quo ex ante*—a Cuba free of missiles. Once he had evidence that the blockade was being effective, his inherent caution would have gone into overdrive and sought to avoid further inflaming the situation. On the other side, Khrushchev, ahead of deploying the missiles, might have imagined himself falling behind his subjective mental benchmark. Installing missiles in Cuba would redress the evident American strategic superiority in terms of missiles and warheads, which the Soviets lacked. This is necessarily speculative. The trouble with using prospect theory as a way of understanding behavior in strategic studies is that we cannot readily gauge in the decision-maker's mind the break-even point at which the domain of gains shifts into a domain of losses, because it is an inherently subjective matter.

This absence of access to the interior mind of decision-makers is a familiar stumbling block for political psychology. In striving to overcome it we risk building a retrospective account to explain what has happened—shoehorning the evidence to fit with the theory and constructing a neat "just so" story that is plausibly convincing at first blush. It is, however, highly likely that decision-makers are subject to the same sort of framing effects as participants in studies of prospect theory. So should we ignore the tendency because we cannot robustly prove it?

Cognitive heuristics evolved to aid rapid decisions, especially in times of stress and danger. President Kennedy's angry and risk-acceptant early reaction to the Soviet provocation is of a piece. Heuristics remain an inescapable part of strategy, even when decision-makers have more time or are considering issues with less immediate danger. To step back and reflect is not to rid oneself of prejudice or bias, especially bias that one is not even aware of possessing. Still, there is a role for deliberate and conscious reflection. An instinctive response to a strong impulsive urge cued by a pressing environmental stimulus is fine for an ant, but not for a human, able to consciously weigh complex choices.

There is an argument from efficiency here: why would our deliberative consciousness exist at cost to the brain, in terms of energy resources, if it did not in fact actually do any deciding for us? Consciousness allows a way of dealing with complexity, notably in situations that involve social interaction and the future beyond the immediate future. Conscious reflection allows us to intuit, dimly, what others might want, and it allows us to grapple with our inclination to heavily discount future goals against immediate gratification. The "strange loop" that is consciousness experience (that is, observing ourselves experiencing, reflecting, and feeling) confers important advantages on humans, allowing us to respond flexibly and imaginatively to new and challenging situations, especially when doing so requires collaboration and forward planning.

The Cuban Missile Crisis demonstrates President Kennedy's ability to do this—drawing back from his initial instincts to snap back at the USSR. More hawkish members of ExComm proved less able to reflect on the challenge. Consider the actions of John McCone, the director of Central Intelligence, on the last Saturday of the crisis, who heard that US reconnaissance jets had come under fire and then insisted that the United States make "the most violent protest, and demand that he stop this business and stop it right away, or we're going to take those SAM sites out immediately" (Dobbs 2008, 368). The hawks persisted with their hawkishness right to the end.

The great triumph of the crisis was that Kennedy, a president with a doubtful record in prior strategic confrontation with the Soviet Union, managed to resist the forceful urgings of his advisers, especially the military ones, to up the ante. We cannot concretely know the extent to which his ability to empathize played a part in this resistance, but he certainly urged his subordinates to imagine themselves in Khrushchev's place. He also urged them to read *Guns of August*, Barbara Tuchman's Pulitzer-winning history, which argued that the Great War had started almost by default, as the antagonists had blundered into conflict without reflecting on the other side's perspective (Tuchman 2014). The president asked his advisers to read the book and discussed it with them. The challenge, as he saw it, was to avoid giving the enemy the choice of escalation or humiliation. Kennedy's empathy, Robert McNamara argued later to Errol Morris in his film *The Fog of War*, was critical in the crisis (Morris 2004). McNamara highlighted the role of Llewellyn Thompson, the US ambassador to the Soviet Union, in helping the president put himself in Khrushchev's shoes. There is an instinctive element to empathy that is evident in humans and other apes (de Waal 2010). But in humans there is also a deliberative element. It takes conscious effort to imagine oneself in the mind of a stranger, especially an adversary who is far away. Kennedy, with the help of his aides and his own reading, managed it on this occasion.

Overall, the lesson for us, as students of the psychological underpinnings of strategy, is that the Cuban Missile Crisis was an altogether emotional process that took place amid great danger and uncertainty. By turns the protagonists were angry and anxious. Fear, stress, and fatigue all played a part in their deliberations, with the president feeling an overwhelming burden of responsibility (Blight

1992). Additionally, Kennedy deliberately sought to add structure to the administration's response—weighing alternative options and striving to empathize with the enemy. There are other psychological dimensions to the decision-making besides these: Kennedy was not a healthy man, and the impact of his chronic underlying condition on his ability to lead can only be speculated (Owen 2008). At the time of the crisis he was taking a cocktail of pills to treat his various ailments, and while we cannot sensibly attribute any of his decisions to the effects of the drugs or his poor health more generally, we may be on safe ground to attribute at least some aspects of his outlook to the effects of a lifelong struggle to overcome some serious medical problems.

Perhaps in the end even Kennedy himself would be unable to articulate precisely why he acted as he had. There was considerable uncertainty and muddle and plenty of scope for miscommunication and miscalculation. It was, in short, a very long way from any consideration of strategy as a theoretically rational response to objectively known courses of action.

The crisis has been a staple example of many political psychology approaches, understood via numerous group-level theories (Allison 1999; Janis 1982), psychological notions about perception (Jervis 1976), and prospect theory (Jervis 1992; Haas 2001). All these theories try to make sense of the complex, messy reality of the negotiations and of strong personalities feeling their way forward amid uncertainty. As attempts to apply rigorous concepts from experimental psychology to the real world of elite-level decision-making they are probably as good as it gets for observers looking on at a distance. The primary record is excellent. We can listen in to the deliberations of the ExComm, which capture a real sense of the drama unfolding through a crackly hissing tape reel, or we can at least read the transcripts (May and Zelikow 1997). We can read the protagonist's memoirs too, either Khrushchev's or perhaps Bobby Kennedy's vivid and emotion-laden account (Kennedy 1969).

The upshot? Both theory-driven and primary-source accounts suggest there is considerable utility in drawing on psychology to understand the strategic decisions taken during the pivotal moments of the crisis. But there are also large methodological problems that limit the ability of political scientist to do more than draw parallels between the findings of the psychology lab and the real world, or rigorously test established concepts against the evidential record. In the end, these difficulties stymie our ability to robustly establish the ways in which psychology shapes strategy—there is too much going on and too many local peculiarities, as the historicist in Clausewitz knew. Nonetheless, the central connection remains: nuclear strategy, as with all other strategies, is an unavoidably human phenomenon susceptible to the same evolved cognitive tendencies as all other forms.

Conclusion: Nuclear Strategy Is Still Human Strategy

The possibility of nuclear Armageddon and the destruction of human society certainly adds an additional dimension to strategy. Robert Jervis in particular is correct in identifying that it shifts the balance between denial and punishment. This is a major change, and some puzzling new phenomena are introduced into strategic theory that, as it happened, were elucidated more by the new generation of civilian theorists rather than by their military counterparts. If you are not trying to deny enemy gains by protecting your territory or citizens (and you cannot readily do so), the weight of strategy shifts to threatening retaliation—certainly this is true once an assured second strike can be secured. This is the conventional logic of deterrence, with many variations (Should you target enemy cities or forces with your retaliation? Fire all your missiles at once, or hold back, threatening further escalation?). It held throughout the Cold War and thereafter. The essential challenge is to make something as incredible as retaliation, which might bring total devastation on the retaliator, seem credible (Quinlan 2009).

How this might be achieved has never been properly elucidated. Strategy in this strange new era could be as much about the credible threat to use force as the actual employment of it. Real fighting might be waged at the periphery—in proxy wars or against allied nonnuclear states. Skirmishing below the level of nuclear threshold did occur, but the prospect of uncontrollable escalation seemed enough to chill even the most excitable statesmen, as with Khrushchev and later Nixon.

There are some theorists, like Kahn, who took a more conventional view of nuclear weapons. They were wrong, insofar as their strategic theories suggested the rational, instrumental use of nuclear weapons as possible. But that was less because the weapons themselves were revolutionary and more because strategy had never been decided in this clinical way—as readers of Thucydides and Clausewitz can readily grasp.

The Cuba crisis reminds me of a line from Clausewitz, that "action can never be based on anything firmer than instinct, a sensing of the truth" (Clausewitz 1993, 125). Kennedy himself offered a similar thought, in his foreword to Ted Sorenson's history of the time: "The essence of ultimate decision remains impenetrable to the observer—often, indeed, to the decider himself" (Sorenson 2005, xxxi). Both men had hit on the essentially psychological basis of strategy.

The Cuban Missile Crisis was perhaps the most serious close call of the Cold War, although there were other moments of tension and at least one, the Able Archer scare of 1983, where nuclear hostilities loomed close because of a misperception (Manchanda 2009). Later, tensions between nuclear-armed Pakistan and India demonstrated that nuclear strategy is not just a matter for superpower blocs. Nuclear weapons change the character of warfare. They raise the destructiveness to the point that protagonists cannot realistically use actual force to achieve their goals and struggle to use the *threat* of it coercively. This is radical and, depending on one's nomenclature, might be considered revolutionary.

With nuclear weapons, the long-established relationship between scale and fighting power posited by Lanchester is redundant, and with it the strategic rationale that drove human evolution: that concentrated force in the right place brings victory. Already, technology and specialization had stretched this basic evolutionary relationship, providing ways to offset the advantages of brute force. Now it was distorted entirely. Might was not always right, as the United States discovered in Vietnam. And with nuclear weapons in their arsenals, the technological capabilities of modern cultures advanced beyond the strategic possibilities that shaped our cognitive evolution. Perhaps, as Kenneth Waltz has argued provocatively, the best thing would be for every state to acquire nuclear weapons. It would maximize the possibilities for a defensive realism, in which the defense would most definitely be stronger than the attack (Waltz 1981).

Yet, for all this, strategy remains an innately psychological phenomenon. Wars continue in the nuclear age, even wars involving the superpowers themselves. As Waltz anticipated, the fear of nuclear weapons may even have encouraged smaller wars around the periphery, and by proxy (Waltz 1959). In nuclear crises, decision-making about the use of violence, as with all other forms of warfare, remains the prerogative of groups of humans—each with their own cognitive attributes. Strategy may have changed in the nuclear era, but it is still recognizably human.

This turned out to be good news in the Cuban Missile Crisis and in later scares too. Certainly there is the potential for error or for a breakdown in communication, as with the Able Archer scare, when Soviet leaders mistook NATO exercises for an impending attack and brought their armed forces to high alert. Just a few months earlier a relatively junior Soviet officer had decided unilaterally that his early warning system was mistaken in signaling an impending NATO attack—again, a major nuclear crisis was only narrowly averted. There is always scope for a hotheaded emotional response, like the initial anger at Cuba in the Kennedy White House. Henry Kissinger used to leave some of President Nixon's more belligerent orders alone, knowing his irascible boss would soon calm down, madman theory notwithstanding (Kissinger 1979). There are grounds for collective shortsightedness, as with the imaginary "missile gap" that preoccupied the defense establishment in the United States in the late 1950s. But deterrence held—by accident or design no one knew. Perhaps, though, one reason for its robustness was that statesmen on both sides were reluctant to instrumentalize the sort of coldly efficient, rational-actor model of nuclear escalation that sees war as a bargaining process susceptible to machine-like calculation.

PART III

Artificial Intelligence and Strategy

CHAPTER **7**

Tactical Artificial Intelligence Arrives

RECENT DEVELOPMENTS IN ARTIFICIAL INTELLIGENCE HAVE AROUSED CON-
siderable alarm, including from prominent scientists like Stephen Hawking and
the hi-tech entrepreneur Elon Musk, who compares AI to the summoning of a
demon and has invested heavily in promoting open approaches to researching AI
and mitigating some of the risks (Gibbs 2014). The philosopher Nick Bostrom
offers the disturbing argument that an artificial "superintelligence" could emerge
unexpectedly and rapidly, surpassing our ability to control it and wreaking huge
destruction, even if it starts out working on a seemingly innocuous task set by
human overseers (Bostrom 2014).

Before we come to the question of a powerful, self-motivated AI enacting its
own strategy, there is the more pressing issue of AI being employed as a tool in
human strategy. This is the immediate challenge posed by AI and is more feasible
than a self-motivated, all-knowing, and hostile AI. Its effects on strategy will be
significant.

Why? AI like this raises the prospect of a radical change in human strategy because intelligent machines will make decisions on a cognitive basis quite different
from evolved human processes. Even an AI that faithfully seeks to follow our instructions is potentially revolutionary. Such an AI poses particular problems beyond those
usually raised by the "agent-principal" dilemma that arises whenever we outsource
the implementation of decisions to *someone* else, not least because of its speed. In
addition, such an AI is problematic for strategic affairs because it will profoundly
destabilize existing power balances between states; indeed, it may even introduce
dramatic changes in the nature of states themselves. Last, AI could recast the balance
of strategic affairs once again back toward the offensive, undercutting what Clausewitz thought was the inherent strength of the defense, and undermining in particular
the defensive basis of nuclear deterrence, the ultimate defensive weapon technology.
All this is possible without the malign, self-motivated AI of Hollywood fiction.

Tactical AI Does Strategy

Tactical weapons systems will utilize the sort of AI not too far distant from the current state of the art. They are already beginning to do so—for example, by controlling the targeting of fast-moving threats, as the *Aegis* system aboard US naval destroyers does, or by controlling the radars and missile interceptors of America's Terminal High-Altitude Area Defense system.

I consider the implications of more advanced AI later. Such an artificial general intelligence (AGI), as it is sometimes known, will be more flexible in its ability to switch between tasks and may experience something akin to intrinsic motivation. It may even possess something like our very human capacities for emotion, consciousness, and empathy. Here, though, the AI in question is a more simple automaton—a sophisticated information processor able to use information well enough to orient a platform in time and space, or to identify and shoot a target. This sort of AI will be able to control fighter aircraft, select its own targets, and communicate with other unmanned vehicles so they can work together as "nodes" in a distributed network. I call this sort of artificial intelligence "tactical AI" because its strengths will be most applicable in the military domain to problems at that level of warfare—including those of maneuver and the application of fires. Higher-level decision-making in warfare demands a more flexible sort of intelligence, including the ability to understand context. Tactical activities, by contrast, demand cognitive abilities of the sort that modern AI is already pretty good at: pattern-recognition, probabilistic reasoning, memory, and, above all, speed.

Calling it "tactical," however, does a disservice to the potential impact of such technologies, which may be profound and reach up into the strategic domain. Among other things this sort of AI will change the utility of scale and concentration in combat, the balance between attack and defense, the utility of surprise, and the way in which defenders seek denial by variously hiding, hardening, or spoofing. It may, up to a point at least, change the way force is used to coerce and deter through the possibility of escalation.

The sorts of platforms that will employ this decision-making technology are starting to become apparent, and in short order dramatic changes may be afoot, both to equipment and to the broader organization of armed forces. For example, much effort in the design of a main battle tank goes into the survivability of the crew. This increases the weight of armor and thus diminishes the speed and maneuverability of the tank. Removing the human opens new possibilities, and not just for weight of armor.

It is very likely that combat will continue to be a combined arms affair involving a range of functionally different AI and legacy platforms. Regardless of the technologies involved, combining them has long been a powerful way of complementing the specialized strengths of individual platforms, especially when the various weapons are working in harmony as part of an integrated system (Biddle 2006). Combined arms warfare greatly complicates the simple logic of Lanchester's square law, with its functionally identical combatants, because now the relative strength of any combination derives not just from scale but also from their specialized skills and the ways they interact. Discerning the balance between competing forces becomes a matter of gauging comparative advantage from among a wide range of skills and attributes that collectively constitute fighting power.

But while combat will remain a combined arms affair, the specifics will differ with the arrival of "tactical AI," perhaps in unexpected ways. For example, one of the key features of modern aerial warfare has been the relative importance of stealth technologies that hide the aircraft by minimizing its signature, especially its radar signature. With AI flying the aircraft, however, platforms will not be constrained by the need to maximize the survivability of their human crew, including in well-defended hostile airspace. Without a pilot, AI aircraft might be smaller and emit a lower radar signal anyway. At the same time, the pattern-recognition abilities of defending AI systems may shift the balance away from the importance of stealth toward other capabilities, like speed and maneuverability. Rather than one large, multirole aircraft that is adept at suppressing enemy defenses while attacking ground targets and engaging in air superiority battles with defending fighters, we might see something very different. Consider: by distributing its capabilities across multiple small platforms, a tactical AI could achieve some measure of redundancy. There would still be an advantage to operating undetected in contested airspace, but even if some of its platforms are detected and destroyed, a mission might still succeed with a swarm of surviving AI still able to prosecute enemy targets.

This tactical AI system would be able to use its distribution as a means of passive defense, since force cannot be readily concentrated against it and it will still be able to retain the ability to rapidly concentrate together in time and space itself. This sort of autonomous, distributed, loosely coordinated "shoal" or "swarm" behavior is one of the key strengths of tactical AI. It is an active area of military research, as with DARPA's experiments with swarms of mini-drones launched from pods attached to larger manned aircraft (US Department of Defense 2017).

Like the "emergent" behavior of social insects, great complexity can emerge from the cumulative behavior of individual agents working as part of a larger, cohesive whole—even when the individual cognitive abilities of such agents might seem rather simple in isolation. This sort of situationalist logic has driven much research in robotics, with machines taking their behavioral cues from immediate environmental stimuli and reacting "instinctively."

This sketch of tactical AI in combat hints at radical changes in prospect, including to weapons design, organizational structures, and the ability of humans to direct the action once under way. To see why that is so, we need to pause and reflect on the underlying decision-making architecture that permits it.

Tactical AI and Machine Learning

Artificial intelligence is a broad term in widespread popular usage that covers a large range of technologies and philosophies. The sorts of technologies that will contribute to "tactical" AI are already sufficiently mature to have begun making their way into military systems, and the pace of progress in research suggests that the capabilities of such systems will mature rapidly. For the most part, the AI referred to here is of the sort termed artificial neural networks (ANN) or "connectionist" AI—a research paradigm that is loosely modeled on the neural structures of human brains.

There is no space here to develop a detailed account of the field of artificial intelligence research. Interested readers would do well to consult one of several excellent overviews of the field, including Margaret Boden's recent *AI*, Nils Nilsson's richly detailed history of the field, and Kevin Warwick's overview (Boden 2016; Nilsson 2010; Warwick 2012). David Vernon's *Artificial Cognitive Systems* is also invaluable, especially his discussion of embodied agents (Vernon 2014). Edge.org recently hosted and then published a lively discussion among experts in the field on the philosophical dimensions of AI (Brockman 2015). Research in the field, especially in "deep learning" within the connectionist paradigm, is voluminous—online Twitter aggregators like Oxford University's Miles Brundage and George Washington University's Adam Elkus provide a good way of filtering the latest developments, especially those with strategic implications.

Several distinctions emerge, as between narrow and broad AI and between weak and strong AI. These are useful categories insofar as they highlight some different characteristics of AI, but they lack specificity and typically oversimplify what may better be thought of as points along a spectrum. Much of the focus here will be on rather narrow or weak AI that can perform really well at one particular task but lacks the ability to flexibly adapt to perform another task or adapt its performance when it encounters a novel situation. Later, I turn to strong, broad, and flexible AI that might be able to do these things better. Rather than being specialized at one function, this sort of generalist AI would be able to turn its hand flexibly to multiple challenges. It would do so by transferring its learning from one domain to another—for example, by recombining concepts in a similar way to human intelligence. AI researchers often talk of "strong" AI as exhibiting these characteristics—and by strong they mean human-like. Yet there is no guarantee that the flexible, strong AI, which sometimes goes by the name artificial general intelligence, will use the same techniques as humans, and in fact it seems unlikely that it will do so. There is, similarly, no particular reason to expect AGI to demonstrate the same sorts of cognitive strengths and weaknesses as human intelligence. It might instead be better at some intellectual skills and worse at others. Or it might supersede human intelligence across a broad range of cognitive skills.

War fighting AI systems would certainly gain from this sort of flexible learning. But tactical systems that can operate without it are entirely feasible. Individual narrow-AI capabilities might be enough to perform a particular military function; while platforms or systems that can combine narrow-AI are also feasible and possible with current AI technologies. This sort of connectionist AI seeks to maximize a reward function programmed in by its designers. It learns by being "trained" on practice data and figuring out the optimal approach in its "universe."

The practical military skills that can be realized with this sort of AI are striking. Already it can, for example, comprehensively outfly an experienced combat pilot in a simulator, even when the performance of its aircraft has been significantly degraded relative to the human pilot's. It can enhance the resolution of blurry images by figuring out what information is probably there. And it can make significant deductions on the basis of analyzing huge complex data sets. The possibilities for control of the air and surveillance should be immediately apparent. All this is possible for an AI that simply maximizes a reward function according to some previously learned processes.

But there is plenty this sort of AI cannot yet do. The simple AI that maximizes its reward function has some powerful advantages over humans—including probabilistic reasoning, pattern recognition, a reliable memory for previous data encountered, and speed of calculation. But a flexible AGI will require some additional attributes. These might include an ability to discern meaning, some level of curiosity, and imagination. These rather underspecified terms are an integral part of human intelligence, and it may be that AGI develops similar proxies. Without these and other abilities, modern AI can seem hyperintelligent in some dimensions and yet incredibly dimwitted in others, as users of Apple's *Siri* personal assistant will know intimately. That personal assistant and others are able to perform impressive feats of speech recognition, transcribing even accented and mumbled delivery nearly instantaneously. But its replies display a rather less-sophisticated grasp of semantics. Alan Turing famously proposed an "imitation game" wherein a machine would be judged intelligent if it could hold a conversation with a human and fool the human into thinking his interlocutor was another human (Turing 1950; Warwick and Shah 2016). Today's AI is a long way short of this sort of intelligence, the occasional brief bluff notwithstanding. So while this may be an overly human yardstick for intelligence, it nevertheless captures the narrow, rather brittle nature of modern machine intelligence: give it a well-bounded problem and plenty of examples to learn from and it will provide an efficient solution. Where military problems can be reduced to this sort of paradigm, AI can contribute, with significant results for strategy.

The AI Renaissance and Deep Learning

To grasp the military strengths and limits of the tactical AI systems I sketched above a brief overview follows. AI is developing rapidly, but its historical progress has been rather uneven, making predictable future developments a haphazard endeavor. The rate of recent progress has generated considerable public attention and some hype. Some breathless accounts see the emergence of an AGI and even "superintelligence" in the coming decades (Kurzweil 2006). Yet many AI researchers remain rather cautious about the possibilities for this sort of general intelligence arising anytime soon.

The stop-start nature of earlier AI research should give some pause. AI has, by now, a long history reaching back in earnest to the mid-twentieth century and the development of computers along the lines envisaged by Turing and John von Neumann; machines able to engage in logical, sequential operations. Pioneering researchers opened lines of inquiry that remain at the forefront of present-day research, including the development of AI modeled loosely on the brain, with networks of interconnected "neurons." From the beginning AI was linked closely with related disciplines—cognitive psychology, philosophy of mind, and more recently neuroscience. And from the start there were military implications to the research—as when early cyberneticists gained experience and inspiration from the wartime struggle to track and target fast-moving aircraft from the ground (Rid 2016; Wiener 1948).

But there followed a series of disappointments, as limits in computing power, along with methodological constraints, stymied the development of AI—a series of AI "winters" has left many of today's researchers cautious even in the face of recent advances. "Connectionist" AI, in particular, entered a long period in the margins, in part because of the skepticism of Marvin Minsky, a leading exponent of the other main approach: logical symbolism (Minsky 1969). This approach modeled cognition at a higher level of abstraction, seeing intelligence as a form of processing of symbols or concepts that might or might not represent real-world objects. That way of thinking about AI has some broad parallels with the way the conscious mind handles concepts—as an intuitive scientist engaged in rough-and-ready cause-and-effect logic. If the connectionist approach drew inspiration from the cellular level of human brains, perhaps the logical symbolic approach was loosely akin to the psychological level of human cognition. In practice, the metaphor seemed to work in the opposite direction: cognitive psychology eagerly borrowed the idea of the brain as a sort of complex computer, with the mind running like software on a neural hardware architecture.

Meanwhile, in computer science "expert systems" became the leading AI sub-field. These were logical processors in the Minsky tradition but which used a database of knowledge about a particular area. There were, however, some large problems for the symbolic approach, not least because of the "combinatorial ex-plosion," as it was termed, that arose from dealing with too many interacting variables. Expert systems were also flummoxed by any changes to their knowledge bases, which could require extensive reprogramming. In a constrained and regi-mented universe like that of a chessboard, this sort of logical AI could function well. Brute force solutions to some problems were eminently feasible, employ-ing the raw computational power of the AI to work out possible future options and calculate the probabilities associated with each outcome. Tree searches could branch out from each present state of the bounded universe, and each possible combination could be explored for its overall likelihood of success. Expert systems could tackle even-more complex problems in richer, less-bounded environments, provided they had input on the sort of relationships that might be expected or were given detailed rules to follow in given situations.

But most real-world situations did not accord to the simple relationships and regulated moves of the "toy universe." Reality was messy and complex—and not readily computable. Whenever novelty was encountered, laborious reprogram-ming of the expertise inherent on the expert system was required. Symbolic processing might bear some relationship to the functional processing of the conscious human brain, but the differences were profound and seemingly insurmountable. The massive parallel processing of the human brain and its dense and richly textured web of associations all contrasted with the comparatively clunky sequential logic of the "good old-fashioned AI" (or GOFAI), as it later became known. By the 1980s the Pentagon was sponsoring work on a pilot's assistant that would reduce the cognitive load on the human operator by monitoring the aircraft's performance, including by responding to voice commands (Roland and Shiman 2002). But the system was hopelessly ambitious given the hardware constraints of the era and the GOFAI employed. Another AI winter beckoned.

The recent revival in AI owes much to the return to prominence of connectionist AI maligned by Minsky and his followers. The idea had never entirely gone away, but its resurgence required the elaboration of new mathematical relationships between the artificial "neurons" in the connectionist system. In particular, the system needed a way of adjusting the weightings attached to each neuron in a layer so that the most effective combinations of neurons could emerge as the network "learned" from data presented to it (LeCun, Bengio, and Hinton 2015). "Backward propagation" through the system to adjust the weightings was one of the breakthroughs; it could be deployed, provided the optimal outcome of the system was known. In effect, the system was trained on one set of data before being set to work on new information applying its newly "trained" neural connections. The process was known, therefore, as supervised learning. There were drawbacks: such systems would require a large volume of structured training data, which was not always possible to obtain in the real world, and the connections might organize themselves to provide a local optimum rather than the theoretically optimal solution. Nonetheless, connectionist AI has rapidly gained ground over the last decade and is now able to tackle hitherto intractable problems like speech recognition and text translation with a high degree of accuracy. It wasn't just a question of concepts; hardware mattered too. Connectionist AI has benefited from the development of powerful hardware able to act as the artificial neurons (the current favorite is the GPU, a graphics processor originally designed for video games consoles).

Perhaps recent AI developments seem limited and prosaic—a view one often finds expressed by longtime AI researchers. Their skepticism contrasts with journalistic hyperbole and may to some extent be a deliberate conceit to counter it. But there is something to it; AI remains very limited when judged against a human yardstick. Still, consider DARPA's autonomous vehicle competition, only a decade past and once considered a formidable challenge that would take many years to solve; today it is viewed as a somewhat prosaic achievement that presages the widespread adoption of automated intelligent vehicles over the next several decades (Thrun et al. 2006). Or consider the achievement of DeepMind, an AI research company that defeated the world champion at Go, the popular board game whose highly structured universe belies a bewildering number of possible combinations. DeepMind's AI, AlphaGo, defied the prediction of many experts that it would take years of effort to surpass human-level performance (Silver et al. 2016). It did so by using a clever two-step process to narrow the scope of its search and then draw on its extensive training, entailing many thousands of games it had played against itself and other adversaries. These are certainly not negligible gains, and they presage others still to come in many disparate fields of human activity—including strategy.

Connectionist AI has permitted highly accurate natural language recognition and translation and the ability to identify features in images (which is especially useful in medical diagnosis) (Schuster et al. 2016; Altman 2017). ANNs can lip read from images of humans talking and can recognize basic emotions in human faces (Chung et al. 2016; Poria et al. 2017). They can even convincingly manipulate video to put words in the mouths of humans (Niessner 2016). This sort of AI can enhance the resolution of existing video imagery by making assumptions about what was likely to be present (Dahl, Norouzi, and Shlens 2017). It can reveal hitherto unknown patterns in vast data sets, as when one AI surveyed street views of all US roads and established predictive relationships between car ownership and voting patterns (Gebru et al. 2017). Two rival AIs rapidly cycled their respective efforts to encrypt information and break the encryption, leading to a new form of secure communication (Abadi and Andersen 2016).

In perhaps the most striking recent development, one AI system has outperformed world-class poker players over an extended run of games (Metz 2017). Poker presented the machine with a game of asymmetric knowledge (unlike board games, where knowledge of the layout and possible options is perfect and mutual). This is starting to get close to strategy—indeed, Clausewitz thought war somewhat analogous to a game of cards. To do this, the poker-playing AI sought to identify statistical patterns in adversary gameplay over an extended run of games while simultaneously searching for and then expunging its own gameplay of patterns that might betray its strategy.

As these and other achievements demonstrate, ANNs have some distinct advantages over human cognition. They are free from biological constraints and evolved heuristics, both of which serve to aid human decision-making amid pressures of time and uncertainty but can also produce systematic errors of judgment. And they have a superior capacity for pattern recognition, probabilistic reasoning, recall, and decision-making speed—all of which have distinct military utility.

Set against that are some fairly profound weaknesses. First, connectionist AI consumes lots of power and requires considerable hardware. And though there have been remarkable increases in computing power (with processing speeds roughly following the rate of increase anticipated by Moore's law), there are still architectural constraints on the complexity of ANN. Moreover, there are indications that we may be approaching the limits of Moore's law, at least when it comes to established materials and methods of organizing computing. Reinforcement-learning ANNs also require large volumes of tagged data because the networks need to be "trained" through exposure to examples of the required end state so that the optimal connections between artificial neurons can be derived.

Perhaps most significant, ANNs evince rather limited cognitive flexibility. Their expertise, once acquired, remains rather domain specific. As with expert systems previously, many of the landmark breakthroughs of connectionist AI have been demonstrated in "toy universes" of board and card games, or in computer-generated worlds, where the only task is to maximize some measure within a strict set of rules. The real universe, of course, is far more complex. For example, in 2013 DeepMind trained an AI on classic 1980s Atari arcade games with impressive results (Mnih et al. 2013). In no time at all the machine was playing the games with superhuman skill and racking up huge scores. This was a problem ideally suited to reinforcement learning: maximize a simple reward function (the score) in a highly structured, two-dimensional universe. The one game that DeepMind's algorithm failed to immediately master, *Montezuma's Revenge,* was challenging because the returns from an action were not immediately derived, which would allow tuning of the algorithm, a problem analogous to "delayed gratification" in humans (Bellemare et al. 2016). DeepMind cracked *Montezuma's Revenge* not long after, building in something loosely analogous to curiosity—the incentive to search without immediate results.

But the essential problem of flexibility remains: deep learning AIs are good at optimizing reward functions in constrained universes but poor at transferring these skills to new tasks. The same basic algorithm can be trained on different tasks using new data to adjust the relative weighting of hierarchical connections between neurons. But, once trained, a network cannot readily adjust to other tasks without complete retraining. Humans, by contrast, are able to apply their learning flexibly across domains, rapidly recombining concepts from existing areas and applying these combinations to others.

One further important weakness is the susceptibility of ANNs to being fooled by adversaries. The odd effect of "adversarial spoofing" on convolutional neural networks (CNNs) illustrates the point. These are a type of ANN that specialize in the categorization of images—famously, for example, learning to recognize pictures of cats on the Internet. But CNNs can produce wildly inaccurate outputs when "spoofed" by the superimposition of noisy information over a target image, though this kind of information is wholly invisible to the human brain (Huang et al. 2017; Gershgorn 2016). The extent to which the algorithm is able to make commonsensical deductions about the images by exploring context is minimal.

Tactical AI Lacks Much Sense of "Meaning"

Perhaps the largest impediment for the sort of AI developed to date has been its inability to grasp meaning with anywhere near the same facility as humans. This is true of logical-processing AI just as it is of connectionist ANNs, and it may be the most prominent impediment to achieving artificial general intelligence. Understanding is an important aspect of cognitive flexibility, allowing skills and associations to be readily applied from one domain to another.

Some, most notably the philosopher John Searle, have argued that machines simply cannot grasp meaning in this way. In his often-cited thought experiment Searle imagined a "Chinese Room" in which information in Chinese script was sent to the room's occupants, who were monoglot English speakers; given rules were applied to the text; and the output, also in Chinese, was duly dispatched onward (Searle 1980). The activity performed was answering questions, but the occupants of the room were none the wiser as to what it all meant—they were just processing abstract symbols via set protocols. The room, of course, stood for an AI machine. As Searle argues, knowledge of syntax does not equate to semantics. Meaning, in the sense we understand it, is beyond AI—indeed, Searle elsewhere suggests that meaning in the human sense is somehow connected to our biological architecture and thus beyond machines.

Limitations in the ability to understand meaning pose problems for military AI, especially when it comes to the ethics of armed conflict. For example, such an AI might correctly be able to assess, via its analysis of video imagery, whether a given person is carrying a weapon and be able to accurately target that person, even avoiding bystanders. But the machine might not grasp the broader context in which the person is holding the weapon out in a gesture of surrender, for example, or has picked it up to inspect it. Contextualizing what it senses on the battlefield would be a challenge for modern AI—even if we allow that it can shoot more accurately and rapidly than a weapon system run by humans.

For humans there are (at least) two dimensions to meaning—one derives from our biological and social ontology. Here, our underlying motivations imbue objects and concepts with a sense of meaning, and then emotions provide a way of navigating our environment that enhances our prospects of satisfying these motivated goals. Machines have reward functions that they seek to optimize, which we might crudely analogize to our motivations. This is where Searle, a materialist, parts company with others who argue for a functionalist account of intelligence. For them, an agent's form follows function rather than stemming from the material that constitutes it. For Searle, the argument is about material—our particular biological makeup constitutes our meaning, and machines cannot share that.

The other dimension of meaning is relational, which refers to the way in which cognitive concepts are either interrelated or distinct. Machines lack our phylogeny and thus the emotional dimension of meaning. But they are capable of relating concepts to one another, and researchers *are* making progress in the categorization of concepts. This is captured in the notion (from Geoffrey Hinton) of "thought vectors" that can relate discrete cognitive ideas (LeCun, Bengio, and Hinton 2015).

These vectors are similar to the idea that we encountered earlier of human consciousness as a "global workspace"—where mental processes can be "broadcast" through a human mind and recombined in new forms (Dehaene 2014). For humans, consciousness does a lot of work in integrating and recombining complex ideas. For an ANN, relational concepts can be established by giving everything a numeric vector or a combination of numbers that represents some aspect of its identity. The more numbers in a vector, the more dimensions along which a concept might vary, and so the greater the granularity in its machine "meaning." Thought vectors suggest that relational meaning, at least, is feasible for AI. Advances in machine translation over recent years demonstrate what's already possible. The more data the machine is exposed to, the richer its understanding of how words and groups of words relate—with the result that clunky, word-for-word translations become progressively more naturalistic.

As with human brains, knowledge in a connectionist AI is distributed across the whole system. The inner workings of the AI, as it trains itself on data and adjusts the weightings between its artificial neurons, are something of a black box. For humans there is some evidence of highly localized knowledge: a so-called and much-rumored grandmother neuron that fires if and only if it receives input pertaining to one's own grandmother. In fact, when they were eventually proved to exist, experimenters found neurons that fired when presented with images of Bill Clinton or characters from the Simpsons (Quiroga et al. 2005). If correct, this finding suggests that individual neurons may be associated with specific bits of real-world information. Nonetheless, in human brains and ANNs alike, complex representations of reality are typically distributed across networks. As an example of the complexity, consider a recent study of the "semantic atlas" of the human brain that imaged the parts of the cortex associated with particular concepts in language (Huth et al. 2016). The authors found that individual words are clustered together with others of similar meaning but also that there are multiple regions associated with each word—suggesting a distributed network with a high degree of redundancy.

There is one last weakness in modern AI worth flagging here: the notions of creativity, curiosity, and imagination. These are again rather anthropocentric terms and somewhat underspecified. We could perhaps imagine an intelligent machine being adept at them if we termed them instead "recombination," "search," and "probabilistic prediction," or something similar. The way in which modern AI approximates any of these terms differs profoundly from the way humans go about it—especially when it comes to imagining the minds of others via our evolved "theory of mind" skills. But modern AI can already demonstrate some of those rough approximations to the extent that humans, ever prone to anthropomorphize, project human-like skills onto them.

During the landmark Go showdown between DeepMind's algorithm and the human world champion, commentators sometimes referred to AlphaGo's "imaginative" or "creative" moves—but they were not creative, at least not in the sense applied to humans. Human players certainly study earlier games, but they cannot feasibly compete with the accurate memory of a powerful computer. Instead, there is a more intuitive and artistic element to human gameplay. At a functional level, radically different processes are involved—embodied emotions and evolved heuristics in the humans make inferences about likely outcomes and intentions of the adversary versus clever probabilistic reasoning allied to a formidably accurate memory in the machine. At times in the gameplay, AlphaGo made moves that seasoned observers saw as radically different and of the sort that humans would not conventionally make. Was the machine "deluded" when it gambled or was it displaying a visionary, risk-loving side to its "character"? Neither: these moves were striking to the humans precisely *because* they employed different methodologies to navigate the vast universe of possible Go moves. This insight offers some pointers for understanding how AI of this sort might shape strategy—the way in which machines make decisions will reflect a fundamentally different underlying cognitive process to ours. The results might be surprising to human onlookers who are conditioned to expect certain behavioral norms.

This summary of AI research leaves plenty still to address, not least from the strategic perspective. But even a brief sketch like this should give an idea of the sorts of military tasks that state-of-the-art AI will be able to take on, and equally of some that will prove more challenging. Later we will consider the questions of autonomy, motivation, and even consciousness in an AGI, and explore their implications for strategy. For now the focus is on the strategic implications of the tactical AI system, constituted of the sorts of AI that are already here or not too far distant.

This sort of AI will be autonomous in a narrow sense of being able to fulfill some tasks without human interaction. Indeed, this ability will be one key attribute since it will allow decision-making and maneuver at blinding speed. Certainly, this autonomy is of a lesser magnitude than an AGI might develop, with something akin to its own motivation. Moreover, the narrow, tactical AI will have a more limited ability to switch between tasks or to respond flexibly to changing circumstances by recombining its basic cognitive skills rapidly and in novel ways. Still, this is a matter of degree rather than a clear-cut distinction. Narrow AIs with specialist skills might be combined in a system that can cumulatively respond more flexibly to the many complexities of operating in the real world. And improvements in the underlying approach to AI might also enhance the ability of such an AI to switch between tasks without laborious retraining. For example, the latest "adversarial networks" of AIs that train in competition against one another are able to greatly reduce the amount of training data required to tune up the network—the loose biological parallel here being of natural selection picking the best-performing AI to advance to the next generation. In short, the distinction between narrow AI and more general AI might ultimately be one of degree rather than an absolute measure. In the interim, there is plenty that even more limited AI can do that will impact strategy.

Tactical AI and Strategy

We can already conceive of tactical warfighting systems assembled using the sort of connectionist AI described above or perhaps employing hybrid techniques that combine with logical processing AI and human cognition. These sorts of systems are broadly feasible with today's state-of-the-art decision-making technologies. Indeed, some fielded platforms already employ AI—as with *Aegis* or the

Patriot antimissile system. Both were originally part of the earlier generation of AI research boosted by the Pentagon in the 1980s and 1990s. Other platforms in development rely more on the new wave of connectionist AI. For example, the United States and other states are experimenting with unmanned fighter aircraft, including using existing legacy platforms, like the F16, that could be repurposed as AI combat platforms. Perhaps the machine pilots will operate with complete autonomy, perhaps they will act in concert with a human pilot in one of the aircraft. Or there are subsystems, like "cognitive radars" that work to rapidly shift wavelengths in a constant battle of detection and evasion with other such systems.

Efforts to discern the effect of these sorts of systems on tactics and strategy alike are in their infancy—perhaps roughly analogous to the first attempts to figure out how nuclear weapons would shape strategy in the early to mid-1950s, when Bernard Brodie and others convinced of their truly revolutionary impact began working through what sort of weapons would best fit the emerging strategy of deterrence. Much of the existing debate on AI and weaponry has focused on the ethics of employing them. While this is an important debate, it's somewhat tangential to our purpose here, except insofar as it reflects on some wider issues, such as the means of command and control, the relationship between armed forces and society, and judgments about risk.

My main focus is on the way in which tactical AI will affect the fundamental relationship between strategy and psychology, and these wider issues will fall out of that discussion. Let's briefly consider some of the enduring strategic principles that have emerged, in part as a reflection of our evolved intelligence.

First, consider the basic underlying driver that scale matters because it can deliver concentrated force against isolated defenders, per Lanchester's square law of armed conflict. Now imagine a tactical AI system operating as a loosely coordinated swarm of platforms, with high redundancy and specialized skills. In this scenario, force can be rapidly concentrated and then dispersed at will. Such a system will have phenomenal pattern recognition skills, giving it excellent situational awareness about the disposition of enemy forces. Under these conditions favorable local force ratios can be established rapidly and reliably. Isolated enemy units will face overwhelming force and the traditional ways in which the defensive side in any confrontation has sought to militate against that will be of little avail. These local imbalances can be exploited in a vanishingly small time frame, as the decision-making speed of the tactical AI allows force to be concentrated in one place and quickly thereafter in another. In between times the attacking tactical AI system can rapidly disperse, limiting its own exposure to counterattack. Mass, in this scenario, remains important—the attacker still needs sufficient weight of fire and numbers of platforms to deal with the vicissitudes of battle, the depth of the battlefield, and the numbers of defenders. Perhaps the most important function of mass here would be to provide some measure of security for the system through redundancy of its individual parts, so that there will be enough platforms on hand to concentrate where required. The mass of an individual platform might matter less—indeed, we could expect that slow-moving, heavy platforms that concentrate a lot of fighting power in one vehicle would be especially vulnerable to the swarm of fast-maneuvering tactical AIs, with their blindingly fast decision-making and relatively cavalier attitude to individual losses.

On the side of the defender, meanwhile, the traditional means of offsetting concentrated assault face some new challenges. Defense via denial has been, at least prior to the arrival of nuclear weapons, the primary way of achieving this. Fortification, disciplined fighting formations, the clever use of terrain and depth, camouflage, and combined arms warfare—all these have allowed defenders to offset the advantages of concentration. The goal is to prevent the attacker from achieving favorable local force ratios and the sort of free-for-all combat idealized in Lanchester's square law. The defender has enjoyed other advantages, too: as the attacker concentrates mass, becoming larger and more cumbersome, the defender can disperse and present a smaller target, achieving more rapid maneuver. Eventually, a mobile defense like this might switch over to the counterattack, in turn exploiting the attacker's weaknesses.

Additionally, there is the broad principle, first identified by Clausewitz, that the defense is stronger than the attack—materially so, since the defense will know the terrain and enjoy shorter internal lines of communication, while the attacker will be progressively ever further from home. But it is also important, psychologically speaking, because of the extra incentive that comes from holding on to possessions relative to accepting risk in order to acquire them. Here, again, tactical AI systems will likely introduce some significant changes. With the distinctive pattern recognition, speed of decision-making, and probabilistic reasoning that are the hallmark of modern AI, the defender's position looks less tenable. Hiding is harder, whether that's attempted by exploiting depth, terrain, or camouflage. Hardening is also problematic: any weaknesses of formation or fortification will be rapidly seized on and exploited. Meanwhile, the attacking force is powerful but is now less cumbersome and slow, with no need to concentrate except in the moments immediately prior to attack. The direction of its attack will be tough to predict since the swarm can maneuver rapidly before concentrating. And the relative psychological advantages of defense will no longer apply: tactical AI will not be susceptible to the same cognitive heuristics as humans—including the sunk cost effect, the endowment effect, and prospect theory, all of which would in some degree enhance the fighting power of a harried defender. Conversely, the attacker would be less susceptible to the psychological forces that underpin culmination. Extended logistical lines and the progressive wear and tear on equipment from sustained campaigning will still factor in, but the attacking AI will be unaffected by fatigue and the mental strain of operating far from home.

Overall it looks like the balance of factors involved in battles and campaigns will favor the attacker, once tactical AI systems can be fielded in numbers. At least one factor might work the other way, however: attackers enjoy the initiative, and in human conflict this has the potential to generate shock and shatter the moral cohesion of the defending force. When the defending force is constituted of un-manned machines, however, it may well be undone by speed but it will not be as susceptible as humans to the psychological effects of shock. Nonetheless, with AI there is still an advantage to going first—indeed, the cumulative advantages accru-ing to the attacker raise the possibility of a decisive, overwhelming "first strike." Moreover, the rapidity of its cognition suggests that once the initiative is ceded, it will be hard for defenders to regain.

This sketch of battle captures some possible features of modern AI operating as a tactical weapon system. It surely overlooks other important aspects, but already there is enough here to suggest that some fairly profound changes in the evolved basis of strategy are possible. This is hardly surprising—strategy is all about choice, and AI is above all a decision-making technology. The sketch also focuses on the action, taking a view of strategy that might have appealed to Clausewitz as being the knitting together of tactical actions. But modern strategy extends further, in both space and time. Modern AI systems may operate at the tactical level, control-ling warfighting machines, but their effect will reach up into the strategic level in its broader sense.

The shifting of balance toward the attacker is an obvious way in which this is true. Strategically astute leaders weigh the relative efficacy of an adversary's de-fensive weapons systems before committing to using armed force. Misjudgments about that can have disastrous consequences—as when the "cult of the offensive" that obtained before the Great War (particularly in France) turned out to be mani-festly unsound. Obviously dominant defensive systems like a viable second-strike nuclear capability may have a stabilizing effect on international relations. Con-versely, a capability that enhances the prospects of a dramatic and effective first strike might encourage adventurism on those who possess it and have faith in its abilities. Such a tendency might further be enhanced by two additional features of tactical AI systems: first, users will not be risking the lives of soldiers, which could change the assessment of risk associated with using force; and second, the ability of the attacking force to rapidly disperse further diminishes the prospect of an effective retaliatory counterattack. Having seized the initiative, the tactical AI then maneuvers rapidly into a loose and widely distributed formation to frustrate defenders shifting over to the counteroffensive. If any attempt to defend through denial is in doubt, or the prospects of their defense through punishment is limited by an elusive adversary, the advantages for the attacker are substantial.

Thus the properties of an ostensibly tactical weapon system will potentially have a profound impact on strategy. Another way tactical AI will shape strategy is by shifting the balance of power in the international system, rather dramatically and over a short period of time. These shifts in relative capabilities could be profoundly destabilizing of the international order, especially when combined with the shifting balance between offense and defense.

Why are such shifts likely? Because the distribution of AI technologies will be uneven and because even very marginal qualitative advantages in tactical AI will be disproportionately important in generating combat power. On horizontal proliferation, this is a familiar story. Rapidly maturing military technologies that have significant barriers to entry and that are unevenly distributed have always had the potential to alter power balances. Onlooking states have some options—they can scramble to acquire the emerging technology through their own indigenous innovation or via industrial espionage or some combination of both. This was the approach of the USSR when faced with the strategic challenge of US atomic weaponry. Alternatively, a state can seek offsetting asymmetric technologies. An example here would be modern China's development of ballistic anti-ship missiles to counter US dominance in carrier aviation. Simultaneously, of course, China is developing its own carrier aviation capability via a blend of indigenous innovation and the acquisition of technologies developed elsewhere. Similar approaches are possible with AI, and many countries are investing heavily in R&D. There are some complicating factors—for one, AI is a decision-making technology rather than a weapon technology, and much of the cutting-edge research lies outside the traditional defense sector, including in corporations that have taken a wary attitude about establishing links with defense. Additionally, there are some critical bottlenecks, including in expertise. The soft power of working for leading Western technology corporations with attractive locations and high wages gives these states a good head start, as does a robust framework of intellectual property rights and civil liberties.

So there may be an efficiency logic to acquiring AI, but not everyone will be able to acquire the most efficient AI. This matters because the key function of a tactical AI is its ability to decide more accurately and more rapidly than an adversary. *Ceteris paribus*, a marginal advantage here will have a dramatic impact on combat performance. John Boyd saw this effect vividly during the Korean War and developed his idea of an "OODA loop" (observe, orient, decide, and act) to explain the stellar performance of US F-86 Sabre pilots against their communist adversaries flying MiG 15 fighters, whose capabilities did not differ all that radically from the American aircraft (J. Boyd 1996). For Boyd, however, the key US advantage was in its pilots' ability to cycle through the OODA loop with greater speed than their communist adversaries. Perhaps one significant difference was the bubble canopy of the American aircraft, which afforded greater all-round visibility than in the MiG. Or perhaps it was the hydraulic controls of the F-86, which allowed the pilot to maneuver the aircraft with less manual effort than the MiG. Regardless, the upshot was a kill ratio that massively favored the Americans, belying the broadly similar capabilities of their respective aircraft.

With tactical AI systems, the key characteristic will also be in decision-making speed, á la Boyd. Individual platform characteristics, like speed, maneuverability, weight of firepower, or armor, might still factor into deciding the outcome, along with numbers. But the speed and the precision of decision-making will exert a disproportionate effect, as in Korea. This effect was recently demonstrated in the simulated aerial combat between an experienced American fighter pilot and a tactical AI called Alpha. Even degrading the physical performance of the aircraft relative to the human pilot's was insufficient to level the field—the computer kept chalking up "kills" (Ernest and Carroll 2016). This vivid demonstration suggests that legacy weapons systems could rapidly become overmatched by new AI systems. An AI that cycles its OODA loop a hundred times faster than a human will easily defeat the human but will fare much less well against one that decides 101 times faster. The arms race to be at the bleeding edge of AI decision-making is likely to be intense, with implications for any efforts to regulate automated weapons.

Once again this sketch suggests that tactical capabilities can have strategic effects. This is particularly true since AI is nondomain specific and we can conceive of its application across warfighting domains. Aerial combat lends itself most readily to the application of modern AI, largely because the environment lacks terrain and clutter, including many human protagonists. Robots and automated land vehicles still face considerable challenges in navigating complex terrain and, while their performance is improving, the state of art exhibited in DARPA's Robot Grand Challenge between 2012 and 2015 demonstrates considerable room for improvement (Sofge 2015). Competing robots there attempted to navigate a complex environment with obstacles but stumbled and fell with comic effect. More problematic still, identifying and prosecuting targets in the land environment might require more of the contextual "understanding" that narrow AI finds difficult.

One final area in which the tactical abilities of narrow AI will have strategic impact is in shaping attitudes to risk. They will further depopulate an already increasingly automated battlefield, and with fewer soldiers exposed to danger we might expect possessing states to be more cavalier about employing force, all other things being equal. This will pose problems for existing alliances. The importance of marginal qualitative advantage offers nonleading states a few unpalatable alternatives: either attempted emulation, which may be hugely costly, socially disruptive, and ultimately fruitless, or the development of asymmetric alternatives to the employment of force—perhaps, for example, via unconventional, normatively disruptive approaches, including terrorism, weapons of mass destruction, or information warfare. When faced with the rapidly rising power of one group in international affairs, two classic approaches are to either balance it through alliances with like-minded groups or to bandwagon with it, seeking security through a close relationship. Military alliances can reflect such narrow cost-benefit analyses but often also include a normative element of shared ideologies. However, states lacking cutting edge AI may find that both balancing and bandwagoning are challenging, notwithstanding any shared sense of community. After all, what meaningful warfighting contribution can a state with legacy weapons or inferior AI make to a coalition that already includes the world leader? Moreover, states with mostly legacy manned platforms are liable to have very different risk parameters than states that can field armies of mostly unmanned platforms. This is especially true of liberal, risk-averse societies with their small, all-volunteer forces. If the AI market leader is set on military action, how far will it tolerate or need more-reticent alliance members? How far will it be willing to share the technologies that underpin its newfound power in the interests of interoperability? Perhaps states that cannot contribute to force will instead make a meaningful contribution through their legitimizing presence in a coalition. But insofar as fighting power is concerned, the rationale for military alliances will be weakened.

Mission Command, Control, and the Agent-Principal Dilemma

One last way in which tactical AI will have strategic impact is worth considering in some detail—the extent to which it will force human-decision makers "out of the loop" of decisions about using force. Concern about this has attracted most attention in the burgeoning literature on autonomous weapons in warfare, particularly by those concerned with the ethics of using robots in life-and-death situations.

Our concern here is more straightforwardly strategic: how far can humans control the action if decisions are being made at blinding speed by machines? Strategy, after all, is about choice, notably how and when to use force. If it ever happens, AGI will theoretically be able to make macro-level decisions about force, most notably about when to escalate or threaten it in order to coerce or deter adversaries. Tactical weapons platforms will be making lower-level decisions than AGI is capable of, but, again, the distinction between AI and AGI is not a binary one. Even a tactical weapons system will be making decisions that reach upward into the domain of strategy.

A tactical weapon system is a composite of narrowly specialized subsystems (one to orient the platform, another to confuse enemy radar, another to locate possible targets, another to search intelligence for salient targeting information, and so on). Collectively, this warfighting system will be making local decisions about what to kill or destroy. The combination of simple cognitive systems will allow more complex behavior and certainly permit significant escalation in force. If the system is simultaneously targeting multiple platforms in multiple dispersed locations, then already it is functioning at the operational level of war, where individual "contacts" are knitted together into sequenced battles that collectively seek to serve overarching strategy. Even a single tactical strike could have a dramatic strategic effect on conflict, especially if it breaks with the preestablished rules of engagement. Thus, an ostensibly "tactical" AI can end up making strategic decisions through its own relatively lowly activities.

This is problematic for military command and control. In particular, it greatly complicates the military concept of "mission command," an enduring principle in some modern armies, especially the British, and increasingly the American armies. This command philosophy relies on the creativity and skill of subordinate agents to carry out a commander's intent in the best way possible. Charles Krulak, an American Marine Corps general, argued for a "strategic corporal" with the skills to sensitively tackle a range of military tasks despite their relatively junior rank (Krulak 1999). With mission command, the commander is supposed to delegate responsibility for determining the best solution to the agents nearer the action, who are in theory better sighted on the problem and can also devote greater attention to the task.

There are problems with mission command in practice, even when it involves only human subordinates. The agent can misinterpret the intent of the commander or new circumstances can arise during the execution of the order that make the commander's order outdated. One problem that receives considerable attention in war college discussions is the tendency of the senior commander to micromanage the subordinate, contrary to the principle—a tendency exacerbated by the arrival of technologies that permit the senior commander greater access to remote tactical events in real time.

The recent film *Eye in the Sky* gives a compelling fictional account of this so-called "long screwdriver" in action, as a drone strike on an enemy terrorist is complicated when a small child selling bread appears near the target (Hood 2016). Discussions spiral quickly up to the level of the defense and foreign secretaries. In reality, this contingency and many others besides would have been anticipated and the ethical dilemma that arose would have been resolved—in this instance by the application of the doctrine of double effect, wherein some number of civilian casualties is weighed against the net gain from killing the target (Whetham 2010). But the broader point is still valid: the real world will throw up unexpected situations, and commanders, feeling well situated and empowered by new technologies, will find it hard to resist the temptation to delve into the tactical execution of their intent. This example is a useful illustration when it comes to considering tactical AI and the agent-principle dilemma.

For the tactical AI system, the speed of decision-making forces the "man in the loop" upward and away from the action. When fighting less technologically sophisticated adversaries, there will still be time to deliberate and intervene to shape the actions of the machines, but in conflict with near-peer adversaries any recourse to human judgment will slow the OODA loop down sufficiently as to ensure defeat, provided the enemy does not feel similarly obliged.

There are two broad sources of difference that together introduce scope for radically different behaviors between a tactical AI system and a legacy human army employing mission command. The first is the human tendency to shift objectives as events unfold, and the second is the comparative understanding of risk in the moment.

On the first difference, Herbert Simon's notions of "satisficing" and "bounded rationality" are relevant, as is Paul Samuelson's theory of "revealed preferences" (Simon 1957; Samuelson 1938). Humans are not strict "rational" actors, at least in any mathematically convenient sense, with neatly ordered and static preferences based on "perfect knowledge" of all available options. Instead, as Simon argues, they adjust their behaviors to roughly optimize preferences between a basket of goals, devoting sufficient cognitive effort to realizing each to a "good enough" level—hence, as we saw, the evolution of labor-saving heuristics that preserve limited conscious resources while delivering "good enough" optimization. More-over, as Samuelson holds, the choices they make are "revealed" to human actors, including to themselves, in the act of doing, rather than being stable and pre-dictable. If this is true of the political goals that guide strategy, the goals that are encoded into a tactical AI at the outset of action are unlikely to reflect all the changing circumstances that arise subsequently. Human goals will shift in time, including as a result of conflict—a point that occurred to Clausewitz, whose fa-mous definition of war as the continuation of politics was immediately followed by a reminder that war itself acts to shape the politics that ostensibly governs it. The machine, meanwhile, will be acting with customary blistering speed and maximum autonomy. The result is scope for a divergence between the goals of humans at $T=1$ and the behavior of the machine following the precepts set at $T=0$.

As for the second difference, the way in which AI systems will navigate tensions in goals given by their designers is unclear, but they are nonetheless unlikely to mimic human satisficing because of the profound differences in cognitive archi-tectures and processes. A human agent will be immersed in the action, navigating in the service of an overarching goal by using evolved cognition, including an evolved capacity to weigh risk. In contrast, the machine will pursue predeter-mined goals in nonhuman ways, including arbitrating any tension between goals. Its reward function may be the same as if it were human, but its approach to optimization will be rather different.

During his work on the OODA loop, John Boyd became acquainted with Kurt Gödel's incompleteness theorems (J. Boyd 1976). Gödel's mathematical logic demonstrates that no algorithm consisting of axioms (truth statements) about the arithmetic of natural numbers can prove all possible truths about them, no matter how many axioms there are. For the imaginative Boyd, the takeaway point was that objective reality is rather slippery; even if we know any number of constituent properties about reality, we will still have an incomplete picture that is in need of continual updating and will only ever obtain an imperfect approximation of it. This fits well with our modern understanding of the way in which the brain acts rather as a naïve scientist, integrating a top-down model of reality with incoming information via the senses, perhaps adjusting the model where there are glaring discrepancies. For Boyd's rapidly maneuvering Sabre pilot over Korea, the goal was to have a good enough approximation of reality and be able to update it rap-idly as events unfolded.

When it comes to tactical AI, the same basic proposition holds: the machine will not be able to model the great complexities of reality and will simplify it away so as to produce effective, timely behaviors that optimize a prespecified reward function. Like humans, it will be making simplifying assumptions and inferences about what is really out there. But the manner in which it makes those inferences is quite different from what a human might do, and the behaviors that result from those inferences may follow suit.

Anticipating just how machines will decide in novel circumstances will be challenging. Even in the toy universe of the Go board, as we saw, AlphaGo made unpredictable decisions that departed from what expert humans considered optimal. Part of this derived from the reward function of the machine, which preferred strategies that would deliver the highest probability of success rather than what looked to humans like the best option; the machine could make seemingly risky moves early in the game yet scrape home with the narrowest of victories. Or so it seemed to the humans watching on. But for AlphaGo a wafer-thin victory margin achieved with a 99.99999 percent probability would be preferred to one with a far bigger victory margin but only a slightly lower likelihood of 99.99 percent. Unlike humans, AlphaGo had the ability to compute those probabilities, based in part on its previous gameplay and in part on its winnowing out of the most improbable moves.

In the more complex Gödel-like real world, a tactical AI system will be unable to compute with anything like the same accuracy. But it will nonetheless surprise with some of its actions, even if we commanders think they have specified *ex ante* reward functions that anticipate many possible contingencies. When it comes to cycling its OODA loop, the snapshots of reality and the probabilistic inferences it draws from them will be inhuman.

We may seek to instill some version of our risk parameters into the tactical AI so that it follows our broad objectives, and we may hope that as the action unfolds it will decide in a broadly similar fashion as we would. But familiar problems arise. For one, we don't know what sort of risk parameters might best satisfy our own reward function in any given moment, since both the function and the risk parameters would be shifting in unexpected ways as events happen. Still less will we know how the machine will see things, even when given a static reward function ahead of time. Our tactical AI need not follow the risk parameters of its superiors—and indeed it is most unlikely to do so. This might even be beneficial, if it removes some of the systematic psychological flaws of human agents, such as the tendency to escalate when angry or to gamble more willingly when in the "domain of losses." The problem with tactical AI, however, is its narrow intelligence, which will be capable of responding to the physical dynamics of conflict but unable to understand context in the same way that human agents will. Human agents have an imperfect view of reality in the way that Boyd anticipated; mistakes are inevitable. But the human ability to interpret and act in a particular context will at least be along the same broad lines as that which their human commander might anticipate. Not so AI.

This is the fundamental challenge of controlling autonomous AI, which may make decisions of strategic import on our behalf. Unpredictability is inherent in conflict, and the performance of subordinates, human or otherwise, is inescapably uncertain, no matter how expertly "mission command" is implemented. Hence Clausewitz's timeless emphasis on the "genius" of the commander, by which he meant his ability to make decisions on the basis of incomplete information amid uncertainty. But tactical AI systems will operate with greater speed and reason via nonhuman processes, undoubtedly challenging the ability of the commander to shape the actions of their machine agents, genius or otherwise.

This is where the ethical dimension in the debate about weaponized AI comes in. Really, this is a subset, albeit a very important one, of that broader issue about control. If control is limited to prior statements of objectives and rules of engagement, and the machine then behaves in unanticipated ways, responding to contingencies in its local environment, who is responsible for the ethical behavior of the machine?

In a narrow sense, tactical AI systems are likely to be more reliable and discriminating in their use of force than even the best-trained and best-equipped humans. Notwithstanding efforts to deceive them (as with spoofing), AI systems are likely to outperform manned platforms at accurately selecting and prosecuting targets—after all, that's one of the principal rationales for deploying them. Unlike humans, the AI won't suffer fatigue or be inclined to respond emotionally to dangerous situations since it does not experience rage, fear, or even the exultant joy of combat that some humans report (Marlantes 2011; Bourke 2000). In the wider sense, however, the machine, at least as we currently conceive of it, will singularly lack the sort of flexible, commonsense judgments that we expect from humans.

For ethical reasons, humans seemingly feel uncomfortable ceding control to machines, and not just in the warfighting domain: self-driving cars and automated surgery offer salient parallels. Humans may be less reliable decision-makers than machines in some contexts, including in steering cars, piloting planes, or carrying out medical diagnoses. But we nonetheless seem more comfortable with a human making such important decisions. Ideally that person would be a trusted member of our in-group, or someone with evident expertise. Where the decision directly affects our own welfare, this is understandable—a lack of control over events that affect us is a notable contributor to stress. Moreover, it is hard to build much feeling of empathy and mutual understanding with a machine.

When humans do not meet the standards we expect, including the ethical standards espoused by our group, we seek justice. But we cannot readily extend the concepts of either restorative or retributive justice to intelligent machines that transgress our social norms. The ethics of warfare are a combination of two fundamentally different philosophical logics (Walzer 2015). On one hand is the consequentialist logic that says the moral good is served by attaining the greatest good for the greatest possible number of individual humans. Ordering a frontal assault that predictably results in the deaths of most attackers may be justified if the greater good is served—for example, by fixing the enemy in place so that a flanking move can break through and bring hostilities to a rapid end. On the other hand there is a deontological approach that stresses the duty to weigh the impact of any decision on each individual person. For humans the balance between those logics can be significantly skewed by the way in which a situation is framed, with scenarios that engage our emotions and empathy toward individuals being more likely to favor a deontological lens.

The well-known philosophical example of the "trolley problem" illustrates the point neatly (Greene 2014). Given the choice between saving one life or saving five lives from being killed by a runaway train, the choice people make will—generally—be determined by the way in which the dilemma is expressed, or "framed." In one scenario, the five lives can be saved only by throwing another person under the runaway train; in another, the five can be saved at the expense of the one by switching the train onto a new track, where only one person loiters unaware of approaching doom. People responding to the scenarios typically find it easier to save the many when they can do so by throwing a switch rather than wrestling a reluctant, panicked individual off a bridge and in front of the train. Yet from a consequentialist standpoint, the scenarios are interchangeable: five lives saved at the expense of one lost. The reason likely has something to do with the emotional and empathetic arousal that comes from actively wrestling someone toward death. Joshua Greene found that different brain systems are active among human participants considering such trolley-like scenarios, depending on how the problem is framed. If the problem is emotionally arousing, people are much more likely to favor a deontological approach; in an abstract calculation, consequentialist logics weighing the greater good are employed. Similar distortions are introduced by having experimental participants think of the victims as in-group members versus outsiders (Cikara et al. 2010). The takeaway for us is that humans apply their ethics in a rather haphazard fashion, depending on, among other things, the way the issue is framed.

With all this subjectivity, what approach should a tactical AI take? Without an evolved moral compass of the sort that shapes human preferences, the machine is again reliant on *ex ante* specification of rules of engagement. This is problematic.

In cool deliberations ahead of time we might fancy using one ethical logic—for example, of course we should drop the bomb to save more lives. So the AI system is programmed accordingly. But in practice the exigencies of the situation may cause us to decide differently. Perhaps the terrorist is about to kill an innocent child. Either way, there may be no time to issue new instructions to an AI that is deciding what to do at inhuman speed.

These ethical dilemmas are only one dimension of a larger problem of changing preferences—both of our overarching goals in war and of the ways in which we use violence to achieve them. While we must specify our goals and rules of engagement to the AI in advance of any action, by the time the machine executes the strategy, matters may have changed. The problem for users of tactical AI is that such preferences can often be revealed only by the action itself.

Conclusion

It is worth pausing for a moment to reiterate that though necessarily speculative, these insights about tactical AI are hugely far-reaching for strategy. To recap: marginal advantages in AI performance, especially in speed of decision-making, are likely to be decisive and render legacy systems redundant. Accordingly, power balances may shift dramatically depending on the pace of development. The offense is likely to dominate because the speed of decision will confer a tremendous advantage on the first mover. That's a different conclusion from some previous analyses of automation in strategic affairs. In a 1987 work on automation and warfare, Frank Barnaby argued that technology favors the defense because it is more cost effective for automated weapons to destroy attacking platforms than it is to deploy them; moreover, the defense itself will be decentralized and so present a difficult target for attacking weapons (Barnaby 1987). Times, and technologies, change. The pattern-recognition abilities of modern ANN give them a better chance at finding and fixing defensive systems and then saturating them with concentrated firepower before dispersing rapidly.

At the extreme this might even undercut the defensive dominance of nuclear weapons, raising the prospect of preemptive first strikes. The possibility of concentrating force rapidly and with devastating precision renews the offensive logic of Lanchester's square law. Additionally, control is difficult given the speed at which tactical AI decides how best to optimize its reward function.

All this makes a concern for relative power balances particularly acute, per the logic of offensive realism (Mearsheimer 2014). The result might be one that a structural realist would predict: a strong security dilemma that feeds arms races and intensifies pressure to bandwagon with leading powers. This is before we come to the broader speculation about the extent to which AI systems shape the basic units of international relations themselves—for example, via the need for collective solutions to large social changes in employment conditions (Ford 2015) or via the impact on the boundary between public and private spheres. Both raise significant questions about the appropriate powers of states to monitor and control their citizens. All this from a tactical weapon system!

Some last thoughts about tactical AI and strategy before moving on to consider the implications of artificial general intelligence operating with true autonomy. First, there is a necessarily speculative dimension to this discussion—AI is developing rapidly, and even if the broad parameters of speed and pattern recognition are visible, much else remains hazy. This is why observers first underestimated AlphaGo's potential and then attributed its unexpected moves to human-like traits like imagination and creativity.

Second, in this instance the efficiency logic of warfare is likely to trump the effects of tradition simply because the impact on fighting power is liable to be so great. Tactical AI need not achieve immediate success across all domains of warfare—land combat is far harder than maneuver in air or at sea, being more cluttered and confused by human and physical geography. It will not, at least as far as war remains a human endeavor, entirely eliminate the moral dimension of fighting power that has allowed less-well-equipped groups to succeed against nominally more powerful adversaries. Nonetheless, the changes that it can reach in the near term are likely to be dramatic enough.

Third, the arrival of AI in society will change many existing institutions and practices, and the organization of armed force is no different. Nuclear weapons and, before their advent, the development of strategic airpower, offer some useful comparisons, as do earlier military-technical innovations. AI is likely to produce changes in the structure of the armed force at least as dramatic as the development of, say, ballistic missile submarines or carrier-based aviation. Autonomous, unmanned, swarming, nano, and other related technologies will further depopulate the battlefield and require new skills of service personnel. They will challenge the long-standing organization of armed forces into separate domains of land, sea, air, and space because they will integrate platforms operating across all of these domains. Alternative bureaucratic distinctions may emerge—perhaps organized along combat functions (intelligence, logistics, and so forth) or perhaps along technical lines (engineer, computer scientist, communications specialist, etc.). They will probably challenge existing notions of the warrior, as has the use of semiautomated, remotely piloted aircraft. And they will alter the relationship between armed forces and the societies that generate them—perhaps exacerbating the estrangement of recent decades where small all-volunteer forces have come to be the norm in many Western liberal societies.

Fourth, speculation remains about which countries will produce the best tactical AI. This requires sustained research in countries with the incentives to attract the best research talent from a limited pool. The usual structural incentives to intellectual creativity—personal freedom, rule of law, and robust property rights—will likely apply. AI research has been concentrated in states that are already militarily powerful: the United States, United Kingdom, France, and China. There are constraints to the proliferation of AI technology—of the hardware on which it runs (which may become even more exclusive with the development of specialist architectures, perhaps neuromorphic chip sets or quantum computing) and of the engineering expertise to train the algorithms.

There are significant caveats to the vision of tactical AI I set out here. One skeptical take on tactical AI is to see it as akin to earlier information-processing technologies: simply a way to reduce, but not eliminate, friction on the battlefield. Even those more limited information technologies were enough to prompt hyperbolic views about an information revolution in military affairs that would "lift the fog of war" (Owens and Offley 2001). It hasn't happened to the extent enthusiasts hoped: war remains bound up with chance and uncertainty. The development of warfighting AI could easily be seen as a simple continuation of this existing era of weaponized information technology. From this perspective tactical AI, like earlier technologies, will further reduce the friction of the battlefield without eliminating it entirely. Perhaps this conservative view is accurate—although, even so, the effect on existing power balances will be dramatic. But autonomy and the capacity to improve performance through learning on the job are qualitatively different phenomena. Unlike other forms of IT, AI is a decision-*making*, not decision-facilitating, technology.

Another possible criticism is that AI will never attain the ability to cope with Gödel-like complexity in unstructured environments, especially those in congested land warfare, where combatants and civilians are intermixed (Coker 2013). Two counters are possible: first, that humans are also imperfect, and second, that this is a problem susceptible to technological progress.

AI employed as a tactical weapon system challenges the evolved psychological basis of decision-making about violence. AI systems will not be shocked by surprise enemy fires or maneuver. They will not suffer fatigue or stress, like a pilot after repeated missions or a hard-pressed battalion staff. Nor will they appraise risk on the basis of prospect theory, commit to sunk costs, or overreact with a flash of anger to a setback or perceived slight—or indeed to any of the multitude of other cognitive heuristics that have proved adaptive for humans. But they will maneuver and concentrate force more rapidly than manned systems. Perhaps most significant, they will respect neither existing organizational structures and prerogatives nor the somewhat artificial distinction between tactical and strategic activities. Skepticism notwithstanding, their employment in combat is inevitable, given their inherent advantages and the acute security dilemma they create. Concerned observers might seek to regulate or even prohibit the development of weaponized AI. With so many different approaches and little tell-tale signature (unlike a nuclear weapons program), this will be difficult if not impossible to do. Rather than a particular weapons technology, AI is a decision-making technology—which is what makes it radically different from earlier military-technological innovations.

CHAPTER **8**

Artificial General Intelligence Does Strategy

IF TACTICAL AI CAN HAVE A DRAMATIC STRATEGIC IMPACT, HOW MUCH more revolutionary will artificial general intelligence prove? Earlier I argued that rather narrow, domain-specific intelligence of the sort currently feasible will change the balance of power between states, enhance the relative strength of the offense, challenge the ability of human commanders to exert control once the action starts, and during conflict behave in ways that are nonhuman and hard to predict. Now we will consider the case of an even more flexible, powerful artificial intelligence This further enlarges the scope for divergence between human designers and agent behavior, which may be particularly problematic when it comes to escalation, deterrence, and coercion—all enduring themes in strategy that have hitherto been weighed via our evolved psychology.

What Is AGI?

Defining AGI is no easy matter, since the concept is rather underspecified. One common approach is anthropocentric: comparing artificial to human intelligence, as with the distinction between "strong" (human-like) and comparatively "weak" AI. This is sometimes done via tests employed to compare humans and machines. Famously, these include Alan Turing's imitation game, but there are others as well, like the Winograd schema challenge, which requires selecting appropriate pronouns in ambiguous circumstances. This is something machines find difficult but which most humans can readily manage. Such a comparison captures the notion that there is something powerfully flexible about human intelligence, but it unduly constrains the possible spaces within which a machine might be said to exhibit "general" intelligence (Shanahan 2015). Human intelligence is the answer to a particular biological challenge, and there is little reason to suppose that a machine, existing outside those biological parameters, will need to follow the human template closely in order to be considered rather intelligent.

Still, human intelligence does exhibit some rather broad features that we might expect to see in general machine intelligence, even if it is not directly modeled on either the physical architecture or functional features of human cognition. Humans have a high degree of cognitive flexibility that allows them to shift rapidly from one task to another with little time spent learning new skills. To do this they can recombine elements of intelligence in new, sometimes innovative ways. Consciousness plays an important part in that recombination of ideas. Perhaps AGI will exhibit something similar—which would be a long way from the laborious training on carefully labeled data sets that typifies today's artificial neural networks. Additionally, humans have inbuilt, or intrinsic, motivations. Our intelligence follows from the need to satisfy these motivations in some optimal way. Earlier we saw that at the deepest level these motivations relate to the evolutionary imperatives to survive and reproduce, which allows the onward propagation of our genes. Other subordinate motivations follow from this—and in humans these take on a rich palate because we have evolved über-cooperation within groups using both dominance and prestige hierarchies.

For AGI there need not be a direct parallel with natural selection, although it would be possible to at least model natural selection's features. "Genetic algorithms" that compete for fitness are already an established part of AI research, but the analogy with natural selection, like that of the artificial neuron to its biological counterpart, is rather loose. Perhaps an AGI competing for "survival" in this manner would develop its own internal motivations in seeking to apply its flexible learning in order to optimize its reward function.

Perhaps an AGI would even need something like consciousness. Consciousness helps us humans to imagine other minds—including (seemingly a uniquely human skill) the minds of those not physically present. And it allows us to reflect with more abstract rationality on the situation at hand rather than the instinctive, often emotional unconscious mind.

These three aspects of general intelligence drive the analysis that follows: the need for cognitive flexibility; the possibility of motivations derived both from the external environment and also intrinsic to the agent; and the scope for machine consciousness. But if these broad categories are somewhat comparable to our human intelligence, there is scope for many differences, some of which could be profound and strategically significant. There are a lot of "mights" and "coulds" in the discussion to come. We do not yet have anything that could fairly be described as an AGI, and there is an inescapably speculative flavor to discussions about it. However, it should be readily apparent that the space for AGI extends much further than the one occupied by human intelligence. But it is worth keeping in mind throughout the potential for large differences between AGI and human intelligence. An AGI that looks like human intelligence is something we can easily imagine (perhaps assisted by our inbuilt tendency to anthropomorphize); but the AGI that eventually emerges need not look much like us at all.

The first difference between human intelligence and AGI, already noted, is the framework of natural selection within which human intelligence evolved. This has shaped our bodies and our minds; without it the intelligence in a machine is likely to be very different. For one thing, the survival imperative present in humans need not be evident in machines—in contrast to the breathless vision of a superintelligent and often malign AI found in science fiction accounts. Even a superintelligent machine need not have any great compulsion to preserve its agency at all costs, since it would not necessarily equate that agency to "life" or have an innate urge to replicate its genes. The artificial intelligence need not be embodied, as we are, in a single organism, with inbuilt senescence. It could be replicated across platforms or even float free of them as part of a diffuse network. If it does not develop consciousness like ours, it need not find itself reflecting on the purpose of its existence or otherwise engage in a search for "meaning," of the sort that has driven much human intellectual endeavor and that some philosophers and psychologists place at the core of human motivation.

A second key difference is the way in which these flexible artificial intelligences might interact. The core strategic themes identified thus far emanate from the overarching advantages of cooperation, as suggested by Lanchester's square law. Indeed, those advantages, I speculated, are an important driver for our intensely cooperative human behavior and perhaps the theory of mind that underpins it. There is no reason to suppose that machines, even ones possessed of AGI, will necessarily develop a theory of mind that is anchored in empathy and über-cooperation in order to coordinate their behaviors socially. In fact, there's little reason to suppose they will if the task at hand is simply coordinating with similar machines. Several possible alternatives are feasible, and more realistic—at least from an engineering perspective. A network of agents could be coordinated by an overarching single intelligence that communicates with, and even controls, "dumb" nodes, like the remote pilot of a modern drone. Or the intelligence could be "cloned" and then distributed into the nodes themselves—perhaps with some specialist modifications, depending on the role each would be expected to fulfill. In either scenario, coordinating among agents as part of the same system would be relatively straightforward. When it comes to coordinating with agents whose interior logic is unknown to the AGI, an alternative approach would be needed, but again, the space for possible solutions is larger than that occupied by human intelligence.

In short, an AGI could develop analogues of human intelligence, and it may even confront some similar challenges that push it, or its designers, along similar lines. If the machine is involved in competitive multi-agent environments, for example, it will need some way of anticipating the behavior of other agents. Clearly this has implications for strategy. Similarly, if a machine is engaged in a complex task or seeks to satisfy multiple reward functions, some of which may be in tension, it will need a way of adjudicating between those goals. Subordinate motivations, some of them internally generated, may provide a solution. Important strategic implications follow from this, quite apart from the fascinating questions about philosophy of (artificial) mind. If a machine's design addresses these challenges in a different way than human minds would, the strategic implications may be profound.

Flexible AGI

Let's consider in more detail some of the features constituting my hypothetical AGI. In common with the doomsday AGI of science fiction, my more conservative version would be a flexible thinker, at least when judged against the narrow AI of today, such as the ANN of DeepMind's AlphaGo. But the boundary between general and domain-specific intelligence is hazily defined. Even completing a task within a narrow domain can require some degree of cognitive flexibility. The tactical AI systems discussed earlier could be constituted of multiple narrow AIs, which would imbue them with a degree of behavioral flexibility. This composite approach suggests that one way to produce AGI is by combining many relatively simple algorithms to produce more sophisticated behaviors. For example, one algorithm could specialize in controlling a weapons platform while another searches for patterns that might constitute a valid target.

We might consider this an inauthentic way of approaching AGI and feel that "true" general intelligence really requires some form of integrated cognition rather than a patchwork assembly. But there is a loose analogy here with the human mind as a massively parallel processing system, much of it operating unconsciously. We have a firm experience of unitary thinking, but much of this is illusory and the product of our narrow-band, sequential consciousness. The underlying brain may be thought of, as many psychologists today do, as a composite of mental "modules." Still, consciousness allows our disparate cognitions to be knitted together into a cohesive-seeming whole, with our attention helping to integrate, recombine, and plan. A composite, or modular, AGI would need some sort of unifying process to coordinate the actions of subordinate intelligences. Indeed, this monitoring and coordinating function might be its distinctive feature. Nonetheless, that function need not look particularly like human consciousness, because the AGI will not be constrained by the embodied features of human cognition. But it might, however, follow the same loose requirement of monitoring the relationship between the system and its environment that Humphrey and others suggest prompts human self-awareness (Humphrey 2011).

As an intermediate step along the road to this sophisticated, highly flexible AGI, researchers are likely to produce flexible, general AIs of more modest abilities—for example, we might plausibly anticipate the first papers to claim creation of "rat-level" general intelligence sometime in the next few years (this is an explicit aim of DeepMind, and likely of others, too). But what does this mean? Rat intelligence, like human intelligence, has evolved to fit a particular environmental niche, and in their ability to adapt to a wide variety of physical environments, rats are remarkably successful. Rats are, for example, intensely social creatures: they like to play and laugh together, which seems to help their ability to solve problems (Forgays and Forgays 1952). Rats are able to navigate a particular physical and social environment in order to secure somatic and reproductive resources. "Rat-like" AGI, by contrast, could doubtless solve some problems of the sort that lab rats have achieved—perhaps being able to navigate a maze in search of a reward whose attainment requires sequential reasoning or spatial memory. But this sort of intelligence is only one facet of the rat's cognitive abilities.

The yardstick for AGI, this logic suggests, is a matter of subjective interpretation rather than a strict criteria. Again, we need to be more imaginative than our anthropomorphic tendency to compare sideways with human cognition. AGI will be marked by a flexible ability to adapt readily to new situations, as with the rat in the maze hunting for food. It will need less training to cope with novelty than do the rather laborious ANNs of today. And it may exhibit flexible behaviors that look ostensibly like human analogs—curiosity, imagination, and so on. But the underlying mechanisms could be radically different and based on, for example, the sort of pattern recognition and probabilistic reasoning of current AI rather than on the affect-laden heuristic reasoning of evolved human cognition.

The distinction between flexible artificial general intelligence and flexible human intelligence also applies to strategy. Humans are decent strategists because they possess a range of cognitive skills, including the capacity to form large groups of nonkin individuals and the ability to communicate through language using abstract ideas and symbolic representation. Both allow for shared ideas and values and for longer-term planning. Although there are numerous systematic glitches in our evolved cognitive abilities, we are still formidable social strategists.

But other strategic intelligences, ones that are flexible but organized along very different lines, are conceivable. As the comparative success of both AlphaGo and the chimpanzees in the two-player strategy game show, human intelligence itself is "domain specific"—good against other groups of humans but not so good when the rules of the game allow the adversary to apply its specialized abilities in probabilistic reasoning or brute-force memory of previous encounters. So human intelligence is just one way of making strategic decisions; under certain circumstances alternative approaches work better.

Perhaps the problem of achieving truly flexible artificial cognition relates to the structure of the artificial "brain"? One approach to AGI is to closely model the physical structure of our human brains in order to "emulate" them. Again, note the comparison is sideways, with human intelligence setting the standard for "strong" AI. But would it work? The prospect is far distant. There are problems mapping the human brain, let alone emulating it. Much about brains remains unknown, notwithstanding the breakthroughs in imaging and computer simulations of recent decades. A newly published atlas found 180 distinct areas of the human cortex, including a staggering 97 newly identified areas (Glasser et al. 2016). Meanwhile, a large-scale European research project on simulating the brain on computers has encountered formidable methodological difficulties and delivered meager results (Theil 2015). Modeling the brain is a science in infancy. Science fiction–like visions of emulation persist nonetheless, even in academic literature. In *The Age of Em*, for example, Robin Hanson describes a world of the near future in which brain emulations are cheap and plentiful, completely reshaping society and what it means to be human (Hanson 2016).

But even the emulation of a human brain, even if done to a molecular level of accuracy, is unlikely to reproduce the cognitive processes that humans experience—brains do not exist separately from their bodily context. In that, at least, Antonio Damasio is surely correct in stating that the material architecture of an intelligence matters, and that it includes both body and brain (Koch et al. 2016). Anything other than total emulation that includes human bodies and even human societies is unlikely to lead to "human-like" intelligence. The human brain, like the rat's, is an answer to a series of particular evolutionary challenges—our conscious deliberation and our unconscious biases and heuristics are likewise distinctively human.

Since human strategy flows from the human condition, an AGI that does not precisely mirror human cognition—embodied and encultured—is unlikely to create strategy in the same way. Still, if we define flexible cognition by its ability to efficiently and successfully orient an agent within complex environments, then machines may plausibly demonstrate it—in fact, they do already. This is the sort of flexibility that contributes to tactical-level AI, as with air superiority fighters discussed earlier. Flexible AGIs like this are likely to be tremendous servants of human agency. But they will not necessarily make the nightmarish adversaries of Hollywood's imagination, not least because they lack intrinsic motivation.

Motivation: What Does AGI Want?

Could an AGI acquire intrinsic motivation? The threat of a malign AI acting in its own interests and against ours has aroused most popular misgivings, fueled, of course, by films like *The Terminator* and *Ex_Machina*. This is the danger that comes most vividly to people's minds when they hear the warnings of Stephen Hawking or Elon Musk that AI poses a grave threat to humanity. It makes for splendid fiction, but is it realistic?

This issue seems critical when thinking about AGI and strategy. In a sense, however, it is a rather conservative view of machine intelligence: if the machine is like us, as are the "replicants" of *Blade Runner*, then we have some pretty solid ideas about how it will act strategically. While it may possess a sort of superintelligence, placing AI within the bounds of human-like intelligence provides a decent guide to its strategic behavior. It suggests, among other things, that it will be motivated by a desire for self-preservation, and possess some means of thinking strategically about how to manipulate, or at least interact, with other agents (including people) to get what it wants. That process of interaction with others and scenario planning about possible futures might also include self-awareness, to the extent that we can talk about consciousness. Of course, being superintelligent, we should expect the AGI to be cognitively sophisticated and able to flexibly combine its ideas and adapt to varied and novel situations. That's the full doomsday package of a highly autonomous, self-aware, and self-motivated AGI with an interest in self-preservation. Such an intelligence might also reflect on meaning and the interior lives of others. Its consciousness might have some emotional hue in which it feels like something to be the machine.

But other dystopian visions are possible that don't rely on human-like AGI. Nick Bostrom's now widely known scenario of the relentless Bayesian paper clip counter is a variation on that doomsday scenario (Bostrom 2014). Here, a superintelligent AI destroys humanity as an inadvertent side effect of its inhuman determination to get the job done at all costs, thwarting all efforts to stop its progress. The AI's probabilistic approach sees it return again and again to its simple task of counting paper clips, Sisyphus-like, because there is always some non-zero possibility that its count is wrong. The machine uses its formidable intellect to garner ever more resources to facilitate its count and blocks all attempts by humans to stop it from doing so. Since there is no point at which the machine can be satisfied beyond all doubt that its count is accurate, the process goes on until the entire universe has been destroyed. This is both superintelligent and yet also sublimely stupid behavior. The AGI lacks both a human-like appreciation of "good enough" outcomes and a way to reconcile its goal with other possible objectives, per the theory of satisficing—not least because it has no other goals. Bostrom dismisses suggestions that an AI like this can be interrupted or ring-fenced from the wider world, mostly because it would be too clever by half. The study of fail-safe mechanisms is a vibrant part of AI research, notwithstanding this objection.

An AI like this would have to be cognitively flexible enough to operate in a complex environment, including interacting with other intelligent agents. Additionally, it would need an intrinsic motivation that runs counter to human intentions. Bostrom's paper clip counter starts out with ostensibly the same intentions that its human controllers had when they gave it the task to complete. They set its reward function and tasked it with optimizing the count. Once it begins, however, the intentions of the humans and the machine part company, with disastrous consequences. The humans specify the machine's task poorly, and lack the means to intercede to correct its course. It may not have had intrinsic motivation initially, but once it gets under way with the count, it is fully autonomous in execution and internalizes a motivation that is not what the humans intend. For the paper clip counting AGI to be malign, Bostrom supposes that its initial reward function becomes all important, such that it cannot be overruled by a new, exogenous reward function calling on it to stop counting. The machine, like the more commonplace science fiction AGIs, has both intrinsic motivation and sufficiently flexible cognition as to pose a grave threat to humans. But why? Why wouldn't the machine be susceptible to interruption? For AGI of this sort to exist, some way must be found for the machine to develop intrinsic motivation and for that motivation to be able to override the extrinsic ones if or when they come into conflict.

An alternative and more conservative vision of a motivated AGI is possible, and to my mind rather more plausible. This version of AGI is closer to the tactical AI that is already with us than to the malign intelligences of Hollywood fame. In this vision of AGI, cognitive flexibility has advanced some way beyond the narrow, brittle AI of today. The machine may also possess additional ability to generate subordinate or proxy motivations in order to help it satisfy its exogenously given reward function, especially where that function is a complex of different goals that might come into tension. Its autonomy and cognitive abilities will be several orders of magnitude greater than an AI existing today. It may even be able to develop itself—writing new code and designing new architectures that allow it to better optimize its given reward function. We might even allow that its intellectual abilities could break into superintelligent territory, so that it is far superior to humans across a range of cognitive abilities.

But there are some critical differences between my vision of AGI and that of Murray Shanahan and Alex Garland's in *Ex_Machina*, or even Bostrom's dreaded paper clip counter. My AGI is autonomous in execution but its ultimate purpose is determined exogenously; this ultimate purpose can be changed by external actors, unlike that of humans, which is given by the logic of natural selection. The "motivations" of this AGI are derived entirely from its pursuit of the externally given reward function.

Difficulties in achieving this will partly reflect the difficulties humans have in deriving a settled, ordered reward function. If we cannot come up with one, how on earth will the machine follow it? Of course, we humans cannot do so, either as individuals or in groups—so we fudge, or "satisfice," to put it more charitably. For example, insofar as political goals in war are complex and shifting, we cannot reasonably expect to craft a definitive reward function for an AGI charged with executing strategy on our behalf. We will likely not even be aware of some of the goals we seek through conflict, nor how much we wish to achieve them or at what cost. At best we will capture a crude approximation of our goals at a particular moment in time. Even then, aspects of that reward function might be in tension: for example, the need to destroy fielded forces in a city while preserving as many civilian lives as possible. The AGI will need some means of balancing these parameters.

One way to do this is for the AGI to develop its own subordinate motivations—figuring out how best to optimize the overall reward function. Humans do this via some evolved heuristics. In the case of ethical dilemmas, the frame of the ethical problem will influence the sorts of heuristics we use. To recap: personalizing the dilemma in a way that stresses individual lives is likely to engage emotional processing, empathy, and deontological logic. Abstracting the problem reinforces the tendency to see it as the sort of cost-benefit issue approached through consequentialist logic. The AGI facing ethical dilemmas is most unlikely to use evolved cognitive heuristics like ours, but it will nonetheless need some way of approaching the issue. It might accordingly develop internal proxy motivations. This sort of internal juggling already happens, in a certain sense. The internal machinations of ANNs are currently something of a mystery to humans—we can see the end result of calculations but cannot easily follow the logic inside the hierarchical stack of artificial neurons that produced it. That's readily apparent when a ConvNet, a type of ANN often used to analyze images, is "spoofed" by the superimposition of noise over an image—instead of a "cat" it sees a pineapple, for example (Moosavi-Dezfooli et al. 2016). Why does this happen? Humans do not yet know. The internal logics of the AGI seeking to optimize the outputs of a complex reward function may be similarly opaque. Given the rather profound differences in architecture and processes between the machine and the human brain, at least for AGIs that are not total brain and body emulations, we can safely assume that its internal process will be rather different from ours.

Would these opaque internal motivations ever amount to the sort of self-directed autonomy we see in science fiction AGI—particularly the urge to survive? The artificial agent might, of course, have exogenously imparted instructions to preserve itself wherever possible in order to carry out its tasks in combat. It could, according to the logic described here, also develop a set of unanticipated interior motivations that enhances its ability to do so. If so, we can start to imagine a very autonomous and possibly malign AGI of the sort that troubles many people. But the sort of autonomy the AGI experiences will inevitably be constrained by its design. The imposition of a new, overarching reward function would immediately change the intermediate, proxy motivations that serve it. Unlike humans, whose ultimate motivation is encoded in our genes and the logic of natural selection, the ultimate motivation of the machine is not. This should make telling it to stop far easier, contra the idea of a relentless, self-motivated, and highly intelligent AI bent on its own survival and advancement.

In fact, the contrast between autonomous human and subservient AGI is overdone. Autonomy is relative for both. As described here, my AGI has rather less autonomy than does a human, given our evolved urge to survive. But humans themselves may not be as autonomous as they imagine. Consider the Japanese kamikaze pilots of the Second World War. These men quite deliberately killed themselves and did so because they derived a higher purpose than self-preservation from their membership of a social group. Their "autonomous" behavior—crashing into

Allied ships—was in reality derived from their membership of a particular culture. They were an extreme manifestation of the human inclination for altruism, prestige, and belonging. To what extent does it make sense to see a kamikaze pilot as wholly autonomous? For humans, then, autonomy is always relative, notwithstanding our inherent confidence in our own agency. For both AGI and humans, in other words, the distinction between exogenous and intrinsic motivation may not be as clear-cut as it initially seems. But the underlying reasons for that constrained autonomy differ radically between human and artificial intelligence.

So, readers of Bostrom's bestselling thesis might fear a future in which an AGI inadvertently obliterates the known universe in the interests of accurate accounting. And if it did, humans could hardly chastise it for failing to show restraint in the face of limited resources and biodiversity. Even so, there are good reasons to suggest that building an AGI will not necessarily result in inadvertent Armageddon while determinedly carrying out a banal task—most notably that it lacks any particular incentive to do so.

The space for possible AGI includes machines that are more closely modeled on human cognition; perhaps some of these *could* develop analogs for human proxy motivations like the drive for prestige or the search for meaning or even the urge to survive. For humans, such goals often come imbued with a sense of meaning and an emotional hue (Csikszentmihalyi 2008; Gilbert 2006). Artificial facsimiles of emotional processing are an ongoing research field but remain unconvincing (Calvo et al. 2015). There is a much larger conceptual space for an AGI that looks decidedly nonhuman. And here, in this larger space, even where there are analogs—curiosity, imagination, and so on—they are just that: analogs, not replications.

So my putative AGI may have an appreciation for meaning, but this would be meaning in the categorical sense of the word, in which mental concepts (including but not limited to linguistic concepts) are interconnected. For humans there are (at least) two dimensions to meaning: one is relational, as in the way in which mental concepts are interrelated or distinct; the other is emotional, deriving from our biological and social ontology. AI developers *are* making rapid progress in the categorization of concepts. This is captured in the notion (from Geoffrey Hinton) of "thought vectors" that can integrate discrete cognitive processes (LeCun, Bengio, and Hinton 2015). It is similar to the idea from neuroscience of human consciousness as a "global workspace" where mental processes can be "broadcast" through a human mind then recombined (Dehaene 2014). But machines lack our phylogeny, and thus the emotional dimension of meaning is absent from AI and difficult to design.

To summarize: my imaginary AGI occupies a very large space in the set of all possible AGIs—it is highly flexible and capable of transfer learning. It is motivated by its exogenously given reward function, although it may develop additional subgoals to help it realize this overarching function, or to balance between competing objectives from multiple reward functions. It will likely outperform humans on a wide range of intelligence tasks—possibly including ones that seemingly require human-type common sense, like the Turing test, where AI is currently stymied by its limited appreciation for irony and other distinctively human abilities. But this AGI is very different from human intelligence. It lacks our phylogeny and the cognitive processes that have evolved within it to help us successfully navigate our environment. On the one hand this is reassuring: the machine will want only what we tell it to want. It will faithfully seek to maximize its reward function, updating that whenever we do, and it will not possess an internal drive to "live" that outweighs our own needs. On the other hand, its attributes will make employing it strategically a formidable challenge.

Why is this? Simply because AGI like this will be able to control a broad spectrum of military activity. An intense security dilemma will likely ensure that this is so, given the degree to which military power will hinge on possessing the best possible AGI. And the flexible AGI will, in theory, possess the ability to escalate all the way up the ladder of escalation, from nonviolent warfare, via the control of information, through small-scale tactical encounters and all the way up to thermonuclear warfare. Additionally, this will be escalation without empathy or a theory of mind like ours. The net result is that strategy will rest on a new form of decision-making that is far different from our evolved psychology.

Consciousness

Before unpacking some of the implications for strategic behavior, some thoughts on machine consciousness round out the discussion of what constitutes an AGI. This is a challenging enough topic when it comes to humans, let alone imaginary machines. But it is important for any discussion of strategy, insofar as it bears on the sort of agency we might expect of an AGI. It also bears on the question of ethics, in determining responsibility for the behavior of the artificial agent and in shaping how we ought to treat an artificial agent. Those are important issues, but my focus here is on the first: the impact of conscious agents on strategy.

Consciousness, prima facie, seems to be one of those processes that an intelligent machine might develop to help it deal with its overall reward function.

Equally though, it is one of those areas where we can anticipate that the analogies with humans will be rather loose. If machines do develop consciousness, that consciousness need not be of the sort that we or even other animals experience. Consciousness is a mongrel concept. The way I have employed it here suggests several key features, including a self-referential quality of monitoring the organism's relationship with its environment; some "broadcast" features that permit the integration and flexible recombination of cognitions; a narrow band quality focusing attention on important information; and an imaginative or scenario-planning function that allows rehearsal of future events, especially in theorizing about the minds of others. We can readily imagine a machine intelligence that can perform some of these functions without the underlying biochemistry or an embodied brain. But the quality of consciousness would be rather different, if so.

It is this biological architecture that gives human consciousness its particular character—the first-person, subjective, often emotional quality. As Antonio Damasio sees it, consciousness for us is the *feeling* of what happens. Perhaps it will feel like something to be a machine as it watches its own cognition in some artificial version of the "thick time" that characterizes the looped dimension of our self-aware conscious minds. But we should be somewhat skeptical, not least because this intelligence will be less closely tied to an equivalent of our physical bodies that generate the subjective sensation of our minds. Machine "consciousness" that is not embodied in the same manner as ours will "feel" rather different—indeed, it might not feel like anything at all. What "bodily" sensations would the machine be self-consciously experiencing?

Still, it should be apparent from the discussion so far that an AGI need not be conscious, yet still qualify as a flexible and adaptive intelligence able to navigate complex environments and realize goals. An unconscious machine can be "curious" in the sense of DeepMind's *Montezuma's Revenge* agent, able to navigate an environment without immediate feedback on its performance; and it can display "imagination" or "creativity" in the useful connections that it makes between separate concepts. And perhaps it can apprehend "meanings," at least in the manner of interconnected concepts. Insofar as these concepts are borrowed from the human world, as with language, the "vectors" of categorical meaning that result will probably even reflect human biases like racism and sexism (Bolukbasi et al. 2016).

When it comes to gauging what others want or intend to do, we humans consciously reflect on their interior minds. But machines can tackle dynamic, adversarial relationships without doing likewise. Unconscious AGIs can win at poker by minimizing "regret"—defined there as the potential for maximum loss (Yakovenko 2015; Metz 2017). This poker-playing AI was actually a compound of narrow AIs—one that could recognize patterns in opponent play over time, another that could filter out patterns in its own play that might give the game away, and a third that could weigh probabilities. Overall, the compound poker-AI beat some leading human players in repeated gameplay (during which it could learn the patterns in their play) without trying to get inside the opponent's head or read "tells," as some amateur human players might. This was a remarkable achievement in a game of asymmetric knowledge, in contrast to Go and chessboards, where information is perfect. Yet, as far as can be ascertained, machine consciousness did not feature.

Unconscious AIs can also be social with other machines, as when they work in a multi-agent environment on tasks that require collaboration and information exchange. Tesla's automated cars, for example, share their experiences in order to maximize the available data for training. DeepMind's engineers created a multi-agent environment with finite resources to be shared in the form of virtual apples. The agents either cooperated when resources were plentiful or competed (by shooting the other agents) when resources got scarce (Leibo et al. 2017). This was very much a "toy universe," but it demonstrated nonetheless a capacity in the agents to optimize their reward function in environments with other independent actors. There was no hint of consciousness from the deep-learning algorithms, which were very much the sort of tactical, domain-specific AI discussed previously. Perhaps, then, AIs will find ways to optimize their reward function in social contexts without somehow acquiring a theory of mind like ours.

Consider some things that a machine would not need consciousness for, but for which it serves a purpose for in humans. For example, consciousness as a way of prioritizing between the multiple parallel networks in the brain, devoting special attention to those that cross some threshold. We can conceive of consciousness as working memory, which points to its limited capacity for handling information and its function as a sequential processor (LeDoux 1999). This limited capacity might be for as few as seven concurrent items of information, according to George Miller (Miller 1956). Machines are also capable of massively parallel processing, and would need some way of arbitrating between the outcomes of processes when they come into conflict, but there is no reason to suppose that narrow-band, sequential human consciousness is the optimal way of doing this. Consciousness also works for us as a satisfying rationalizer for decisions that are reached by unconscious processes. We can rapidly confabulate plausible narratives to explain events, serving our need for esteem and consistency, albeit sometimes at the expense of accuracy. Machines, lacking ego, need not play the same game. Lastly, we might think of consciousness as imposing a linearity and unity on cognition—the "thick time" of our inner lives in which sensory perception and memory are seamlessly integrated to produce a unified experience of reality that is, in actuality, a sophisticated construction of different sensations arriving at different times. This helps us model reality and also rehearse and anticipate how our actions will shape the world around us. An AGI able to inhabit dispersed platforms simultaneously would not need this sensation of unity, even if it has to engage in functionally similar modeling of its interactions with the world. In short, AGI that is flexible and motivated to achieve goals would not necessarily need to emulate human consciousness.

Still, this has not stopped computer scientists and philosophers from wondering about sentient machines. All these characteristics of consciousness are susceptible to modeling, albeit with considerable abstraction. Long-standing cognitive architectures in AI research like ACT-R and SOAR possess some of the functional attributes that I ascribe to consciousness (Laird 2012; Anderson 2005). In SOAR, for example, overarching tasks are broken down into subtasks. Then memories, whether semantic, procedural, or episodic, are "chunked," or combined together, and recruited into working memory by the current problem, based on an earlier utility in dealing with similar problems. In humans we would call that analogical reasoning (Nilsson 2010).

The "modularity" of these artificial cognitive architectures in some senses mirrors what we understand about modularity of the mind, in Fodor's evocative phrase, even if the actual constitution of the modules differs (Fodor 1983). Many psychologists see the brain as containing multiple functional modules that link together to form a complex and sophisticated cognitive package. The philosopher Daniel Dennett evocatively uses the language of modern smartphones to talk about cognitive "apps" (Dennett 2017). AI like SOAR and ACT-R does something similar. Yet, despite these broad functional similarities, all the modeling in the world hasn't manifestly produced the qualitative sensation of consciousness.

In its absence, profound difficulties exist in imagining something as alien as conscious AGI. If the artificial "agent" is not embodied in the same way—indeed, especially if it is distributed across a system—why would it need such an integrationist illusion of a single "self"? Human consciousness is intimately connected to biology and to the sensations that are associated with it, whose read-out constitutes emotion. The self-aware AI in the famous manga film *Ghost in the Shell* exists in a disembodied sense, though it can inhabit corporeal form at will (Oshii 1996). Sci-fi speculation about the self-awareness of the internet follows a similar logic—a self-referential intelligence, even (in some fictional accounts) an affective intelligence. Bostrom refers to a "singleton"—a solitary superintelligence able to draw on an extensive and widely distributed architecture (Bostrom 2006). This would be a lonely existence, perhaps, but only if a machine experienced loneliness—and there is no a priori reason to suppose it would, since the function of emotions is to orient a biological agent, including in its relations with others. If the agent *is* the environment, or if the agent floats across the environment in disembodied fashion, the logic for evolved emotions fails.

In short, an AI might theoretically evolve consciousness, at least according to the materialist logic of Gerald Edelman and Guilio Tononi, which holds that consciousness is simply a quality of the integration and differentiation of any information system (Edelman 2001). But any such consciousness need not look much like ours; indeed, it might be a long way farther from our experience than the oft-compared subjective experience of Thomas Nagel's bat (Nagel 1974). In sum, a self-motivated, flexible, and superintelligent AI that has nothing like our motivations or consciousness is conceivable. If anything, this is a far more likely outcome for AGI, given the rather peculiar circumstances in which our own intelligence emerged. The tendency to anthropomorphize is strong, aided by our love of storytelling and movie special effects. Still, even if the AGI that eventually emerges looks more like my version than the more-threatening one that Hollywood prefers, there will be some profound implications for strategy. In fact, the implications are likely to be *more* profound because of the radical differences in underlying cognition.

AGI and Strategy

Our AGI might not inadvertently destroy humanity or do so on behalf of internally motivated goals—but it certainly has the potential to do so as a tool of human societies charged with the execution of strategy. Tactical AI, we saw, will have a significant impact on strategy, even if using only the limited technologies available today. This sort of narrow AI is fairly basic compared to the AGI sketched here. It lacks the degree of cognitive flexibility to switch easily between tasks and adapt swiftly to novel circumstances. It can be combined with other domain-specific AIs to produce complex, remarkable cognition—as with the poker-playing machine or the group intelligence of the insect "hive mind." An AGI, by contrast, would be an integrated package capable of managing all the discrete tasks of the constituent poker AIs, and many more besides—a souped-up version of tactical AI. In its military guise, such an AGI would be able to integrate the activities of the many nodes in the distributed, swarm-like system sketched earlier. It would possess the ability to employ force at all levels of intensity. This AGI would, of course, retain the significant attributes of the more limited AI precursor, notably in pattern recognition, memory, and speed, which translate well into military power. Moreover, the AGI would be able to generate internal motivations that are unanticipated by its designers. In combination with speed and the capacity to escalate, this makes for a dangerous and unpredictable package.

The strategic impact of the tactical AI came via its effect on the basic parameters of combat, as expressed in the abstract by Lanchester's laws. An AGI will possess the same attributes: its nodes will maneuver at speed and it will concentrate force rapidly, outcycling any lesser adversary. Additionally, however, an AGI would have the ability to coordinate force across the entire spectrum. Its major impact would therefore come via its effect on the existing parameters of escalation, coercion, and deterrence in strategy. In the nascent military thinking on AI, much attention has been given to the notion of human-machine teaming. If humans cannot realistically remain "in the loop" because of the need for speed, then they might at least remain "*on* the loop," with the power to intervene and stop actions already under way, especially escalatory actions.

That's the theory. Some element of human control could remain in this theoretical human-machine system. When the AI wants to target something that might be escalatory or unethical, humans could step in. There would be limits, especially at the tactical level, where speed in combat is of the essence, as with missile defense or air defense more broadly. But where it can be employed, human-machine teaming could employ the strengths of the two types of cognition in complimentary fashion; with humans adding contextual understanding of the sort that the fast-deciding, pattern-recognizing AI cannot.

But with an AGI, the scope for the humans to even remain "on the loop" in this way is limited. The integration of weapons as part of an AGI system will allow the machine to coordinate not just tactical encounters but to knit these together into operational activities. Whereas the decisions of a tactical AI can inadvertently have operational and strategic effect, the AGI warfighter will intentionally craft its behaviors to prevail at higher levels of war. This is radically different from strategy as it has been conducted hitherto. With an integrated AGI, the sequencing of violence, especially the decision to escalate, will be taken by nonhuman intelligence that weighs the risks of doing so in a way very different from humans.

AGI Gauges Adversary Behavior Differently

How will such an AGI decide to escalate? When deciding how best to use violence the AGI, like humans, will seek to understand how its adversary will respond. To do that, it will need to know something about the adversary's cognitive processes, even if it does not share them. AGIs in a strategic context pitted against human adversaries will inevitably ask the same questions as do humans of their enemies: What do they intend? How might they be deceived, coerced, or deterred?

To answer these questions, humans rely on innate empathy, observations of behavior, and conscious reasoning, then combine the three to imagine the others' perspective. Of these methods, AI has a clear lead only in the observation of behaviors, given our notoriously subjective powers of observation. AI excels at pattern recognition, and a strategic AGI would be able to learn from previous examples of human behavior. But it would face similar problems there to human strategists: the small n size in international affairs that has impeded generalization by human scholars means that even a highly intelligent AGI would ultimately be uncertain about how humans will react in a particular circumstance.

Short of generalizations like the democratic peace theory (which itself obscures large areas of contention, e.g., what is a democracy? what is war? what is the chain of causation?), there are few robust empirical findings about the behavior of states in international society, especially when it comes to war (Lebow 2010; Levy 2010). A machine could be very well informed and possess a rich understanding of human behavior yet still come up short in gauging strategy in the moment. There is no perfect knowledge to be had in strategic affairs, and the intelligent machine would still have a limited ability to know whether a particular human adversary would escalate or concede.

At the tactical level, a military AI might be able to anticipate enemy behavior based on some generalizations about earlier activity. This is how the poker champion AI overcame its human adversaries: it recognized repeated patterns in their play while obscuring the same in its own approach. There was no attempt at theory of mind, still less at empathy. Breaking free of those regularities might offer humans who are pitted against the formidable memory- and pattern-recognition abilities of tactical AI some chance of success. Perhaps if human adversaries make radical, unexpected moves, the machine can be caught out; but it's a fine balance, since moves that are wildly unlikely are liable also to be poor choices within the rules of the game. I'm reminded, writing this, of Austin Powers sticking with five in a game of blackjack, declaring that he likes to live dangerously (Roach 1997).

In the real world, complexity increases the scope for radical and unexpected moves by humans that might catch an AI unaware. Tactical AI might be less adept at coping with such erratic behaviors, and this would allow a role for humans. But what about an AGI? Given complexity and the sui generis problem—where every event has unique qualities—the strategic AGI might attempt some technique other than probabilistic reasoning based on past performance. Perhaps at this elevated level humans could retain a place in strategizing, bringing empathetic and emotionally informed reasoning to bear to help the AGI understand adversary behavior—but only if they have time to do so, a liberty that would be unavailable if the AGI-human team is pitted against a rival AGI that makes its decisions more quickly, without human input.

Could the AGI use another approach to predict the behavior of rivals? It might, depending on the features of its intelligence. It may, for example, possess a sophisticated grasp of meaning in the sense of related concepts—perhaps via some "thought vector" abilities of the sort discussed earlier. This would amount to a theory of mind of sorts. But it would be a rather different sort of "theory" than the one that comes naturally to (most) humans.

You might think that an AGI wouldn't need a rich, human-like theory of mind anyway since it possesses the ability to overwhelm human adversaries at all levels of violence. That's close to the classic notion of escalation dominance (Kahn 1960). Here, the machine's abilities, especially its speed, will force *its own* humans out of the loop, while if the enemy attempts to employ humans, the AGI could simply achieve escalation dominance by rapidly upping the ante until such time as it spots the enemy's will to match that escalation weaken. And if an enemy system is managed solely by computers, theory of (human) mind would anyway be of little use: the problem of how much escalation would be needed to coerce its computer enemy could be addressed instead by modeling its machine logic.

Yet in all these scenarios there is still the inescapable need for informed guesswork about enemy intentions. The underlying architecture of the enemy AGI might be very different from its own. And if there are any humans involved in commanding the enemy system at any level, the AGI will need to be able to anticipate what they are thinking, no matter how fast it is by comparison: observing their behaviors might not be enough.

In the possible spaces for an AGI outlined above, there is scope for an AGI to be more human-like in its cognition, perhaps even self-conscious. Here is a rationale for such a development. After all, as I have argued, the evolution of intelligence in humans was driven very much by the need to gauge what others were thinking, the better to behave strategically around them. Perhaps such consciousness could emerge from the sort of pattern-recognition attributes that underpin the remarkable cognitive abilities of narrow AI. War would provide a catalyst for the development of machine consciousness, just as it did for humans.

Consciousness aside, this scenario, of a strategic AGI, seems rather terrifying. The need for an edge in war will make the introduction of AI systems all but inevitable; AI regulation through treaty will be very difficult, if not impossible, given the possibilities of proliferation and defection. There are some barriers to entry, including bottlenecks of expertise, but there is also an acute security dilemma and pressure to develop autonomous weapon systems.

There is no need to imagine a sentient, human-like AGI with our sort of self-awareness. All that is needed is a flexible intelligence capable of adapting to novelty and controlling a wide range of nodes across a spectrum of force. This is beyond current abilities, certainly, but not so far as to be inconceivable in the near future. This AGI would seek to optimize our goals, as a faithful servant, and it will try to gauge how adversaries will respond. Yet its willingness to escalate within conflict will depend on a different, nonhuman logic, which may be rather opaque to us. And when it comes up against a comparable system, there will be a distinct advantage in acting first.

Getting to AGI

AGI seemingly remains far off, notwithstanding recent gains in ANNs. Perhaps these speculations about a warfighting AGI won't come to pass in our lifetimes, and I am being unduly concerned. AI skeptics, especially those working in the field, have seen previous bursts of enthusiasm come and go. Machine learning promises tremendous changes to human society—including in the realm of strategy. But there are marked limits to its abilities, and even deep learning is unlikely to unlock them in short order. AI's recent achievements against humans have drawn on its inherent strengths—most notably its prodigious memory for previous experience, its ability to recognize patterns in large data sets, and its ability to calculate probabilities. Yet truly flexible learning, to say nothing of intrinsic motivation and consciousness, are more distant prospects.

Connectionist AI has made solid advances in some aspects of human cognition, visual and natural language recognition, most notably. But rapid developments of recent years notwithstanding, it remains fairly primitive when set against human cognition in its capacity for gauging meaning and for generalizing across tasks. IBM Watson's achievements in the TV show *Jeopardy* showed some capacity for natural-language processing—a human-like skill but one that required no great understanding of its competitors, who simply had to be beaten to the buzzer (Ferrucci 2012). The tactical control problems of dogfighting are about maneuver in three dimensions—and again these play to AI strengths. Even poker resolves to learning probabilities of cards and, perhaps, to seeking patterns in an opponent's behavior in what is still a fairly constrained universe, compared to the rich and complex world away from the card table. DARPA's recent robot challenge, featuring autonomous robots trying to navigate a simulated emergency situation, demonstrates the limitations of current technology: robots stumbled and fell and struggled to rise again, with comic effect (Simon 2015).

Narrow AI is one thing; broad AI with a semblance of "common sense" (as with curiosity or imagination, a rather underspecified term) is something altogether more complicated. It's here that AI remains notoriously weak, struggling to discern meaning in ambiguous sentences, of the sort that even a toddler would understand—suggesting that its grasp of semantics is lacking. And that's before it gets to tone, emphasis, or even body language, each of which can radically transform meaning in spoken language. There have been embarrassing missteps, as when Microsoft's Twitter-based AI sought to learn from the online interactions of teenagers: it ended up spewing forth a torrent of racist and sexist swearing—which may, however, say more about humans than it says about the AI (Alba 2016).

On the whole, connectionist AI still requires large volumes of carefully labeled data from which to learn; this rather limits its applicability to situations where data is scarce. As for creativity, AI can write a good haiku, perhaps because the enigmatic form lends an aura of profundity to its efforts. It can produce basic reporting, with data-rich financial articles being a particular forte and sports as a sideline. But its novels and comedy scripts are execrable (Vincent 2016).

Some leading AI researchers, including Facebook's Yann Le Cunn and Baidu's Andrew Ng, take pains to point out the limitations in ANNs and act as a break on more breathless journalistic hyperbole. Deep learning has rejuvenated AI research and produced dazzling breakthroughs in information processing, but the intelligence produced is of a particular constrained type. More broadly, computer scientist Michael Littman argues that the prospect of a superintelligence is constrained by both the impending limitations in computing power (as Moore's law runs out of steam, given limitations on conventional processing power) and more fundamentally by the different philosophical approaches that underpin human and machine cognition (Littman 2015). Humans model reality on a "good enough" basis as naïve scientists, making probabilistic inferences about what incoming information means. Machines, by contrast, seek mathematical solutions and model reality in a more literal way. This constrains them because of the richness of reality (outside toy universes) where some problems may have no mathematical solution, à la Gödel's theorem. Of these two problems, the end of Moore's law is the more tractable: alternative processors, including, for example, "neuromorphic" chips modeled on human brains, or quantum computing may overcome any impending bottleneck in conventional processing power. Other nascent technologies—more realistic artificial neurons, for example, or even the use of biological neurons—may also contribute (Tuma et al. 2016).

But that still leaves the other, more profound, problem: AI is an excellent processor of huge quantities of information but much less adept at making inferences on the basis of incomplete information. Some of these difficulties may be more readily solvable than others. Autonomous cars still struggle with cluttered environments and rain, but here rapid improvements are possible because the problem plays to AI strengths (Gomes 2016). Less solvable are those problems that involve meaningful relations with humans. That's why many of the books and journalistic articles about the sorts of jobs under threat from automation stress generalizable social skills as being most resistant to change (Ford 2015). Insofar as strategy is a social activity conducted by groups of humans against other groups of humans, we might consider this a disadvantage for machines and conclude that humans are likely to be the best arbiters of how to use violence instrumentally, even in an age where many of their weapons are autonomous. Certainly that's a logic that appeals to enthusiasts for human-machine teaming in the Pentagon.

But warfare might not allow such a sanguine view. Regardless of progress toward AGI, tactical AIs, computational limitations notwithstanding, will shortly be able to act with precision and speed, dominating combat by concentrating fighting power. As that begins to happen, humans will increasingly have to outsource strategy to machines that do not reason in the same way that we do.

Conclusion

Landmark breakthroughs in AI rapidly come to seem mundane, not least to experts aware of previous generations of unfulfilled hype. A gulf remains between the evolved capabilities of the human brain, all eighty billion neurons and half a trillion synaptic connections, and those of even the most sophisticated neural network.

Still, notwithstanding the skepticism of some seasoned observers, the pace of change in recent years has been impressive. Starting with the most tactical of weapons systems, AIs soon will be making real-world decisions on violence. We will seek to match those decisions as best we can to our intentions, slippery though those intentions are. From these humble tactical beginnings AIs will engage in functional activities at ever-higher levels of military activities: coordinating sorties and operations as a battlespace manager, opening new fronts, ratcheting force upward in a bid for escalation dominance. We may seek to confine intelligent machines to the lower reaches of military activity or we may seek to use their higher-level thinking as a sort of "oracle" to help human strategists decide the best way ahead (Ayoub and Payne 2016). Initially, while such systems remain in their infancy, doing so will be possible, but the competitive advantages to be gained from integration, speed, and discrimination will gradually force ever-more elevated decisions on rival AGIs.

We need not fear the demon of an AI with a mind and motivations of its own to grasp just how revolutionary these changes are. We need not even fear the determinedly moronic paper clip counter. But we ought at least to be apprehensive about strategic AIs misinterpreting our intentions or calculating action in nonhuman ways, with results that may surprise and disappoint. Even with machines making strategic decisions, aspects of friction, uncertainty, and chance—those psychological forces so well apprehended by Clausewitz—will remain integral features of human conflict because reality is so complex as to be incomputable without abstraction and estimation. But the friction will, for the first time in human history, be addressed by machines that make strategy via an altogether alien form of cognition.

CONCLUSION

Strategy Evolves beyond AI

IN THE INTRODUCTION I ARGUED FOR TWO MACRO-REVOLUTIONS IN STRA-
tegic affairs. The first was associated with evolutionary developments that gave humans a different sort of social cognition from the one experienced by their near relations among the other great apes. Violence, a staple feature of prehistoric existence, necessitated (and probably selected for) close cooperation in large, non-kin groups. Perhaps this process catalyzed the development of language—that's certainly compatible with the gossip theory of Robin Dunbar. An abstract mathematical relationship posited by Frederick Lanchester suggests that larger groups gain disproportionately in combat where it is possible to concentrate force, all other things being equal. Dominic Johnson and Niall MacKay persuasively applied Lanchester's law to understand human evolution as a product of conflict.

A second revolution is now under way as the result of information-processing technologies that are accelerating. In this second macro-revolution the biological basis of decision-making is challenged. Plenty of other technologies have been described as "revolutionary," including any number of weapon systems—from composite bows and spoke-wheeled chariots to nuclear-powered submarines and ballistic missiles. Such weapons are the products of advanced cultures and can dramatically change the character of warfare and of the societies that wage it. Fair enough. These weapons require careful thinking in each local context about how best to enact strategy. They certainly complicate the business of extracting useful and enduring strategic concepts from the rich detail of history.

But at the most fundamental level such abstraction is possible precisely because strategy is a psychological activity, and our psychology evolves very slowly. Recognizing as much was Clausewitz's enduring triumph. Later, when game theory was in vogue, Thomas Schelling's analysis provided a timely reminder that human psychology is not reducible to the modeling of rational-actor theory. Emotion and other heuristics are all products of our evolved psychology—and while misperception and miscalculation might ensue, there is no inevitability to this, as demonstrated by the Cuban Missile Crisis.

One technology in particular has already altered this evolved psychological basis of strategy: writing. Artificial intelligence promises an even more radical transformation. The connection between the two is that both technologies alter our evolved psychological ways of making decisions. The development of writing, independently several times in human history, provided a way of externalizing cognition and sharing information across time and space, thus facilitating specialization. Writing allowed reflection on strategy and catalyzed technological innovation. Information technologies were extremely limited until very recently in human history. When they sped up with the development of computers, information technologies created an expectation of a radical change in strategy. This was premature. The information revolution in military affairs, as it was known, changed the parameters of strategy in some respects. It enhanced situational awareness and permitted greater speed and precision when it came to concentrating force. The countries that developed it most fully experienced greatly enhanced fighting power relative to legacy militaries—as the United States demonstrated in 1990–91 against the hitherto formidable Iraqi army. But there were limits—not just limits imposed by the available technology but also at the conceptual level, where strategy remained resolutely psychological. All the smart munitions and networked sensors in the world could not determine how vigorously Serbia's strongman Slobodan Milosevic would resist the NATO air campaign against him in Kosovo or ascertain how effective a "surge" of new troops into Afghanistan would be in defeating the Taliban insurgency there. Even a "smart" bomb needed a human to select the target.

On one hand the development of artificial intelligence can be seen as simply an extension of this ongoing information processing "revolution," albeit one that accelerates the changes already unleashed. This view accords with a certain skepticism on the part of AI researchers about the limitations of their efforts. Seen this way, AI is just another information-processing tool for humans. Claims for "revolutions" in military affairs deserve to be treated skeptically—the bar is often set far too low, and concepts come and go with bewildering speed (as with hybrid warfare, the indirect approach, the comprehensive approach, fourth-generation warfare, effects-based operations, and many more in recent years alone). Perhaps my claim for a revolution in strategy as a consequence of AI will be seen as similarly breathless and hyperbolic.

But AI is more than just another information-processing tool. Friction and chance will remain staples of strategy, and the alarmist conception of AI as a malign, self-motivated actor will likely remain the stuff of Hollywood fiction. But

AI will represent a radical departure in strategic affairs nonetheless because it will be making strategic decisions on our behalf and enacting them autonomously on the basis of calculations that are not human. This may have far-reaching consequences—changing the societies that wield it, changing the relative power between them, and changing the character of conflict. Other technologies have done as much. AI is more radical because it changes the very basis of strategic decisions themselves. Machines do not employ the cognitive heuristics that inform our decisions, still less the conscious reflection that we use to imagine a future or intuit what others might want. And while machines will certainly be acting to fulfill our goals, something will inevitably be lost in translation. Moreover, while the action will remain tactical for the near future, the competitive advantages to be gained from machine intelligence will produce decision-making at ever-more elevated levels. AI is not a weapons technology per se; it is a decision-making technology, which makes it inevitably strategic. Though strategy has emerged from human evolution, in the future it will be the evolution of machines rather than humans that shapes it most.

Even this, however, is not the end of the story, for either intelligence or for strategy. At present, most debate about AI is largely focused on machine learning and artificial neural networks. These techniques have certainly made remarkable advances. But there are other approaches to artificial intelligence that may yet have important contributions to make, perhaps in concert with ANNs. In addition, the architecture on which artificial intelligence currently operates will continue to develop. A computer today is recognizably the same sort of machine as it was decades ago—containing a set of microchips and switches that are able to process data in binary fashion and conceptually organized along lines originally conceived by John von Neumann, with data shuttling between a central processor and memory. Alternatives are readily conceivable, such as quantum computing, which replaces the definitive ones and zeros of binary code with an indeterminate quantum state. This is an immature technology but it offers the tantalizing prospect of far-greater processing speeds than at present are achievable, enabling calculations that are simply unfeasible on even the fastest binary machines. "Neuromorphic" chipsets that are modeled on the massively parallel processes of the brain rather than on the sequential processing of a von Neumann machine also promise to dramatically enhance computer power, this time using conventional binary processing.

A more profound change in the nature of artificial intelligence will come with the increasing integration of biological and artificial intelligence systems. One way this might be achieved is to use real neurons as the architecture for AI. Kevin Warwick's pioneering work used cultured rat neurons to control a robot in conjunction with a more traditional computer (Warwick et al. 2010). We can imagine biological-synthetic hybrid intelligences as lying along a spectrum, with this sort of thing at one end—a computer that uses living brain tissue as its processor, albeit in a disembodied manner. Perhaps some attempts to emulate the human brain will proceed along these lines, since the neurons already have the distinctive electrochemical means of communication that materially gives rise to our emotions and perhaps our consciousness.

But this is not the only possibility. At the other end of the spectrum are humans using synthetic AI technologies to enhance their own cognitive abilities. We have long done this, starting with writing and primitive calculating machines. Today's smartphones, with their personal assistants, are just the latest iteration; next might be virtual reality technologies that augment the real world with additional overlaid information. This is a rapidly maturing technology now on the cusp of commercial takeoff. For all these technologies, the computing power remains outside the human body but transforms the user's sense of reality. Even closer integration is not far away, bringing the artificial part of intelligence across the sensory organ divide and into the biological brain.

Prostheses can already interpret signals from the human body, including via the nervous system, and translate that into motion; in the other direction, the limb can feed back real-world information from the prosthesis into the brain (Tyler 2016; Flesher et al. 2016). Thought control of computers is already feasible, with computers sensing and interpreting brain signals via the scalp (Salazar-Gomez et al. 2017). Paralyzed people are already able to control robots and even their own limbs using their thoughts (Ajiboye et al. 2017; Wodlinger et al. 2015). These, however, remain immature technologies, as do ones allowing information to travel in the other direction, with computer inputs feeding directly into visual and other cortices.

The combination of these technologies promises to blur the boundary between human and computer cognition. Even more dramatic changes are feasible. "Mind merging," where thought processes from one biological brain are transmitted into another, has already been demonstrated in rats (Pais-Vieira et al. 2013). These synthetic approaches to modified human intelligence might be combined with others, such as "optogenetics," where light triggers responses in neurons that have been genetically engineered. Biotechnologies, including CRISPR gene editing, raise additional possibilities to alter evolved cognition, perhaps shaping capacities for attention or recall. The scope for an individual human mind to act in concert with others' is already apparent, even if the precise manner in which it might do so remains unclear. These technologies and others besides challenge the essence of what it means to be human and even what it means to be an individual. The moniker "AI" does insufficient justice to the human part of this intelligence, but "cyborg" sounds altogether too science fiction. Still, the science fiction of my youth again points the way. Think of humans uploading themselves to the grid or cyberspace in *Tron* and *Neuromancer* (Gibson 2016; Lisberger 1982).

At present, real-life cyborgs are, in the main, people with prostheses, computer scientists, or performance artists. Warwick, for example, made himself into a cyborg, with implants in his arm able to control a robotic hand. There may be an understandable reluctance to become a cyborg when that entails invasive and obtrusive technology. The demise of Google Glass and the slow uptake of "smart clothing" demonstrate the limits of public enthusiasm. But any reluctance could be ameliorated by nano technologies, and in the cases of military activity or the health sector, any gains will provide a powerful incentive to do so.

This brings us to the final point: the strategic implications of technologies like these that blur the boundaries between biological and machine intelligence and even between individual humans. The notion seems so exotic as to render any deductions about strategy wildly speculative. Nonetheless, some very broad points can already be made by following the broad themes that have animated this book. The first is that while AI might presage dramatic changes in strategy and war, along the lines discussed in the last two chapters, this is not inevitably the end of the story. Intelligence will continue to develop in the age of AI, and biological intelligences of some sort may be part of that picture. Strategy will perforce continue to evolve alongside the entities that make and enact it. Blurred human-AI hybrids will necessarily relate to one another; in an environment with limited resources, this will necessitate a blend of competitive and cooperative approaches, with violence remaining one possible means of interaction.

Second, a human-AI hybrid will have authentically intrinsic motivations and its cognition will be influenced by evolved heuristics, including emotion. The AGI described in the previous chapter was issued a reward function by its designers, and it worked to optimize that, whereas the new hybrid would have more autonomy and its intrinsic motivations would be informed by the search for meaning in a richly human sense.

This hybrid AI may also be a conscious intelligence. For one thing, it is not obvious that human consciousness could be somehow unpackaged from the other constituent elements of our intelligence. Evolution sometimes has a sedimentary quality, with successive developments layered one atop the other and making use of existing abilities, albeit sometimes adapted for novel purposes. Such was the picture of human consciousness previously sketched: able to deliver new abilities by developing existing processes of monitoring the organism's interaction with its environment. It is harder to imagine consciousness arising in a biological AI that uses cultured neurons simply as a processor, but comparatively easy to imagine at the other end of the spectrum, where nonbiological AI merges with already conscious humans. The resultant conscious experience may look very different, however: "jacked," in Gibson's term from *Neuromancer*, in ways that are as hard to imagine as it is to conceive of the conscious experience of a bat or octopus (Godfrey-Smith 2017).

Third, if there is a "mind" involved in weighing the use of force—whether that's a merged mind of a suprahuman society or the enhanced mind of a hybrid human—then strategy will retain its psychological basis. Strategists will attempt to fathom reality, including by reflecting on the minds of others. The organization of such intelligences into new societies and the means through which these societies might seek to instrumentalize force are wholly opaque. This is the realm where science fiction will have as much to contribute as science itself, and for a long time to come. We will have passed far beyond the simple logic of mass and cooperation that are captured in Lanchester's calculus. Material power will reside in the generation of complex warfighting technologies. But with biological, emotionally informed intelligences shaping strategy, power will inevitably retain its psychological dimensions. How badly will those intelligences want their goals, and how tenaciously will they hold on to their gains? What degree of escalation might coerce them into backing down?

ACKNOWLEDGMENTS

FOR ABSORBING DISCUSSIONS AND HIS CONSIDERABLE EXPERTISE ON artificial intelligence, neuroscience, and the philosophy of mind, my thanks go first to Kareem Ayoub, wunderkind of DeepMind.

At KCL I'm grateful to Ned Lebow, whose prolific writing, deep knowledge, and generous spirit is inspirational. Dave Houghton, my former supervisor and sometime departmental colleague, set me off on this path and has kept me hugely entertained ever since. Wyn Bowen's interest in the relationship between technology and strategy has undoubtedly catalyzed the development of a center of excellence at King's College. Thomas Rid is both an enviably stylish writer and an authority on technology and warfare. His somewhat skeptical take on AI has challenged me throughout to think more deeply about the subject. Where we disagree we do so with a warmness of spirit. David Betz continues to be a friend, mentor, and collaborator—and I'm grateful for all of these. Jon Hill's obdurate technophobia should make him invulnerable when the machines come for us and has made him an excellent sounding board.

There is a small community of scholars working in related areas, many of whom have been generous with their support for my own work. Adam Elkus and Miles Brundage have been a great aid to my understanding of AI and its impact on politics. At Oxford, Dominic Johnson's writing was very influential in shaping my own ideas. He is as comfortable in the world of evolutionary biology as he is with international relations theory; he continually produces groundbreaking research that crosses the disciplines, to the distinct advantage of strategic studies.

My thanks to the excellent team at Georgetown University Press, especially to Donald Jacobs for his support and enthusiasm. Thanks also to the anonymous reviewers, whose insights have undoubtedly sharpened my argument.

I wrote this book while training for an ironman—classic midlife crisis. Stephanie Jones, Richard Exley, and Anders Holmberg were my training buddies, and we endured much pain and many good times together. Thanks, I think.

The book is dedicated to my wonderful mother, who has given me unstinting love and support in my writing career, both as a journalist and as an academic.

REFERENCES

Abadi, Martín, and David G. Andersen. 2016. "Learning to Protect Communications with Adversarial Neural Cryptography." *ArXiv* 1610.06918 [Cs] (October). http://arxiv.org /abs/1610.06918.

Ajiboye, A. Bolu, Francis R. Willett, Daniel R. Young, William D. Memberg, Brian A. Murphy, Jonathan P. Miller, Benjamin L. Walter, et al. 2017. "Restoration of Reaching and Grasping Movements through Brain-Controlled Muscle Stimulation in a Person with Tetraplegia: A Proof-of-Concept Demonstration." *Lancet* 389 (10081): 1821–30. doi:10.1016/S0140-6736(17)30601-3.

Alba, Davey. 2016. "It's Your Fault Microsoft's Teen AI Turned into Such a Jerk." *Wired.* March 25. http://www.wired.com/2016/03/fault-microsofts-teen-ai-turned-jerk/.

Allison, Graham T. 1999. *Essence of Decision: Explaining the Cuban Missile Crisis.* New York: Harlow, Longman.

Altman, R. B. 2017. "Artificial Intelligence (AI) Systems for Interpreting Complex Medical Datasets." *Clinical Pharmacology and Therapeutics* 101 (5): 585–86. doi:10.1002/cpt.650.

Anderson, John R. 2005. "Human Symbol Manipulation within an Integrated Cognitive Architecture." *Cognitive Science* 29 (3): 313–41. doi:10.1207/s15516709cog0000_22.

Ardrey, Robert. 1976. *The Hunting Hypothesis: A Personal Conclusion concerning the Evolutionary Nature of Man.* London: Collins.

Ariely, Dan. 2009. *Predictably Irrational: The Hidden Forces That Shape Our Decisions.* London: Harper.

———. 2012. *The (Honest) Truth about Dishonesty: How We Lie to Everyone, Especially Ourselves.* London: HarperCollins.

Aristotle. 2000. *The Politics.* Translated by T. A. Sinclair, revised by Trevor Saunders. Harmondsworth: Pearson.

Ayoub, Kareem, and Kenneth Payne. 2016. "Strategy in the Age of Artificial Intelligence." *Journal of Strategic Studies* 39 (5–6): 793–819. doi:10.1080/01402390.2015.1088838.

Baars, Bernard J. 1993. *A Cognitive Theory of Consciousness.* Cambridge: Cambridge University Press.

———. 1997. *In the Theater of Consciousness: The Workspace of the Mind.* New York: Oxford University Press.

Baggini, Julian. 2015. *Freedom Regained: The Possibility of Free Will*. London: Granta.

Baker, Peter. 2009. "How Obama Came to Plan for 'Surge' in Afghanistan." *New York Times*, December 5. http://www.nytimes.com/2009/12/06/world/asia/06reconstruct.html.

Bal, P. Matthijs, and Martijn Veltkamp. 2013. "How Does Fiction Reading Influence Empathy? An Experimental Investigation on the Role of Emotional Transportation." *PLOS ONE* 8 (1): e55341. doi:10.1371/journal.pone.0055341.

Baragwanath, Emily, and Mathieu de Bakker. 2012. *Myth, Truth, and Narrative in Herodotus*. Oxford: Oxford University Press.

Barkow, Jerome H., Leda Cosmides, and John Tooby. 1992. *The Adapted Mind: Evolutionary Psychology and the Generation of Culture*. New York: Oxford University Press.

Barnaby, Frank. 1987. *The Automated Battlefield: New Technology in Modern Warfare*. Oxford: Oxford University Press.

Barron, Andrew B., and Colin Klein. 2016. "What Insects Can Tell Us about the Origins of Consciousness." *Proceedings of the National Academy of Sciences* 113 (18): 4900–4908. doi:10.1073/pnas.1520084113.

Baumeister, Roy F. 2012. *Willpower: Rediscovering Our Greatest Strength*. London: Allen Lane.

BBC Earth. 2011. *The Chimpanzee's Monkey Ambush*. YouTube video, https://www.youtube.com/watch?v=40SEMy4Z_zM.

Bellemare, Marc G., Sriram Srinivasan, Georg Ostrovski, Tom Schaul, David Saxton, and Remi Munos. 2016. "Unifying Count-Based Exploration and Intrinsic Motivation." *ArXiv* 1610.06918 [Cs] (June). http://arxiv.org/abs/1606.01868.

Berger, Peter L., and Thomas Luckmann. 1991. *The Social Construction of Reality: A Treatise in the Sociology of Knowledge*. London: Penguin UK.

Berna, Francesco, Paul Goldberg, Liora Kolska Horwitz, James Brink, Sharon Holt, Marion Bamford, and Michael Chazan. 2012. "Microstratigraphic Evidence of In Situ Fire in the Acheulean Strata of Wonderwerk Cave, Northern Cape Province, South Africa." *Proceedings of the National Academy of Sciences* 109 (20): E1215–20. doi:10.1073/pnas.1117620109.

Betts, Richard K. 2000. "Is Strategy an Illusion?" *International Security* 25 (2): 5–50. doi:10.1162/016228800560444.

Biddle, Stephen. 2006. *Military Power: Explaining Victory and Defeat in Modern Battle*. New ed. Princeton, NJ: Princeton University Press.

Blight, James G. 1992. *The Shattered Crystal Ball: Fear and Learning in the Cuban Missile Crisis*. Lanham, MD: Rowman & Littlefield.

Block, Ned. 2002. "Some Concepts of Consciousness." In *Philosophy of Mind: Classical and Contemporary Readings*, edited by D. Chalmers, 206–19. Oxford: Oxford University Press.

Block, Ned Joel, Owen J. Flanagan, and Güven Güzeldere. 1997. *The Nature of Consciousness: Philosophical Debates*. Cambridge, MA: MIT Press.

Bobbitt, Philip. 2013. *The Garments of Court and Palace: Machiavelli and the World That He Made*. New York: Grove.

Boden, Margaret A. 2016. *AI: Its Nature and Future*. Oxford: Oxford University Press.

Bolukbasi, Tolga, Kai-Wei Chang, James Zou, Venkatesh Saligrama, and Adam Kalai. 2016. "Man Is to Computer Programmer as Woman Is to Homemaker? Debiasing Word Embeddings." *ArXiv* 1607.06520 [Cs, Stat] (July). http://arxiv.org/abs/1607.06520.

Bostrom, Nick. 2006. "What Is a Singleton?" *Linguistic and Philosophical Investigations* 5 (2): 48–54.

———. 2014. *Superintelligence: Paths, Dangers, Strategies*. Oxford: Oxford University Press.

Botvinick, Matthew M., Jonathan D. Cohen, and Cameron S. Carter. 2004. "Conflict Monitoring and Anterior Cingulate Cortex: An Update." *Trends in Cognitive Sciences* 8 (12): 539–46. doi:10.1016/j.tics.2004.10.003.

Bourke, Joanna. 2000. *An Intimate History of Killing: Face-to-Face Killing in Twentieth-Century Warfare*. London: Granta.

Bowden, Rory, Tammie S. MacFie, Simon Myers, Garrett Hellenthal, Eric Nerrienet, Ronald E. Bontrop, Colin Freeman, Peter Donnelly, and Nicholas I. Mundy. 2012. "Genomic Tools for Evolution and Conservation in the Chimpanzee: Pan Troglodytes Ellioti Is a Genetically Distinct Population." *PLOS Genetics* 8 (3): e1002504. doi:10.1371/journal.pgen.1002504.

Bower, Gordon H. 1981. "Mood and Memory." *American Psychologist* 36 (2): 129–48. doi:10.1037/0003-066X.36.2.129.

Bowles, Samuel. 2009. "Did Warfare among Ancestral Hunter-Gatherers Affect the Evolution of Human Social Behaviors?" *Science* 324 (5932): 1293–98. doi:10.1126/science.1168112.

Boyd, Brian. 2010. *On the Origin of Stories*. Cambridge, MA: Harvard University Press.

Boyd, John R. 1976. *Destruction and Creation*. US Army Command and General Staff College. https://pdfs.semanticscholar.org/fe11/06ea0359da21082be64fc315a696b1d71528.pdf.

———. 1996. "The Essence of Winning and Losing." Unpublished lecture notes, originally circulated on the Defense in the National Interest website, now archived at https://www.danford.net/boyd/essence.htm.

Bräuer, Juliane, Josep Call, and Michael Tomasello. 2007. "Chimpanzees Really Know What Others Can See in a Competitive Situation." *Animal Cognition* 10 (4): 439–48. doi:10.1007/s10071-007-0088-1.

Brewer, Marilynn B. 1999. "The Psychology of Prejudice: Ingroup Love and Outgroup Hate?" *Journal of Social Issues* 55 (3): 429–44. doi:10.1111/0022-4537.00126.

Brockman, John, ed. 2015. *What to Think about Machines That Think: Today's Leading Thinkers on the Age of Machine Intelligence*. New York: Harper Perennial.

Brodie, Bernard. 1959. *Strategy in the Missile Age*. Princeton, NJ: Princeton University Press.

Broks, Paul. 2003. *Into the Silent Land: Travels in Neuropsychology*. London: Atlantic.

Burgess, Darren J. 2016. "Evolutionary Genetics: Haunted by the Past—Modern Consequences of Neanderthal DNA." *Nature Reviews Genetics* 17 (4): 191. doi:10.1038/nrg.2016.26.

Burr, William. 2015. *Nixon's Nuclear Specter: The Secret Alert of 1969, Madman Diplomacy, and the Vietnam War*. Lawrence, KS: University Press of Kansas.

Butler, Robin, Baron of Brockwell, et al. 2004. *Review of Intelligence on Weapons of Mass Destruction: Report of a Committee of Privy Counsellors*. HC 898. London: Stationery Office.

Byrne, Richard, ed. 1989. *Machiavellian Intelligence: Social Expertise and the Evolution of Intellect in Monkeys, Apes, and Humans*. Oxford: Oxford University Press.

Calvo, Rafael A., Sidney D'Mello, Jonathan Gratch, and Arvid Kappas. 2015. *The Oxford Handbook of Affective Computing*. New York: Oxford University Press.

Carney, Dana R., Amy J. C. Cuddy, and Andy J. Yap. 2010. "Power Posing Brief Nonverbal Displays Affect Neuroendocrine Levels and Risk Tolerance." *Psychological Science* 21 (10): 1363–68.

Carrier, L. Mark, Larry D. Rosen, Nancy A. Cheever, and Alex F. Lim. 2015. "Causes, Effects, and Practicalities of Everyday Multitasking." *Developmental Review* special issue: *Living in the "Net" Generation: Multitasking, Learning, and Development* 35 (March): 64–78. doi:10.1016/j.dr.2014.12.005.

Carstairs-McCarthy, Andrew, and Derek Bickerton. 2007. "Language Evolution: A Brief Guide for Linguists." *Lingua* 117 (3): 510–26. doi:10.1016/j.lingua.2005.02.006.

Cartledge, Paul. 2003. *Spartan Reflections*. Berkeley: University of California Press.

Cawkwell, G. L. 1983. "The Decline of Sparta." *Classical Quarterly* 33 (2): 385–400.

Cellan-Jones, Rory. 2014. "Stephen Hawking Warns Artificial Intelligence Could End Mankind." *BBC News*, 2 December. http://www.bbc.co.uk/news/technology-30290540.

Chagnon, Napoleon A. 1988. "Life Histories, Blood Revenge, and Warfare in a Tribal Population." *Science* 237 (4843): 985–92.

———. 2014. *Noble Savages: My Life among Two Dangerous Tribes—The Yanomamö and the Anthropologists*. New York: Simon & Schuster.

Chalmers, D. J. 1995. "Facing Up to the Problem of Consciousness." *Journal of Consciousness Studies* 2 (3): 200–219.

Chandler, David G. 1993. *The Campaigns of Napoleon*. London: Weidenfeld.

Chomsky, Noam. 2015. *Aspects of the Theory of Syntax*. Cambridge, MA: MIT Press.

Chung, Joon Son, Andrew Senior, Oriol Vinyals, and Andrew Zisserman. 2016. "Lip Reading Sentences in the Wild." *ArXiv* 1611.05358 [Cs] (November). http://arxiv.org/abs/1611.05358.

Cialdini, Robert B. 2014. *Influence: Science and Practice*. Harlow: Pearson Education.

Cieri, Robert L., Steven E. Churchill, Robert G. Franciscus, Jingzhi Tan, and Brian Hare. 2014. "Craniofacial Feminization, Social Tolerance, and the Origins of Behavioral Modernity." *Current Anthropology* 55 (4): 419–43. doi:10.1086/677209.

Cikara, Mina, Rachel A. Farnsworth, Lasana T. Harris, and Susan T. Fiske. 2010. "On the Wrong Side of the Trolley Track: Neural Correlates of Relative Social Valuation." *Social Cognitive and Affective Neuroscience* 5 (4): 404–13. doi:10.1093/scan/nsq011.

Clausewitz, Carl von. 1993. *On War*. Edited by M. Howard. New York: David Campbell.

Clodfelter, Mark. 1989. *The Limits of Air Power: The American Bombing of North Vietnam*. New York: Free Press.

Coker, Christopher. 2009. *War in an Age of Risk*. Cambridge: Polity.

———. 2010. *Barbarous Philosophers: Reflections on the Nature of War from Heraclitus to Heisenberg*. New York: Columbia University Press.

———. 2013. *Warrior Geeks: How Twenty-First-Century Technology Is Changing the Way We Fight and Think about War*. London: Hurst.

Collins, Sarah A. 2000. "Men's Voices and Women's Choices." *Animal Behaviour* 60 (6): 773–80. doi:10.1006/anbe.2000.1523.

Cornell, Heather N., John M. Marzluff, and Shannon Pecoraro. 2012. "Social Learning Spreads Knowledge about Dangerous Humans among American Crows." *Proceedings of the Royal Society of London B: Biological Sciences* 279 (1728): 499–508. doi:10.1098/rspb.2011.0957.

Crockett, Molly J., Luke Clark, Matthew D. Lieberman, Golnaz Tabibnia, and Trevor W. Robbins. 2010. "Impulsive Choice and Altruistic Punishment Are Correlated and Increase in Tandem with Serotonin Depletion." *Emotion* 10 (6): 855–62. doi:10.1037/a0019861.

Csikszentmihalyi, Mihaly. 2008. *Flow: The Psychology of Optimal Experience*. New York: Harper Perennial.

Cunning, David. 2014. *The Cambridge Companion to Descartes' Meditations*. Cambridge: Cambridge University Press.

Dahl, Ryan, Mohammad Norouzi, and Jonathon Shlens. 2017. "Pixel Recursive Super Resolution." *ArXiv* 1702.00783 [Cs] (February). http://arxiv.org/abs/1702.00783.

Dallek, Robert. 2008. *Nixon and Kissinger: Partners in Power*. London: Penguin.

Damasio, Antonio R. 1999. *The Feeling of What Happens: Body and Emotion in the Making of Consciousness*. New York: Harcourt Brace.

———. 2006. *Descartes' Error: Emotion, Reason, and the Human Brain*. London: Vintage.

Dawkins, Richard. 1987. *The Blind Watchmaker: Why the Evidence of Evolution Reveals a Universe without Design*. New York: Norton.

Dehaene, Stanislas. 2014. *Consciousness and the Brain: Deciphering How the Brain Codes Our Thoughts*. London: Penguin.

Dennett, Daniel C. 1993. *Consciousness Explained*. London: Penguin.

———. 2017. *From Bacteria to Bach and Back: The Evolution of Minds*. London: Allen Lane.

de Waal, F. B. M. 2007. *Chimpanzee Politics: Power and Sex among Apes*. Baltimore: Johns Hopkins University Press.

———. 2010. *The Age of Empathy: Nature's Lessons for a Kinder Society*. London: Souvenir.

———. 2012. "The Antiquity of Empathy." *Science* 336 (6083): 874–76. doi:10.1126/science.1220999.

———. 2013. *The Bonobo and the Atheist: In Search of Humanism among the Primates.* New York: W. W. Norton.

———. 2017. *Are We Smart Enough to Know How Smart Animals Are?* London: Granta.

Diamond, Jared M. 2005. *Guns, Germs, and Steel: The Fates of Human Societies.* London: Norton.

———. 2013. *The World until Yesterday: What Can We Learn from Traditional Societies?* London: Penguin.

Dobbs, Michael. 2008. *One Minute to Midnight: Kennedy, Khrushchev, and Castro on the Brink of Nuclear War.* London: Hutchinson.

Dobelli, Rolf. 2014. *The Art of Thinking Clearly: Better Thinking, Better Decisions.* London: Sceptre.

Dunbar, Robin. 1992. "Neocortex Size as a Constraint on Group Size in Primates." *Journal of Human Evolution* 22 (6): 469–93. doi:10.1016/0047-2484(92)90081-J.

———. 2004. *Grooming, Gossip, and the Evolution of Language.* London: Faber and Faber.

———. 2014. *Human Evolution.* London: Pelican.

Dutton, Denis. 2010. *The Art Instinct: Beauty, Pleasure, and Human Evolution.* Oxford: Oxford University Press.

Eagleman, David. 2011. *Incognito: The Secret Lives of the Brain.* Edinburgh: Canongate.

Edelman, Gerald M. 2001. *Consciousness: How Matter Becomes Imagination.* London: Penguin.

Eisenberger, Naomi I., and Matthew D. Lieberman. 2004. "Why Rejection Hurts: A Common Neural Alarm System for Physical and Social Pain." *Trends in Cognitive Sciences* 8 (7): 294–300. doi:10.1016/j.tics.2004.05.010.

Ekman, Paul, and Daniel Cordaro. 2011. "What Is Meant by Calling Emotions Basic." *Emotion Review* 3 (4): 364–70. doi:10.1177/1754073911410740.

Ellsberg, Daniel. 2002. *Secrets: A Memoir of Vietnam and the Pentagon Papers.* New York: Viking.

Epley, Nicholas. 2014. *Mindwise: How We Understand What Others Think, Believe, Feel, and Want.* London: Allen Lane.

Ernest, Nicholas, and David Carroll. 2016. "Genetic Fuzzy Based Artificial Intelligence for Unmanned Combat Aerial Vehicle Control in Simulated Air Combat Missions." *Journal of Defense Management* 6 (1). doi:10.4172/2167-0374.1000144.

Fearon, James D. 1995. "Rationalist Explanations for War." *International Organization* 49 (3): 379–414. doi:10.1017/S0020818300033324.

Ferrucci, D. A. 2012. "Introduction to 'This Is Watson.'" *IBM Journal of Research and Development* 56 (3.4): 1–15. doi:10.1147/JRD.2012.2184356.

Fichte, Johann Gottlieb. 2000. *Foundations of Natural Right: According to the Principles of the Wissenschaftslehre.* Cambridge: Cambridge University Press.

Fiske, Susan T. 2008. *Social Cognition: From Brains to Culture*. Boston: McGraw-Hill Higher Education.

Flesher, Sharlene N., Jennifer L. Collinger, Stephen T. Foldes, Jeffrey M. Weiss, John E. Downey, Elizabeth C. Tyler-Kabara, Sliman J. Bensmaia, Andrew B. Schwartz, Michael L. Boninger, and Robert A. Gaunt. 2016. "Intracortical Microstimulation of Human Somatosensory Cortex." *Science Translational Medicine* 8 (361): 361ra141. doi:10.1126/scitranslmed.aaf8083.

Fodor, Jerry A. 1983. *The Modularity of Mind: An Essay on Faculty Psychology*. Cambridge, MA: MIT Press.

Ford, Martin. 2015. *Rise of the Robots: Technology and the Threat of a Jobless Future*. New York: Basic Books.

Forgays, Donald G., and Janet W. Forgays. 1952. "The Nature of the Effect of Free-Environmental Experience in the Rat." *Journal of Comparative and Physiological Psychology* 45 (4): 322–28. doi:10.1037/h0053731.

Frankl, Viktor E. 2011 (1946). *Man's Search for Meaning*. London: Rider.

Freedman, Lawrence. 2000. *Kennedy's Wars: Berlin, Cuba, Laos, and Vietnam*. New York: Oxford University Press.

———. 2003. *The Evolution of Nuclear Strategy*. Basingstoke: Palgrave Macmillan.

———. 2013. *Strategy: A History*. New York: Oxford University Press.

Fry, Douglas P. 2007. *Beyond War: The Human Potential for Peace*. New York: Oxford University Press.

———. 2015. *War, Peace, and Human Nature: The Convergence of Evolutionary and Cultural Views*. New York: Oxford University Press.

Fukuyama, Francis. 1992. *The End of History and the Last Man*. London: Hamish Hamilton.

Fuller, John Frederick Charles. 1946. *Armament and History: A Study of the Influence of Armament on History from the Dawn of Classical Warfare to the Second World War*. London: Eyre & Spottiswoode.

Fursenko, Aleksandr, and Timothy Naftali. 2001. *One Hell of a Gamble*. New York: W. W. Norton.

Gaddis, John Lewis. 1982. *Strategies of Containment: A Critical Appraisal of Postwar American National Security Policy*. New York: Oxford University Press.

———. 2007. *The Cold War*. London: Penguin.

Gallese, Vittorio, and Alvin Goldman. 1998. "Mirror Neurons and the Simulation Theory of Mind-Reading." *Trends in Cognitive Sciences* 2 (12): 493–501. doi:10.1016/S1364-6613(98)01262-5.

Gallup, Gordon G. 1970. "Chimpanzees: Self-Recognition." *Science* 167 (3914): 86–87. doi:10.1126/science.167.3914.86.

Gamble, Clive, John Gowlett, and R. I. M. Dunbar. 2014. *Thinking Big: How the Evolution of Social Life Shaped the Human Mind*. London: Thames & Hudson.

Gannon, Patrick J., Ralph L. Holloway, Douglas C. Broadfield, and Allen R. Braun. 1998. "Asymmetry of Chimpanzee Planum Temporale: Humanlike Pattern of Wernicke's Brain Language Area Homolog." *Science* 279 (5348): 220–22. doi:10.1126/science.279.5348.220.

Gardner, R. Allen, and Beatrice T. Gardner. 1969. "Teaching Sign Language to a Chimpanzee." *Science* 165 (3894): 664–72.

Gardner, Robert. 1963. *Dead Birds*. Documentary film. Cambridge, MA: Peabody Museum.

———. 2007. *Making "Dead Birds": Chronicle of a Film*. Cambridge, MA: Peabody Museum Press.

Gat, Azar. 2001. *A History of Military Thought: From the Enlightenment to the Cold War*. Oxford: Oxford University Press.

———. 2006. *War in Human Civilization*. Oxford: Oxford University Press.

Gazzaniga, Michael S. 2011. *Who's In Charge? Free Will and the Science of the Brain*. New York: HarperCollins.

Gebru, Timnit, Jonathan Krause, Yilun Wang, Duyun Chen, Jia Deng, Erez Lieberman Aiden, and Li Fei-Fei. 2017. "Using Deep Learning and Google Street View to Estimate the Demographic Makeup of the US." *ArXiv* 1702.06683 [Cs] (February). http://arxiv.org/abs/1702.06683.

Geertz, Clifford. 2010. *The Interpretation of Cultures*. London: Fontana.

George, Alexander L. 1969. "The 'Operational Code': A Neglected Approach to the Study of Political Leaders and Decision-Making." *International Studies Quarterly* 13 (2): 190–222.

Gershgorn, Dave. 2016. "Fooling the Machine." *Popular Science*, March 30. http://www.popsci.com/byzantine-science-deceiving-artificial-intelligence.

Gibbs, Samuel. 2014. "Elon Musk: Artificial Intelligence Is Our Biggest Existential Threat." *Guardian*, October 27. https://www.theguardian.com/technology/2014/oct/27/elon-musk-artificial-intelligence-ai-biggest-existential-threat.

Gibson, William. 2016. *Neuromancer*. London: Gollancz.

Gilbert, Daniel Todd. 2006. *Stumbling on Happiness*. London: Harper.

Gladwell, Malcolm. 2005. *Blink: The Power of Thinking without Thinking*. London: Allen Lane.

Glasser, Matthew F., Timothy S. Coalson, Emma C. Robinson, Carl D. Hacker, John Harwell, Essa Yacoub, Kamil Ugurbil, et al. 2016. "A Multi-Modal Parcellation of Human Cerebral Cortex." *Nature* 536 (7615): 171–78. doi:10.1038/nature18933.

Godfrey-Smith, Peter. 2017. *Other Minds: The Octopus, the Sea, and the Deep Origins of Consciousness*. New York: Farrar, Straus and Giroux.

Gomes, Lee. 2014. "Hidden Obstacles for Google's Self-Driving Cars." *MIT Technology Review*, August 28. https://www.technologyreview.com/s/530276/hidden-obstacles-for-googles-self-driving-cars/.

Gómez-Robles, Aida, William D. Hopkins, and Chet C. Sherwood. 2013. "Increased Morphological Asymmetry, Evolvability, and Plasticity in Human Brain Evolution." *Proceedings of the Royal Society B* 280 (1761): 575. doi:10.1098/rspb.2013.0575.

Goodall, Jane. 1991. *Through a Window: Thirty Years with the Chimpanzees of Gombe*. Harmondsworth: Penguin.

Gordon, Deborah. 2011. *Ants at Work: How an Insect Society Is Organized*. New York: Free Press.

Gottschall, Jonathan. 2013. *The Storytelling Animal: How Stories Make Us Human*. Boston: Mariner.

Gray, Colin S. 2016. *Perspectives on Strategy*. Oxford: Oxford University Press.

Greene, Joshua. 2014. *Moral Tribes: Emotion, Reason, and the Gap between Us and Them*. New York: Atlantic.

Griffin, Donald R. 2001. *Animal Minds: Beyond Cognition to Consciousness*. Chicago: University of Chicago Press.

Haas, Mark L. 2001. "Prospect Theory and the Cuban Missile Crisis." *International Studies Quarterly* 45 (2): 241–70. doi:10.1111/0020-8833.00190.

Hameroff, Stuart, and Roger Penrose. 1996. "Orchestrated Reduction of Quantum Coherence in Brain Microtubules: A Model for Consciousness." *Mathematics and Computers in Simulation* 40 (3): 453–80. doi:10.1016/0378-4754(96)80476-9.

Hamilton, W. D. 1964. "The Genetical Evolution of Social Behaviour 1." *Journal of Theoretical Biology* 7 (1): 1–16. doi:10.1016/0022-5193(64)90038-4.

Hanson, Robin. 2016. *The Age of Em: Work, Love, and Life When Robots Rule the Earth*. Oxford: Oxford University Press.

Hanson, Victor Davis. 1998. *Warfare and Agriculture in Classical Greece*. Berkeley: University of California Press.

———. 1999. *The Other Greeks: The Family Farm and the Agrarian Roots of Western Civilization*. Berkeley: University of California Press.

———. 2005. *A War like No Other: How the Athenians and Sparta Fought the Peloponnesian War*. London: Methuen.

Hardy, Bruce L. 2004. "Neanderthal Behaviour and Stone Tool Function at the Middle Palaeolithic Site of La Quina, France." *Antiquity* 78 (301): 547–65. doi:10.1017/S0003598X00113213.

Hare, Brian, Victoria Wobber, and Richard Wrangham. 2012. "The Self-Domestication Hypothesis: Evolution of Bonobo Psychology Is Due to Selection against Aggression." *Animal Behaviour* 83 (3): 573–85. doi:10.1016/j.anbehav.2011.12.007.

Hariri, Yuval Noah. 2015. *Sapiens: A Brief History of Humankind*. London: Vintage.

Harris, Eugene E. 2015. *Ancestors in Our Genome: The New Science of Human Evolution*. New York: Oxford University Press.

Harris, Sam. 2012. *Free Will*. New York: Free Press.

Hatemi, Peter K., and Rose McDermott. 2011. *Man Is By Nature a Political Animal*. Chicago, IL: University of Chicago Press.

Henrich, Joseph, Robert Boyd, Samuel Bowles, Colin Camerer, Ernst Fehr, Herbert Gintis, and Richard McElreath. 2001. "In Search of Homo Economicus: Behavioral Experiments in Fifteen Small-Scale Societies." *American Economic Review* 91 (2): 73–78.

Herodotus. 1996. *The Histories*. Translated by Aubrey de Sélincourt. London: Penguin.

Herrnstein, Richard J. 1994. *The Bell Curve: Intelligence and Class Structure in American Life*. New York: Free Press.

Heuser, Beatrice. 2002. *Reading Clausewitz*. London: Pimlico.

———. 2010. *The Evolution of Strategy: Thinking War from Antiquity to the Present*. Cambridge: Cambridge University Press.

Heyes, C. M. 1994. "Reflections on Self-Recognition in Primates." *Animal Behaviour* 47 (4): 909–19. doi:10.1006/anbe.1994.1123.

Higham, Thomas, Laura Basell, Roger Jacobi, Rachel Wood, Christopher Bronk Ramsey, and Nicholas J. Conard. 2012. "Testing Models for the Beginnings of the Aurignacian and the Advent of Figurative Art and Music: The Radiocarbon Chronology of Geißenklösterle." *Journal of Human Evolution* 62 (6): 664–76. doi:10.1016/j.jhevol.2012.03.003.

Hill, Christopher. 2016. "Insects: Still Looking like Zombies." *Animal Sentience* 1 (9).

Hobbes, Thomas. 1982. *Leviathan*. Harmondsworth: Penguin.

Homer. 1991. *The Iliad*. Translated by Robert Fagles. London: Penguin Books.

Hood, Gavin. 2016. *Eye in the Sky*. Feature film. Raindog Films and Production One.

Hornblower, Simon. 1992. "The Religious Dimension to the Peloponnesian War, or, What Thucydides Does Not Tell Us." *Harvard Studies in Classical Philology* 94: 169–97. doi:10.2307/311424.

Horns, Joshua, Rebekah Jung, and David R. Carrier. 2015. "In Vitro Strain in Human Metacarpal Bones during Striking: Testing the Pugilism Hypothesis of Hominin Hand Evolution." *Journal of Experimental Biology* 218 (20): 3215–21. doi:10.1242/jeb.125831.

Houghton, David Patrick. 2001. *US Foreign Policy and the Iran Hostage Crisis*. Cambridge: Cambridge University Press.

———. 2009. "Analogical Reasoning, Neuroscience, and Emotion: Towards a Hot Cognitive Approach." Paper presented at the annual meeting of the International Studies Association's Fiftieth Annual Convention, New York. February 15. http://citation.allacademic.com/meta/p_mla_apa_research_citation/3/1/2/3/6/p312366_index.html.

Howard, Michael. 2002. *The Invention of Peace and the Reinvention of War: Reflections on War and International Order*. London: Profile.

Hrdy, Sarah Blaffer. 2009. *Mothers and Others: The Evolutionary Origins of Mutual Understanding*. Cambridge, MA: Harvard University Press.

Huang, Sandy, Nicolas Papernot, Ian Goodfellow, Yan Duan, and Pieter Abbeel. 2017. "Adversarial Attacks on Neural Network Policies." *ArXiv* 1702.02284 [Cs, Stat], (February). http://arxiv.org/abs/1702.02284.

Hublin, Jean-Jacques, Abdelouahed Ben-Ncer, Shara E. Bailey, Sarah E. Freidline, Simon Neubauer, Matthew M. Skinner, Inga Bergmann, et al. 2017. "New Fossils from Jebel Irhoud, Morocco, and the Pan-African Origin of *Homo Sapiens*." *Nature* 546 (7657): 289–92. doi:10.1038/nature22336.

Hugill, Nadine, Bernhard Fink, Nick Neave, and Hanna Seydel. 2009. "Men's Physical Strength Is Associated with Women's Perceptions of Their Dancing Ability." *Personality and Individual Differences* 47 (5): 527–30. doi:10.1016/j.paid.2009.04.009.

Humphrey, Nicholas. 2011. *Soul Dust: The Magic of Consciousness.* London: Quercus.

Huth, Alexander G., Wendy A. de Heer, Thomas L. Griffiths, Frédéric E. Theunissen, and Jack L. Gallant. 2016. "Natural Speech Reveals the Semantic Maps That Tile Human Cerebral Cortex." *Nature* 532 (7600): 453–58. doi:10.1038/nature17637.

Janis, Irving L. 1982. *Groupthink: Psychological Studies of Policy Decisions and Fiascoes.* Boston: Houghton Mifflin.

Jervis, Robert. 1976. *Perception and Misperception in International Politics.* Princeton, NJ: Princeton University Press.

———. 1989. *The Meaning of the Nuclear Revolution: Statecraft and the Prospect of Armageddon.* Ithaca, NY: Cornell University Press.

———. 1992. "Political Implications of Loss Aversion." *Political Psychology* 13 (2): 187–204. doi:10.2307/3791678.

Johnson, Dominic. 2016. *God Is Watching You: How the Fear of God Makes Us Human.* New York: Oxford University Press.

Johnson, Dominic D. P., and Niall J. MacKay. 2015. "Fight the Power: Lanchester's Laws of Combat in Human Evolution." *Evolution and Human Behavior* 36 (2): 152–63. doi:10.1016/j.evolhumbehav.2014.11.001.

Jomini, Antoine-Henri. 1992. *The Art of War.* London: Greenhill.

Jordan, Borimir. 1986. "Religion in Thucydides." *Transactions of the American Philological Association (1974–)* 116: 119–47. doi:10.2307/283914.

Junger, Sebastian. 2011. *War.* London: Fourth Estate.

Kagan, Donald. 2009. *Thucydides: The Reinvention of History.* New York: Viking.

Kagan, Donald, and Gregory F. Viggiano. 2013. *Men of Bronze: Hoplite Warfare in Ancient Greece.* Princeton, NJ: Princeton University Press.

Kahn, Herman. 1960. *On Thermonuclear War.* Princeton, NJ: Princeton University Press.

Kahneman, Daniel. 2011. *Thinking, Fast and Slow.* London: Allen Lane.

Kahneman, Daniel, Jack L. Knetsch, and Richard H. Thaler. 1990. "Experimental Tests of the Endowment Effect and the Coase Theorem." *Journal of Political Economy* 98 (6): 1325–48. doi:10.1086/261737.

Kahneman, Daniel, Paul Slovic, and Amos Tversky. 1982. *Judgment under Uncertainty: Heuristics and Biases.* Cambridge: Cambridge University Press.

Kahneman, Daniel, and Amos Tversky. 1979. "Prospect Theory: An Analysis of Decision under Risk." *Econometrica* 47 (2): 263–91. doi:10.2307/1914185.

Kant, Immanuel. 2007. *Critique of Pure Reason.* London: Penguin.

Kaplan, Fred M. 1991. *The Wizards of Armageddon.* Stanford, CA: Stanford University Press.

Keeley, Lawrence H. 1996. *War before Civilization.* New York: Oxford University Press.

Keller, Laurent, and Elisabeth Gordon. 2009. *The Lives of Ants.* Oxford: Oxford University Press.

Kennedy, Robert F. 1969. *Thirteen Days: A Memoir of the Cuban Missile Crisis*. New York: W. W. Norton.

Khong, Yuen Foong. 1992. *Analogies at War: Korea, Munich, Dien Bien Phu, and the Vietnam Decisions of 1965*. Princeton, NJ: Princeton University Press.

Kissinger, Henry. 1979. *The White House Years*. London: Weidenfeld & Nicolson and Michael Joseph.

Kiyonari, Toko, Shigehito Tanida, and Toshio Yamagishi. 2000. "Social Exchange and Reciprocity: Confusion or a Heuristic?" *Evolution and Human Behavior* 21 (6): 411–27. doi:10.1016/S1090-5138(00)00055-6.

Koch, Christof, et al. 2016. "Exclusive: Oliver Sacks, Antonio Damasio and Others Debate Christof Koch on the Nature of Consciousness." *Scientific American Blog Network*, accessed June 17. http://blogs.scientificamerican.com/mind-guest-blog/exclusive-oliver-sacks-antonio-damasio-and-others-debate-christof-koch-on-the-nature-of-consciousness/.

Krulak, Charles C. 1999. "The Strategic Corporal: Leadership in the Three Block War." *US Marine Corps Gazette* 83 (1) (January).

Kühl, Hjalmar S., Ammie K. Kalan, Mimi Arandjelovic, Floris Aubert, Lucy D'Auvergne, Annemarie Goedmakers, Sorrel Jones, et al. 2016. "Chimpanzee Accumulative Stone Throwing." *Scientific Reports* 6 (February): 22219. doi:10.1038/srep22219.

Kurzweil, Raymond. 2006. *The Singularity Is Near*. London: Gerald Duckworth.

Laird, John E. 2012. *The Soar Cognitive Architecture*. Cambridge, MA: MIT Press.

Lameira, Adriano R., Madeleine E. Hardus, Alexander Mielke, Serge A. Wich, and Robert W. Shumaker. 2016. "Vocal Fold Control beyond the Species-Specific Repertoire in an Orang-Utan." *Scientific Reports* 6 (July): 30315. doi:10.1038/srep30315.

Lanchester, Frederick William. 1916. *Aircraft in Warfare: The Dawn of the Fourth Arm*. London: Constable.

Lebow, Richard Ned. 1984. *Between Peace and War: The Nature of International Crisis*. Baltimore, MD: Johns Hopkins University Press.

———. 2001. "Thucydides the Constructivist." *American Political Science Review* 95 (3): 547–60. doi:10.1017/S0003055401003112.

———. 2003. *The Tragic Vision of Politics: Ethics, Interests, and Orders*. Cambridge: Cambridge University Press.

———. 2006. "Fear, Interest, and Honour: Outlines of a Theory of International Relations." *International Affairs* 82 (3): 431–48. doi:10.1111/j.1468-2346.2006.00543.x.

———. 2008. *A Cultural Theory of International Relations*. Cambridge: Cambridge University Press.

———. 2010. *Why Nations Fight: Past and Future Motives for War*. New York: Cambridge University Press.

LeCun, Yann, Yoshua Bengio, and Geoffrey Hinton. 2015. "Deep Learning." *Nature* 521 (7553): 436–44. doi:10.1038/nature14539.

LeDoux, Joseph E. 1999. *The Emotional Brain: The Mysterious Underpinnings of Emotional Life*. London: Phoenix.

———. 2002. *Synaptic Self: How Our Brains Become Who We Are.* London: Macmillan.

Leibo, Joel Z., Vinicius Zambaldi, Marc Lanctot, Janusz Marecki, and Thore Graepel. 2017. "Multi-Agent Reinforcement Learning in Sequential Social Dilemmas." *ArXiv* 1702.03037 [Cs] (February). http://arxiv.org/abs/1702.03037.

Levy, Jack S. 1997. "Prospect Theory, Rational Choice, and International Relations." *International Studies Quarterly* 41 (1): 87–112. doi:10.1111/0020-8833.00034.

———. 2010. *Causes of War.* Chichester: Wiley-Blackwell.

Libet, B. 1999. "Do We Have Free Will?" *Journal of Consciousness Studies* 6 (8–9): 47–57.

Liddell Hart, Basil Henry. 1967. *Strategy: The Indirect Approach.* London: Faber and Faber.

Lieberman, Matthew D. 2015. *Social: Why Our Brains Are Wired to Connect.* Oxford: Oxford University Press.

Lincoln, Tim. 2005. "Animal Behaviour: Congo's Art." *Nature* 435 (7045): 1040. doi:10.1038/4351040b.

Lisberger, Steven. 1982. *TRON.* Feature film. http://www.imdb.com/title/tt0084827/.

Littman, Michael. 2015. "'Rise of the Machines' Is Not a Likely Future." *Live Science*, January 28. http://www.livescience.com/49625-robots-will-not-conquer-humanity.html.

Locke, John. 2008. *An Essay concerning Human Understanding.* New York: Oxford University Press.

Loftus, Elizabeth F., and John C. Palmer. 1974. "Reconstruction of Automobile Destruction: An Example of the Interaction between Language and Memory." *Journal of Verbal Learning and Verbal Behavior* 13 (5): 585–89. doi:10.1016/S0022-5371(74)80011-3.

MacKay, N. J. 2006. "Lanchester Combat Models." *ArXiv* Math/0606300 (June). http://arxiv.org/abs/math/0606300.

Mackinlay, John. 2009. *The Insurgent Archipelago: From Mao to Bin Laden.* London: Hurst.

Makari, George. 2015. *Soul Machine: The Invention of the Modern Mind.* New York: W. W. Norton.

Manchanda, Arnav. 2009. "When Truth Is Stranger Than Fiction: The Able Archer Incident." *Cold War History* 9 (1): 111–33. doi:10.1080/14682740802490315.

Manoogian, John. 2016. "Cognitive Bias Codex Poster." *Design Hacks Posters.* https://www.designhacks.co/products/cognitive-bias-codex-poster.

Mar, Raymond A., Keith Oatley, and Jordan B. Peterson. 2009. "Exploring the Link between Reading Fiction and Empathy: Ruling Out Individual Differences and Examining Outcomes." *Communications* 34 (4): 407–28. doi:10.1515/COMM.2009.025.

Marlantes, Karl. 2011. *What It Is like to Go to War.* London: Corvus.

Martin, Alia, and Laurie R. Santos. 2016. "What Cognitive Representations Support Primate Theory of Mind?" *Trends in Cognitive Sciences* 20 (5): 375–82. doi:10.1016/j.tics.2016.03.005.

Martin, Christopher Flynn, Rahul Bhui, Peter Bossaerts, Tetsuro Matsuzawa, and Colin Camerer. 2014. "Chimpanzee Choice Rates in Competitive Games Match Equilibrium Game Theory Predictions." *Scientific Reports* 4 (June). doi:10.1038/srep05182.

Maslow, Abraham H. 1968. *Toward a Psychology of Being.* Princeton, NJ: Van Nostrand.

May, Ernest R., and Philip Zelikow. 1997. *The Kennedy Tapes: Inside the White House during the Cuban Missile Crisis*. Cambridge, MA: Belknap.

McConachy, Bruce. 2001. "The Roots of Artillery Doctrine: Napoleonic Artillery Tactics Reconsidered." *Journal of Military History* 65 (3): 617.

McCullough, Michael. 2008. *Beyond Revenge: The Evolution of the Forgiveness Instinct*. San Francisco: Jossey-Bass.

McDermott, Rose. 2001. *Risk-Taking in International Politics: Prospect Theory in American Foreign Policy*. Ann Arbor: University of Michigan Press.

McGlynn, Terrence P. 2000. "Do Lanchester's Laws of Combat Describe Competition in Ants?" *Behavioral Ecology* 11 (6): 686–90. doi:10.1093/beheco/11.6.686.

McNeill, William H. 2008. *The Pursuit of Power: Technology, Armed Force, and Society since A.D. 1000*. New York: ACLS Humanities.

Mearsheimer, John J. 2014. *The Tragedy of Great Power Politics*. Updated ed. Norton Series in World Politics. New York: Norton.

Mercer, Jonathan. 1996. *Reputation and International Politics*. Ithaca, NY: Cornell University Press.

———. 2005. "Rationality and Psychology in International Politics." *International Organization* 59 (1): 77–106. doi:10.1017/S0020818305050058.

Metz, Cade. 2017. "Inside the Poker AI That Out-Bluffed the Best Humans." *Wired*, February 1. https://www.wired.com/2017/02/libratus/.

Miller, George A. 1956. "The Magical Number Seven, Plus or Minus Two: Some Limits on Our Capacity for Processing Information." *Psychological Review* 63 (2): 81–97. doi:10.1037/h0043158.

Minsky, Marvin. 1969. *Perceptrons: An Introduction to Computational Geometry*. Cambridge, MA: MIT Press.

Miritello, Giovanna, Esteban Moro, Rubén Lara, Rocío Martínez-López, John Belchamber, Sam G. B. Roberts, and Robin I. M. Dunbar. 2013. "Time as a Limited Resource: Communication Strategy in Mobile Phone Networks." *Social Networks* 35 (1): 89–95. doi:10.1016/j.socnet.2013.01.003.

Mnih, Volodymyr, Koray Kavukcuoglu, David Silver, Alex Graves, Ioannis Antonoglou, Daan Wierstra, and Martin Riedmiller. 2013. "Playing Atari with Deep Reinforcement Learning." *ArXiv*1312.5602 [Cs] (December). http://arxiv.org/abs/1312.5602.

Moosavi-Dezfooli, Seyed-Mohsen, Alhussein Fawzi, Omar Fawzi, and Pascal Frossard. 2016. "Universal Adversarial Perturbations." *ArXiv* 1610.08401 [Cs, Stat] (October). http://arxiv.org/abs/1610.08401.

Morgenthau, Hans J. 1954. *Politics among Nations: The Struggle for Power and Peace*. New York: Knopf.

Morris, Errol. 2004. *The Fog of War: Eleven Lessons from the Life of Robert S. McNamara*. Documentary film. http://www.imdb.com/title/tt0317910/.

Muir, Rory. 2000. *Tactics and the Experience of Battle in the Age of Napoleon*. New Haven, CT: Yale University Press.

Nagel, Thomas. 1974. "What Is It like to Be a Bat?" *Philosophical Review* 83 (4): 435–50. doi:10.2307/2183914.

Nguyen, Anh, Jason Yosinski, and Jeff Clune. 2014. "Deep Neural Networks Are Easily Fooled: High Confidence Predictions for Unrecognizable Images." *ArXiv* 1412.1897 [Cs] (December). http://arxiv.org/abs/1412.1897.

Nicolson, Adam. 2014. *The Mighty Dead: Why Homer Matters*. London: William Collins.

Niebuhr, Reinhold. 1932. *Moral Man and Immoral Society: A Study in Ethics and Politics*. New York: Charles Scribner's Sons.

Niessner, Matthias. 2016. *Face2Face: Real-Time Face Capture and Reenactment of RGB Videos*. YouTube. https://www.youtube.com/watch?v=ohmajJTcpNk.

Nilsson, Nils J. 2010. *The Quest for Artificial Intelligence: A History of Ideas and Achievements*. Cambridge: Cambridge University Press.

Nosworthy, Brent. 1995. *Battle Tactics of Napoleon and His Enemies*. London: Constable.

Oshii, Mamoru. 1996. *Ghost in the Shell*. Animated film. http://www.imdb.com/title/tt0113568/.

Overy, R. J. 2013. *The Bombing War: Europe, 1939–1945*. London: Allen Lane.

Owen, David. 2008. *In Sickness and In Power: Illness in Heads of Government during the Last One Hundred Years*. London: Methuen.

Owens, William A., and Ed Offley. 2001. *Lifting the Fog of War*. Baltimore, MD: Johns Hopkins University Press.

Pais-Vieira, Miguel, Mikhail Lebedev, Carolina Kunicki, Jing Wang, and Miguel A. L. Nicolelis. 2013. "A Brain-to-Brain Interface for Real-Time Sharing of Sensorimotor Information." *Scientific Reports* 3 (February): 1319. doi:10.1038/srep01319.

Panksepp, Jaak. 1998. *Affective Neuroscience: The Foundations of Human and Animal Emotions*. New York: Oxford University Press.

Pape, Robert Anthony. 1996. *Bombing to Win: Air Power and Coercion in War*. Ithaca, NY: Cornell University Press.

Paret, Peter. 2007. *Clausewitz and the State: The Man, His Theories, and His Times*. Princeton, NJ: Princeton University Press.

———. 2009. *The Cognitive Challenge of War: Prussia, 1806*. Princeton, NJ: Princeton University Press.

Parry, Milman. 1987. *The Making of Homeric Verse: The Collected Papers of Milman Parry*. Edited by Adam Parry. Oxford University Press.

Patterson, Francine G. 1978. "The Gestures of a Gorilla: Language Acquisition in Another Pongid." *Brain and Language* 5 (1): 72–97. doi:10.1016/0093-934X(78)90008-1.

Payne, Kenneth. 2011. "Building the Base: Al Qaeda's Focoist Strategy." *Studies in Conflict and Terrorism* 34 (2): 124–43.

———. 2015a. *The Psychology of Modern Conflict: Evolutionary Theory, Human Nature, and a Liberal Approach to War*. Basingstoke: Palgrave Macmillan.

———. 2015b. *The Psychology of Strategy: Exploring Rationality in the Vietnam War*. London: Hurst.

―――. 2015c. "Fighting On: Emotion and Conflict Termination." *Cambridge Review of International Affairs* 28 (3): 480–97. doi:10.1080/09557571.2014.888539.

―――. 2016. "Prospect Theory and the Defence in Clausewitz's *On War*." Paper presented to the annual meeting of the International Studies Association, Atlanta, Georgia. March 16. http://web.isanet.org/Web/Conferences/Atlanta%202016/Archive/968b741d-130c-4912-a4ee-997345a57ce1.pdf.

Pinker, Steven. 2003. *The Blank Slate: The Modern Denial of Human Nature*. London: Penguin.

―――. 2012. *The Better Angels of Our Nature: A History of Violence and Humanity*. London: Penguin.

Pinker, Steven, and Paul Bloom. 1990. "Natural Language and Natural Selection." *Behavioral and Brain Sciences* 13 (4): 707–27. doi:10.1017/S0140525X00081061.

Pitman, George R. 2010. "The Evolution of Human Warfare." *Philosophy of the Social Sciences* 41 (3): 352–79. doi:10.1177/0048393110371380.

Poria, Soujanya, Erik Cambria, Rajiv Bajpai, and Amir Hussain. 2017. "A Review of Affective Computing: From Unimodal Analysis to Multimodal Fusion." *Information Fusion* 37 (September): 98–125. doi:10.1016/j.inffus.2017.02.003.

Postgate, Nicholas. 2014. *Bronze Age Bureaucracy: Writing and the Practice of Government in Assyria*. Cambridge: Cambridge University Press.

Puts, David A., Alexander K. Hill, Drew H. Bailey, Robert S. Walker, Drew Rendall, John R. Wheatley, Lisa L. M. Welling, et al. 2016. "Sexual Selection on Male Vocal Fundamental Frequency in Humans and Other Anthropoids." *Proceedings of the Royal Society B* 283 (1829): 2830. doi:10.1098/rspb.2015.2830.

Pyszczynski, Thomas A., Jeff Greenberg, and Sheldon Solomon. 2003. *In the Wake of 9/11: The Psychology of Terror*. Washington, DC: American Psychological Association.

Quester, George H. 1977. *Offence and Defense in the International System*. London: John Wiley.

Quinlan, Michael. 2009. *Thinking about Nuclear Weapons: Principles, Problems, Prospects*. Oxford: Oxford University Press.

Quiroga, R. Quian, L. Reddy, G. Kreiman, C. Koch, and I. Fried. 2005. "Invariant Visual Representation by Single Neurons in the Human Brain." *Nature* 435 (7045): 1102–7. doi:10.1038/nature03687.

Ranehill, Eva, Anna Dreber, Magnus Johannesson, Susanne Leiberg, Sunhae Sul, and Roberto A. Weber. 2015. "Assessing the Robustness of Power Posing No Effect on Hormones and Risk Tolerance in a Large Sample of Men and Women." *Psychological Science* 26 (5): 653–56. doi:10.1177/0956797614553946.

Reiterman, Tim. 2008. *Raven: The Untold Story of the Rev. Jim Jones and His People*. New York: Tarcher.

Rid, Thomas. 2016. *Rise of the Machines: The Lost History of Cybernetics*. Melbourne: Scribe.

Roach, Jay. 1997. *Austin Powers: International Man of Mystery*. Feature film. http://www.imdb.com/title/tt0118655/.

Roach, Neil T., Madhusudhan Venkadesan, Michael J. Rainbow, and Daniel E. Lieberman. 2013. "Elastic Energy Storage in the Shoulder and the Evolution of High-Speed Throwing in *Homo*." *Nature* 498 (7455): 483–86. doi:10.1038/nature12267.

Rodríguez-Vidal, Joaquín, Francesco d'Errico, Francisco Giles Pacheco, Ruth Blasco, Jordi Rosell, Richard P. Jennings, Alain Queffelec, et al. 2014. "A Rock Engraving Made by Neanderthals in Gibraltar." *Proceedings of the National Academy of Sciences* 111 (37): 13301–6. doi:10.1073/pnas.1411529111.

Roland, Alex, and Philip Shiman. 2002. *Strategic Computing: DARPA and the Quest for Machine Intelligence, 1983–1993*. Cambridge, MA: MIT Press.

Rosen, Stephen Peter. 2005. *War and Human Nature*. Princeton, NJ: Princeton University Press.

Roser, Max. 2016. "Visual History of the Rise of Political Freedom and the Decrease in Violence." *Our World in Data*. Online Resource. https://ourworldindata.org/VisualHistoryOf/Violence.html#/1.

Ross, Lee. 1977. "The Intuitive Psychologist and His Shortcomings: Distortions in the Attribution Process." *Advances in Experimental Social Psychology* 10: 173–220. doi.org/10.1016/S0065-2601(08)60357-3.

Rousseau, Jean-Jacques. 1984. *A Discourse on Inequality*. Harmondsworth: Penguin.

Rowlands, Mark. 1999. *The Body in Mind: Understanding Cognitive Processes*. Cambridge: Cambridge University Press.

Rusch, Hannes. 2014. "The Evolutionary Interplay of Intergroup Conflict and Altruism in Humans: A Review of Parochial Altruism Theory and Prospects for Its Extension." *Proceedings of the Royal Society of London B* 281 (1794): 20141539. doi:10.1098/rspb.2014.1539.

Rutherford, Adam. 2016. *A Brief History of Everyone Who Ever Lived: The Stories in Our Genes*. London: Weidenfeld & Nicolson.

Salazar-Gomez, Andres F., Joseph DelPreto, Stephanie Gil, Frank H. Guenther, and Daniela Rus. 2017. "Correcting Robot Mistakes in Real Time Using EEG Signals." Paper presented at the *IEEE International Conference on Robotics and Automation,* Singapore. May 29–June 3. http://groups.csail.mit.edu/drl/wiki/images/e/ec/correcting_robot_mistakes_in_real_time_using_EEG_signals.pdf.

Samuelson, P. A. 1938. "A Note on the Pure Theory of Consumer's Behaviour." *Economica* 5 (17): 61–71. doi:10.2307/2548836.

Schelling, Thomas C. 2008. *Arms and Influence*. New Haven, CT: Yale University Press.

Schuster, Mike, Melvin Johnson, and Nikhil Thorat. 2016. "Zero-Shot Translation with Google's Multilingual Neural Machine Translation System." *Google Research Blog*. November 22. https://research.googleblog.com/2016/11/zero-shot-translation-with-googles.html.

Searle, John R. 1980. "Minds, Brains, and Programs." *Behavioral and Brain Sciences* 3 (3): 417–24. doi:10.1017/S0140525X00005756.

Sémelin, Jacques. 2007. *Purify and Destroy: The Political Uses of Massacre and Genocide*. London: Hurst.

Seyfarth, Robert M., Dorothy L. Cheney, and Thore J. Bergman. 2005. "Primate Social Cognition and the Origins of Language." *Trends in Cognitive Sciences* 9 (6): 264–66. doi:10.1016/j.tics.2005.04.001.

Shanahan, Murray. 2010. *Embodiment and the Inner Life: Cognition and Consciousness in the Space of Possible Minds*. Oxford: Oxford University Press.

———. 2015. *The Technological Singularity*. Cambridge, MA: MIT Press.

Sharot, Tali. 2012. *The Optimism Bias*. London: Robinson.

Shiv, Baba, and Alexander Fedorikhin. 1999. "Heart and Mind in Conflict: The Interplay of Affect and Cognition in Consumer Decision Making." *Journal of Consumer Research* 26 (3): 278–92. doi:10.1086/209563.

Shumaker, Robert W., Kristina R. Walkup, and Benjamin B. Beck 2011. *Animal Tool Behavior: The Use and Manufacture of Tools by Animals*. Baltimore, MD: Johns Hopkins University Press.

Sidwell, Keith. 2009. *Aristophanes the Democrat: The Politics of Satirical Comedy during the Peloponnesian War*. Cambridge: Cambridge University Press.

Silver, David, Aja Huang, Chris J. Maddison, Arthur Guez, Laurent Sifre, George van den Driessche, Julian Schrittwieser, et al. 2016. "Mastering the Game of Go with Deep Neural Networks and Tree Search." *Nature* 529 (7587): 484–89. doi:10.1038/nature 16961.

Simon, Herbert A. 1957. *Models of Man: Social and Rational; Mathematical Essays on Rational Human Behavior in a Social Setting*. New York: John Wiley.

Simon, Matt. 2015. "Stop Laughing at Those Clumsy Humanoid Robots." *Wired*, June 11. http://www.wired.com/2015/06/stop-laughing-clumsy-humanoid-robots/.

Singer, Peter. 2011. *The Expanding Circle: Ethics, Evolution, and Moral Progress*. Princeton, NJ: Princeton University Press.

Singer, P. W. 2011. *Wired for War: The Robotics Revolution and Conflict in the Twenty-First Century*. London: Penguin.

Slovic, Paul. 2010. *The Feeling of Risk: New Perspectives on Risk Perception*. Earthscan Risk in Society Series. London: Earthscan.

Slovic, Paul, Melissa L. Finucane, Ellen Peters, and Donald G. MacGregor. 2007. "The Affect Heuristic." *European Journal of Operational Research* 177 (3): 1333–52. doi:10.1016/j.ejor.2005.04.006.

Sofge, Eric. 2015. "The DARPA Robotics Challenge Was a Bust." *Popular Science,* July 6. http://www.popsci.com/darpa-robotics-challenge-was-bust-why-darpa-needs-try-again.

Solomon, Sheldon, Jeff Greenberg, and Tom Pyszczynski. 1991. "A Terror Management Theory of Social Behavior: The Psychological Functions of Self-Esteem and Cultural Worldviews." *Advances in Experimental Social Psychology* 24: 93–159.

Soman, Dilip, George Ainslie, Shane Frederick, Xiuping Li, John Lynch, Page Moreau, Andrew Mitchell, et al. 2005. "The Psychology of Intertemporal Discounting: Why Are Distant Events Valued Differently from Proximal Ones?" *Marketing Letters* 16 (3–4): 347–60. doi:10.1007/s11002-005-5897-x.

Sorenson, Theodore C. 2005. *Decision-Making in the White House: The Olive Branch or the Arrows*. Foreword by John F. Kennedy. New York: Columbia University Press.

Soutschek, Alexander, Christian C. Ruff, Tina Strombach, Tobias Kalenscher, and Philippe N. Tobler. 2016. "Brain Stimulation Reveals Crucial Role of Overcoming Self-Centeredness in Self-Control." *Science Advances* 2 (10): e1600992. doi:10.1126/sciadv.1600992.

Steiner, Deborah Tarn. 2015. *The Tyrant's Writ: Myths and Images of Writing in Ancient Greece*. Princeton, NJ: Princeton University Press.

Stevenson, Robert Louis. 2012. *Dr Jekyll and Mr Hyde*. London: Penguin.

Strachan, Hew. 2005. "The Lost Meaning of Strategy." *Survival* 47 (3): 33–54. doi:10.1080/00396330500248102.

Strack, Fritz, Leonard L. Martin, and Sabine Stepper. 1988. "Inhibiting and Facilitating Conditions of the Human Smile: A Nonobtrusive Test of the Facial Feedback Hypothesis." *Journal of Personality and Social Psychology* 54 (5): 768.

Sun Tzu. 2014. *The Art of War*. Translated by John Minford. London: Penguin.

Tacitus. 2003. *The Annals of Imperial Rome*. Translated by Michael Grant. Harmondsworth: Penguin Classics.

Tajfel, Henri. 2010. *Social Identity and Intergroup Relations*. Cambridge: Cambridge University Press.

Tannenwald, Nina. 1999. "The Nuclear Taboo: The United States and the Normative Basis of Nuclear Non-Use." *International Organization* 53 (3): 433–68.

Team Fighting Championship Fight. 2014. *Fight One of the TFC Event One: LPH (Poznan, Poland) vs Wisemen (Gothenburg, Sweden)*. YouTube video. https://www.youtube.com/watch?v=GixDXD44_yA.

Tetlock, Philip E. 2005. *Expert Political Judgment: How Good Is It? How Can We Know?* Princeton, NJ: Princeton University Press.

Tetlock, Philip, and Dan Gardner. 2016. *Superforecasting: The Art and Science of Prediction*. London: Random House.

Thaler, Richard H. 1980. "Toward a Positive Theory of Consumer Choice." *Journal of Economic Behavior & Organization* 1 (1): 39–60. doi:10.1016/0167-2681(80)90051-7.

———. 2009. *Nudge: Improving Decisions about Health, Wealth and Happiness*. London: Penguin.

Theil, Stefan. 2015. "Why the Human Brain Project Went Wrong—and How to Fix It." *Scientific American*, October 1. https://www.scientificamerican.com/article/why-the-human-brain-project-went-wrong-and-how-to-fix-it/.

Thrun, Sebastian, Mike Montemerlo, Hendrik Dahlkamp, David Stavens, Andrei Aron, James Diebel, Philip Fong, et al. 2006. "Stanley: The Robot That Won the DARPA Grand Challenge." *Journal of Field Robotics* 23 (9): 661–92. doi:10.1002/rob.20147.

Thucydides. 2008. *The Landmark Thucydides: A Comprehensive Guide to the Peloponnesian War*. Translated by Richard Crawley. Edited by Robert B. Strassler. Introduction by Victor David Hanson. New York: Free Press.

Toffler, Alvin. 1980. *The Third Wave*. London: Collins.

Tomasello, M., S. Savage-Rumbaugh, and A. C. Kruger. 1993. "Imitative Learning of Actions on Objects by Children, Chimpanzees, and Enculturated Chimpanzees." *Child Development* 64 (6): 1688–1705.

Tomasello, Michael, Malinda Carpenter, Josep Call, Tanya Behne, and Henrike Moll. 2005. "Understanding and Sharing Intentions: The Origins of Cultural Cognition." *Behavioral and Brain Sciences* 28 (5): 675–91. doi:10.1017/S0140525X05000129.

Trivers, Robert L. 1971. "The Evolution of Reciprocal Altruism." *Quarterly Review of Biology* 46 (1): 35–57.

———. 2013. *Deceit and Self-Deception: Fooling Yourself the Better to Fool Others*. London: Penguin.

Tromp, John, and Gunnar Farnebäck. "Combinatorics of Go." *Computers and Games* (2007): 84–99. doi:10.1007/978-3-540-75538-8_8.

Trundle, Matthew. 2001. "The Spartan Revolution: Hoplite Warfare in the Late Archaic Period." *War and Society* 19 (2): 1–17. doi:10.1179/072924701791201495.

Tuchman, Barbara. 2014. *The Guns of August*. London: Penguin.

Tuma, Tomas, Angeliki Pantazi, Manuel Le Gallo, Abu Sebastian, and Evangelos Eleftheriou. 2016. "Stochastic Phase-Change Neurons." *Nature Nanotechnology* 11 (8): 693–99. doi:10.1038/nnano.2016.70.

Turchin, Peter. 2015. *Ultrasociety: How Ten Thousand Years of War Made Humans the Greatest Cooperators on Earth*. Chaplin, CT: Beresta.

Turing, A. M. 1950. "Computing Machinery and Intelligence." *Mind* 59 (236): 433–60.

Turner, John C. 1987. *Rediscovering the Social Group: A Self-Categorization Theory*. Oxford: Basil Blackwell.

Turney-High, Harry H. 1971 *Primitive War: Its Practice and Concepts*. Columbia: University of South Carolina Press.

Tyler, Dustin J. 2016. "Creating a Prosthetic Hand That Can Feel." *IEEE Spectrum: Technology, Engineering, and Science News*, April 28. http://spectrum.ieee.org/biomedical/bionics/creating-a-prosthetic-hand-that-can-feel.

US Department of Defense. 2017. "Department of Defense Announces Successful Micro-Drone Demonstration," January 9. https://www.defense.gov/News/News-Releases/News-Release-View/Article/1044811/department-of-defense-announces-successful-micro-drone-demonstration/.

van Creveld, Martin L. 1991. *The Transformation of War*. New York: Free Press.

Vegetius Renatus, Publius Flavius. 1993. *Epitome of Military Science*. Liverpool: Liverpool University Press.

Vernon, David. 2014. *Artificial Cognitive Systems: A Primer*. Cambridge, MA: MIT Press.

Vincent, James. 2016. "Writing New Episodes of Friends Is Easy If You Use a Neural Network." *Verge*, January 21. http://www.theverge.com/2016/1/21/10805398/friends-neural-network-scripts.

Vinge, Vernor. 1993. "The Coming Technological Singularity." *Whole Earth Review* 81: 88–95.

Wagenmakers, E.-J., T. Beek, L. Dijkhoff, Q. F. Gronau, A. Acosta, R. B. Adams, D. N. Albohn, et al. 2016. "Registered Replication Report: Strack, Martin, & Stepper (1988)." *Perspectives on Psychological Science* 11 (6): 917–28. doi:10.1177/1745691616674458.

Waltz, Kenneth N. 1959. *Man, the State, and War: A Theoretical Analysis*. New York: Columbia University Press.

———. 1981. "The Spread of Nuclear Weapons: More May Be Better: Introduction." *Adelphi Papers* 21 (171): 1. doi:10.1080/05679328108457394.

Walzer, Michael. 2015. *Just and Unjust Wars: A Moral Argument with Historical Illustrations*. New York: Basic.

Warneken, Felix, and Alexandra G. Rosati. 2015. "Cognitive Capacities for Cooking in Chimpanzees." *Proceedings of the Royal Society B* 282 (1809): 20150229. doi:10.1098/rspb.2015.0229.

Warwick, K. 2012. *Artificial Intelligence: The Basics*. London: Routledge.

Warwick, Kevin, and Huma Shah. 2016. *Turing's Imitation Game: Conversations with the Unknown*. Cambridge: Cambridge University Press.

Warwick, Kevin, Dimitris Xydas, Slawomir J. Nasuto, Victor M. Becerra, Mark W. Hammond, Julia H. Downes, Simon Marshall, and Benjamin J. Whalley. 2010. "Controlling a Mobile Robot with a Biological Brain." *Defence Science Journal* 60 (1): 5–14. doi:10.14429/dsj.60.11.

Weigley, Russell Frank. 1973. *The American Way of War: A History of United States Military Strategy and Policy*. New York: Macmillan.

Weinstein, Neil D. 1980. "Unrealistic Optimism about Future Life Events." *Journal of Personality and Social Psychology* 39 (5): 806–20. doi:10.1037/0022-3514.39.5.806.

Whetham, David. 2010. *Ethics, Law and Military Operations*. Basingstoke: Palgrave Macmillan.

White, Ralph K. 1984. *Fearful Warriors: A Psychological Profile of U.S.-Soviet Relations*. New York: Free Press.

Whitehead, Hal. 2015. *The Cultural Lives of Whales and Dolphins*. Chicago: University of Chicago Press.

Wiener, Norbert. 1948. *Cybernetics: Or Control and Communication in the Animal and the Machine*. New York: Wiley.

Wilson, Edward O. 1980. *Sociobiology*. Cambridge, MA: Belknap.

Wodlinger, B., J. E. Downey, E. C. Tyler-Kabara, A. B. Schwartz, M. L. Boninger, and J. L. Collinger. 2015. "Ten-Dimensional Anthropomorphic Arm Control in a Human Brain–Machine Interface: Difficulties, Solutions, and Limitations." *Journal of Neural Engineering* 12 (1): 016011. doi:10.1088/1741-2560/12/1/016011.

Wohlstetter, Albert. 1959. "The Delicate Balance of Terror." *Survival* 1 (1): 8–17. doi:10.1080/00396335908440116.

Wood, Noelle, and Nelson Cowan. 1995. "The Cocktail Party Phenomenon Revisited: How Frequent Are Attention Shifts to One's Name in an Irrelevant Auditory Channel?" *Journal of Experimental Psychology* 21 (1): 255–60. doi:10.1037/0278–7393.21.1.255.

Wrangham, Richard W. 1996. *Demonic Males: Apes and the Origins of Human Violence.* Boston: Houghton Mifflin.

———. 2009. *Catching Fire: How Cooking Made Us Human.* London: Profile.

Wrangham, Richard W., and Luke Glowacki. 2012. "Intergroup Aggression in Chimpanzees and War in Nomadic Hunter-Gatherers." *Human Nature* 23 (1): 5–29. doi:10.1007/s12110-012-9132-1.

Wrangham, Richard W., Michael L. Wilson, and Martin N. Muller. 2005. "Comparative Rates of Violence in Chimpanzees and Humans." *Primates* 47 (1): 14–26. doi:10.1007/s10329-005-0140-1.

Yakovenko, Nikolai. 2015. "Artificial Intelligence and Hold 'Em, Part 1: Counter-Factual Regret Minimization." *Poker News*, October 23. https://www.pokernews.com/strategy/artificial-intelligence-hold-em-1-23152.htm.

Yunis, Harvey. 2003. *Written Texts and the Rise of Literate Culture in Ancient Greece.* Cambridge: Cambridge University Press.

Zellen, Barry Scott. 2012. *State of Doom: Bernard Brodie, the Bomb, and the Birth of the Bipolar World.* London: Continuum.

INDEX

heads, evolution of, 47

Hegel, Georg, 90

helot underclass, 107, 111

Henrich, Joseph, 93

Herodotus, 98, 99, 113, 129

heuristics, 73–86; adaptive glitches and, 81–83; artificial general intelligence and, 201–2; cognitive, 81, 115, 154, 192, 202, 218; decision-making and, 83–85, 130, 154; emotions as, 78–79; errors of, 83–84, 86; incompatible goals and, 84–85; prospect theory and, 130; strategic, 77–78; unconscious mind and, 75–77, 82

Heuser, Beatrice, 103, 114

Hinton, Geoffrey, 174, 203

hippocampus, 60

Hiroshima, 136

historicism, vs. theory, 131–32

History of the Peloponnesian War (Thucydides), 91, 98, 112, 131–32

Hobbes, Thomas, 44, 102, 128

Homer, 95; on hoplite warfare, 108; *Iliad*, 94, 96–98, 111, 112; vs. Thucydides, 102

Homo erectus, 11, 64, 72, 116

homunculus, fallacy of, 57

honor, 39, 104, 113

hoplite warfare, 67, 106–10; Aristotle on, 108–9, 114; emergence of, 95, 96; Lanchester's square law and, 111–13; offense and, 15

horsemen, 110–11, 118

Houghton, David, 79

Howard, Michael, 102–3

human-AI hybrids, 218–21

human nature, 43–44, 98, 101

humiliation, vs. escalation, 155

Humphrey, Nicholas, 60, 197

hunter-gatherer societies: battles between, 5, 68; egalitarianism of, 105, 106–7; fission-fusion society of, 44; kinship bands and, 9, 45, 65; resource availability and, 82; warfare in, 3, 14, 43, 102, 127; weapons development by, 64

hunting, 4, 64

IBM, 212

identity: group, 24, 31, 35; of out-groups, 35; referent, 133; social, 53, 60, 77, 101, 117, 133

Iliad (Homer), 94, 96–98, 111, 112

images, 171, 173, 202

imagination: art and, 40; artificial intelligence and, 175, 205; in decision-making, 30; of the future, 56–57; social networks and, 10; theory of mind and, 4, 7, 50

imitation game, 168, 193

imitative learning, 4, 48

improvisation, 32, 39, 40, 57

incompleteness theorems, of Gödel, 185

India, 158

indirect way of war, 7–8

industrial warfare, 28, 127, 133–34

infantry: in ancient Greece, 96, 106, 109, 110–11, 131; in Napoleonic warfare, 121, 123–24

inferences, 175, 186, 213, 214

information, 57–58, 95, 101, 103

information-processing technologies, 94, 191, 213, 216, 217

in-groups, 35, 62, 82, 104, 133, 187–88

insects, social, 29, 166

instinctive decision-making, 77, 92, 121–22, 153, 154, 157

instincts, 40, 54

The Insurgent Archipelago (Mackinlay), 104

intelligence (human): vs. artificial general intelligence, 23, 193–96, 198, 204; biological-synthetic hybrid intelligence and, 218–21; cognitive flexibility and, 194, 198; distributed, 37–38; domain-specific, 198; evolution of, 211; mind-merging technologies for, 23–24; social theory of, 4, 9; sociobiology and, 43; theory of mind and, 23

intelligence analysis, 83

intentionality: artificial general intelligence and, 211; consciousness and, 53–55; Cuban Missile Crisis and, 135, 152; learning and, 49–50; levels of, 45; mind-reading abilities and, 51; observation of, 145; theory of mind on, 8

interests, 19, 34–35, 90, 104, 199, 203

intergroup conflict: chimpanzees and, 13; cooperation and, 3–4, 90; human nature and, 43–44; large groups and, 4; life-threatening, 130; in prehistoric societies, 3–4, 68–69, 82. *See also* warfare

international relations: balance of power in, 180, 182; emotions in, 79; "madman" theory of, 142, 143, 159; prospect theory and, 132; psychological factors in, 34; tactical AI and, 190

ABOUT THE AUTHOR

DR. KENNETH PAYNE IS A SENIOR LECTURER IN THE SCHOOL OF SECURITY Studies at King's College, London. He is also a senior member of St. Antony's College, Oxford, having earlier been a visiting fellow in the Department of International Relations there. Payne's research is broadly in the field of political psychology and strategic studies. This is his third book. His first, *The Psychology of Strategy: Exploring Rationality in the Vietnam War* (OUP; Hurst & Co., 2015), considers the psychological dimension of US strategy. His second, *The Psychology of Modern Conflict* (Palgrave, 2015), explores the relationship between liberal ways of warfare and our violent human prehistory.